Tipping

Tipping

*An American
Social History of Gratuities*

by
Kerry Segrave

McFarland & Company, Inc., Publishers
Jefferson, North Carolina and London

British Library Cataloguing-in-Publication data are available

Library of Congress Cataloguing-in-Publication Data

Segrave, Kerry, 1944–
    Tipping : an American social history of gratuities / by Kerry
Segrave.
        p.   cm.
    Includes bibliographical references.
    ISBN 0-7864-0347-0 (library binding : 50# alkaline paper) ∞
    1. Tipping — United States — History.   I. Title.
HD4928.T58S44   1998
395.5 — dc21   97-48412
                                                                      CIP

HD 4928
T58 S44
1998

Manufactured in the United States of America

*McFarland & Company, Inc., Publishers
  Box 611, Jefferson, North Carolina 28640*

Contents

Preface

In its early years, tipping was a much-hated custom, branded as un–American and undemocratic. Much opposition rose against it from labor, from clubs formed specifically to fight it, and from state and city governments, which in some cases went so far as to pass laws prohibiting tipping. None, of course, succeeded. As time passed, this opposition faded; tipping eventually became more entrenched in American life than in any other country. Although the government was fairly quick to recognize tips as taxable income, it was much slower to include tips as income in the calculation of unemployment insurance payments, social security benefits, and so forth.

Though organized opposition to tipping has failed, the custom remains in disfavor with much of the population. Many people are uncomfortable in tipping situations; they are unsure of whom to tip and how much. This uncertainty has led to a seemingly endless series of media guides to the custom. In the last few decades there has been a huge increase in the number of psychological studies done on tipping. One notable result is that the standard belief about tipping — that a tip is given as a reward for good service — is not substantiated. From its beginnings as a European custom, tipping soon immigrated to America, and finally became a quintessential American trait.

This book examines the history of tipping, primarily in the United States, over the last 120 years. Following a brief overview in the first chapter, the book is organized along the line of action and reaction; that is, after each chapter discussing how tipping evolved and was practiced in a given period, there follows a chapter relating how consumers responded. Responses ran the gamut from weary acquiescence to ordinances banning the practice. Some of these ordinances — long since repealed — are reproduced in Appendix 2. Research for this book was conducted at the University of British Columbia, Simon Fraser University, and the Vancouver Public Library.

Chapter 1

Tipping Begins,
Then Moves to America

"The dirty scrub of a waiter grumbled about his allowance, which I reckoned liberal. I added sixpence to it, and produced a bow which I was near rewarding with a kick. Accursed be the race of flunkeys!"
—Thomas Carlyle

The origins of the practice of tipping are vague, but it may have begun in the late Middle Ages. During an age of paternalism and wardship, the master or lord of the manor might give his servant or laborer a few extra coins, from either compassion or appreciation of a good deed. Such gestures may have occurred because of exceptional hardship arising from a large family, illness, or other social disadvantages befalling the servant and his family. By the time of Tudor England (1485–1603), a shift had taken place in that visitors to private homes were expected to give sums of money (known as vails) at the end of a visit for service rendered by the host's servants above and beyond their usual duties. Thus was established the idea that a tip was given for something extra—either services or effort.[1]

Vails soon became expected from every guest that dined at the master's table and slept in one of his beds. This custom grew increasingly irksome for the givers. One account from the 1760s noted that footmen, valets, and gentlemen's servants all expected vails with the practice having spread

> to a most distressing and exhaustive tune. Is it not upon record that poor Goldy [Oliver Goldsmith] could not attend the evening parties of some of his titled patrons, because he had not a guinea to spare wherewith to fee the lacquey in attendance, who took charge of his cloak or his sword? Did not the great Doctor [Samuel] Johnson himself give up the satisfaction he derived from visiting some of his noble friends for the same reason?

By then at least one unnamed master was in the habit of "sharing" the vails received by his servants and giving large parties with sparse entertainment to supplement his income.[2]

1

Guests who visited private homes found servants flanking the door at departure time, with the departee expected to satisfy them. Even British royalty complained about the high cost of visiting friends. An ungenerous guest supposedly might find his horse injured, or he might hear a footman mutter that on the next visit he would receive a plate of gravy on his breeches. The system of vails became so hated that groups of masters attempted to abolish it. At a meeting of the gentry and nobility in 1760 in Edinburgh, Scotland, it was unanimously agreed to abolish the practice of giving vails to servants. They also decided, with less enthusiasm, that it would be more "honourable," for both master and servant, to raise wages. The attempt to abolish vails was taken up in London, where in 1764 a disturbance broke out at Ranelagh House in that city, in which the coachmen, footmen, and other servants of masters who wouldn't allow their servants to accept vails ran amok. Those servants

> began by hissing their masters, they then broke all the lamps and outside windows with stones; and afterwards putting out their flambeaus, pelted the company in a most audacious manner, with brick-bats, etc., whereby several were greatly hurt, so as to render the use of swords necessary.

Several servants were injured when they were run through with those swords. A few years later vails were reportedly abolished in Shropshire, Shrewsbury.[3]

The practice, however, did not stop. During the first decade of the twentieth century, tipping servants in private houses in Britain was still a hot topic. One claim was that a guest staying at a friend's manor for a one-week hunting visit could expect to lay out around $100 to the servants. Englishmen were said to yearn for a host who would veto tips to servants. One such savior was Lord Sefton, who banned the practice on his estate. All his guest rooms displayed a notice that no gratuities should be given to any servant. Although it may have been considered a start, one observer complained that "every man who visits the noble Lord has his own valet and every woman guest a maid of her own. Such guests are not in the habit of giving tips, and poorer members of society will have to go on making gratuities as heretofore unless the example of Lord Sefton is generally followed."[4]

At the same time, Americans were blamed for increasing the size of tips given servants in private British homes. (Generally, Americans abroad were blamed for tipping too much throughout Europe. Perhaps it could be viewed as a subconscious revenge for the very practice of tipping, which was imported from Europe. In America, that situation was condemned regularly.) Those "liberal but misguided" Americans were blamed for spoiling the servants to the extent that English people of modest means were not able to accept as many invitations as before "for fear of being insulted by the servants in case they undertip." One Englishman remarked that when he went to visit a house, his host took him aside to warn him not to overtip. The host explained that he had discharged all his previous servants because "they had been spoiled to such an extent by American visitors that he was afraid that his home would get something of the reputation of a hotel." When that same Englishman visited another country house, he tipped more conservatively but "was positively insulted by a servant for offering a tip that gladly would have been accepted at a country house in America."[5]

In America the practice of tipping servants took hold, and was reported as fairly widespread in the private homes of the gentry by 1900. Assessing the situation in 1907, a *New York Times* editorial remarked that the custom of tipping servants was borrowed from Britain "where it has grown lately to be a positive nuisance.... A week-end at a hotel might not be more expensive." In this article, no blame was attached to Americans traveling abroad. Regarding Lord Sefton's example, the editor said, "He is a man of influence, and he may make the prohibition of tips in private houses an English fashion. Then it will speedily become an American fashion, and one of the most sensible England has passed over to us."[6]

The question of whether to tip servants in private houses became a quieter issue after World War I. The practice had not been abolished, but the private manor with a retinue of live-in servants and the hosting of large parties had become largely a thing of the past for all but the super-rich. The expense of sustaining huge estates and all those servants was too great. Still, tipping survived. Letitia Baldrige, former White House social secretary to Jacqueline Kennedy and the co-author of *The Amy Vanderbilt Complete Book of Etiquette*, noted in the 1980s that if she stayed in a friend's private home she left $10 if she was alone and one person made her bed and ironed her dress; $15 for the night if her husband was with her. If the house had a cook, Baldrige left $10 for that servant. During the same period, conservative pundit William F. Buckley, Jr., rented a château in Switzerland each year with a staff of five. One year, his son and daughter-in-law invited a couple to stay for a week. At the end of the period, his son Christopher explained, "My dad took me aside and discreetly said, I think you should tell your guests they ought to leave a 'propina.' Dad never says tip. He always says propina. Since it's money, you know, it's best not to discuss it directly. So he always lapses into Spanish." Buckley suggested $150 for the cook, $100 each for the concierge, butler, and scullery maid, and $50 for the underchef. It fell to Christopher to tell his friends to hand over $500. "They were very sweet about it but clearly shocked to the depths of their souls, as well they should have been."[7]

Some time after vails was an established practice it evolved to a new form whereby employees of commercial enterprises such as restaurants and hotels were tipped. Samuel Pepys mentioned tipping in 1668 with such references as "June 1, dinner and servants, £1 0s. 6d." and "June 11, reckoning, £2 5s. 6d.; servants, 1s. 6d." From the daily expenditure accounts kept by Gilbert White in the 1770s came the following: "gave the Drawer at the Blue Boar, 1s; gave Mr. Parker's man of Trin. Coll. 1s; servants at Chilgrove and Chichester, 6s." From these accounts, it seems these men were tipping in both private homes and commercial establishments. Thomas Carlyle found himself at the Bell Inn at Gloucester, sometime in the early to mid–1800s. When he departed, he left something for the waiter. "The dirty scrub of a waiter grumbled about his allowance, which I reckoned liberal. I added sixpence to it, and produced a bow which I was near rewarding with a kick. Accursed be the race of flunkeys!" grumbled Carlyle.[8]

By 1795, tipping was common enough that one journalist remarked, in reference to hotels,

> If a man who has a horse puts up at an inn, besides his usual bill, he must give at least one shilling to the waiter, sixpence each to the chambermaid, the ostler and the jackboot, making together half a crown. If the traveler only puts up to have refreshment, besides paying for his horse's standing, he has to give away in the day another half-crown, which makes five shillings in the day to the servants.[9]

It is unclear when the word *tip* made its way into the English language. Many accounts have it that the word originated in a London coffeehouse on Fleet Street frequented by Samuel Johnson and his cronies, such as Oliver Goldsmith. (The time was probably between 1756, when Goldsmith came to London, and 1774 when he died.) On the table was a bowl with the words "To Insure Promptitude" printed around it. Taking the first letter of each word, the phrase, it is said, was shortened to *tip*. Patrons like Johnson would put a coin in the bowl from time to time throughout the evening. A variation on that story holds that in the eighteenth century, London coffeehouse patrons sometimes handed the waiter a coin wrapped in a piece of paper printed with the words "to insure promptness," or, merely "T.I.P." According to Johnson biographer James Boswell, the doctor visited a restaurant and reported: "I had a cut of meat for sixpence and bread for a penny, and gave the waiter a penny; so that I was quite well served — nay, better than the rest, for they gave the waiter nothing."[10]

Other theories hold that the word *tip* comes from the Dutch *tippen,* meaning "to tap," and referring to the sound of a coin being clicked against a glass to catch a waiter's attention; or that the word tip derives from the Latin "stips," meaning gift. In many foreign languages, words for "tip" are associated with drinking, because in many countries the tip began as a gratuity to enable the tippee to buy himself a drink. In French "pourboire" means literally "for drink;" the German "trinkgeld" is "drink money;" the Spanish "propina" is from "propinar," meaning invite to drink; Russia's "nachai" is the equivalent of "for tea;" and the Chinese "cumshaw" is "tea money." It may be reasonable to surmise the word *tip* is a short form of "tipple" — to drink.[11]

"Tip" was apparently in use even before the time of Johnson, Goldsmith, and Fleet Street coffeehouses. In Jonathan Swift's 1733 poem "The Legion Club" are found the lines: "When I saw the keeper frown, / Tipping him with half-a-crown...." The *Oxford English Dictionary* gives four uses of the word *tip* prior to 1753. The 1933 issue of the *OED* defined tip as "a small present of money given to an inferior, especially to a servant or employee of another for a service rendered or expected." In its 1989 edition the *OED* used the same definition.[12]

Thus, tipping seems to have started with the traveling aristocracy and spread downward class by class. With the rise of wage labor in industrial capitalism, the number and position of servants declined. That same rise of industrial capitalism brought with it an increase in commercial eating and drinking establishments, hotels, and mass transportation wherein those who received tips — maids, valets, waiters, and so forth were found in large numbers. As a greater proportion of people dined out, stayed in hotels, traveled on trains, and so on, they found themselves in tipping situations. All of those who received tips in the past were regarded as social inferiors at a time when such distinctions were felt to be normal and natural — God's will. All the services for which tips were given — serving meals, carrying luggage, making beds, drawing drinks, and so forth — were regarded as menial labor. Those legacies of who was tipped for what services remain with us today. Toward the end of the 1800s, tipping was pervasive enough in society to involve most people in a tipping situation from time to time. Up until the present, it has remained a controversial issue.

Today tipping is perhaps more entrenched in the United States than in any other nation. Yet it flew in the face of supposedly American values of the era when it came into prominence. As one writer noted, "What, may I ask, is more un–American than tipping? It doesn't belong in American society; it doesn't belong in a democracy. It is a product of lands where for centuries there has been a servile class." According to this account, there was no tipping in the United States prior to 1840, with European travel writers and visitors often expressing amazement that they were not expected to tip. English traveler John Fowler visited a town in New York State in 1830, where he recorded the following expenditure: "total 81 cents; waiter 0; chambermaid and boots, ditto; and civility and thanks into the bargain. Will this be credited in England? It will be some time before it is a practice there, at all events." It was newly rich Americans who brought the habit back, to prove they had been abroad and knew the rules. A second account agreed there was little or no tipping in America prior to the Civil War and blamed U.S. travelers abroad for bringing the custom home.[13]

Viewing the situation differently was a *Gunton's Magazine* article in 1896 that remarked that in the United States "we have been comparatively free from this offensive semi-mendicancy." However, tipping was a growing custom among a certain class of laborers such as domestic servants, coachmen, barbers, waiters, and railroad porters: "It will be observed that these occupations are nearly all filled by foreigners and negroes who for the most part have been reared under the patronizing and semi-feudal influences of paternal or ante-wage condition." Centuries of slavery had left blacks in menial jobs while Europeans were menial workers due to the "aristocratic, patronizing conditions of Europe." Thus, in this account, the tip takers (not the givers) were primarily responsible for the spread of the custom in America, due to their servile nature. How they had the power to accomplish this while being menial, went unexplained.[14]

Toward the end of the 1890s, reports commented that tipping was established in America, evidence of "degeneracy" with the result that "now there is in this country as there has been for centuries in Europe a conscienceless, servile, but insolent class which bows to nothing but money, and a careless class of spendthrifts who are long on money and short on common honesty and self respect." A *New York Times* editor stated that once tipping got a hold in the United States it spread rapidly like "evil insects and weeds."[15]

Ladies Home Journal publisher Edward Bok felt that something had to be done about the habit, either abolishing or regulating it, because "tipping in America has gone beyond all rhyme or reason." Only Americans abroad were subjected to the practice at first, then "the evil came over here, and with our characteristic extravagance, we abused it until the amount of an English or Continental tip is reasonable in comparison with the average American tip." Bok didn't explain exactly how tipping crossed the Atlantic.[16]

In 1908 it was glumly announced that the only parts of the United States free of tipping were the Kentucky Hill district, the Smoky Mountains, and the "still uncivilized" parts of the Hudson Bay district. Another observer was resigned to the fact the tip had come to stay with the only change likely to occur being a "broadening of the territory infested by it." Reportedly, around 1905 it was not uncommon in restaurants in cities as large as St. Louis to see signs proclaiming, "No Tipping! Tipping is not American!"[17]

Comparisons were often made between the custom in America and Europe. Much of it had to do with who tipped the most. An 1897 report had it that one could get by with leaving smaller tips in England than in the United States. While no American would think of leaving a two-cent tip at home, he could do so safely in Europe without being scorned by the receiver. A decade later it was reported that tipping in America was worse than in England because the tips were larger, although a greater variety of occupations expected to be tipped in England.[18]

On the other hand, Americans were blamed in 1908 for spoiling English railway porters by overtipping them. *Travel* magazine noted in 1913 that Americans overtipped in foreign nations. However, a European in a New York City hotel reportedly got excellent attention from a grill chef without leaving a single tip, while at the same time Americans were slighted. This anomaly was explained by the fact that the chef said to the European, "Oh sir, you appreciate what I do for you, while on many of these others our thoughtfulness is lost." That caused *Travel* to conclude the foreigner knew how to treat a servant: "He knows when to be friendly, and yet where to draw the line."[19]

American Federation of Labor president Samuel Gompers had a chapter titled "Nuisances of European Travel" in his book *Labor in Europe and America* in which he complained, "I wish to say something about the almost hourly sufferings of American travelers in Europe from mosquito bites [tipping]. To the sharp probes from these insects, with the resultant pain, fever and disgust, the traveler is obliged to submit continually — at hotels and restaurants, on the railroad and often elsewhere." He was pestered everywhere, he said. Although he felt it was a bad system, he concluded pervasive tipping "is in Europe universal and accepted by all classes of travelers as an inevitable nuisance. It often borders on blackmail. Tippers go raving mad in recounting their wrongs under the tyrannies of the system."[20]

Chapter 2

"Illegal and Un-American": Tipping Practices 1880–1919

"I, good American as I consider myself, do look down upon certain persons as my inferiors, and those persons are the ones who accept tips from me, and I expect and demand that they shall treat me as their superior."
— Elizabeth Banks

Class, race, and gender all played a part in the early discussions of tipping. According to one observer, it was well known that waiters in Europe generally did not come from the upper classes of society, nor did they have much formal education. Those few who did were "generally above accepting tips and fees." Furthermore, the European waiters usually had more education than their American counterparts, making them more likely to refuse tips, "temptations that prove too strong for the low-bred and unintelligent," such as American tip takers. To eliminate the custom, agitation was necessary, to be aimed at hotel and restaurant owners:

> We are unwilling to believe that the moral sense of American landlords and waiters will not respond to sentiments of honor and self-respect as quickly as the manhood of the landlords and waiters of Vienna and Lucerne. Free American citizens ought not to be shamed into the practices of minor morals by the example of caste-bound Europeans.

In 1891, journalist Arthur Gaye wrote that a tip was bestowed upon a person "who is presumed to be inferior to the donor, not only in worldly wealth, but in social position also."[1]

At the turn of the century, one foreign-born American waiter had managed to put his son through college and law school on his salary and tips over 20 years. "It probably never occurred to him that there was anything debasing in taking a tip. And for him there was nothing debasing in it. He lived and acted in harmony with the sphere of life into which he

9

was born," reported the account. Yet it would be a completely different thing for the son, a beneficiary of tips, to receive them. "He is an American and must take fees only."[2]

In Portland, Maine, in 1905, Mayor Baxter assailed the practice of college students receiving tips as waiters at summer hotels. Public reaction was said to be on the mayor's side. Baxter felt the thousands of students working in summer hotels could, if they chose, get summer jobs not subject to the "degrading conditions of tipping."[3]

Reporter Elizabeth Banks also complained at that time about the effect of tipping on college girls who waitressed.

> Mark the servility of the girl's attitude and her meek and lowly "Yes, Sirs" and "No, Sirs!" Why should a college student, baking buckwheat cakes in the interests of education, address Mr. Hopkinson Smith or any other man as a superior, say "Sir" to him and accept his pity and his tips?—Why, I'll tell you why—because the man to whom she handed the cakes was her superior! She makes him her superior by kow-towing to him and accepting a tip.

If a college girl accepted the tip, then "she will never be able to lift her head high in the true pride of self-supporting America womanhood. She will go through life saying 'Yes, Sir,' and 'No, Sir.'" Calling the custom un–American, Banks felt self-respecting Americans had to tip in order to secure their rights, for which they had already paid. Again attacking college students who took tips on their summer jobs, Banks said "they are selling not only their self-respect, but are throwing away their glorious birthright as American citizens, and they certainly have no right to complain if they are 'looked down upon.'" Regarding the argument that tips were necessary because hotel wages were so low, Banks believed college girls had plenty of other job opportunities in the summer. "If they cannot get a decent wage without tips let them take to household service, comforting themselves with the knowledge that no one whose respect is worth having will think any less of them for doing housework."[4]

Banks herself solidly believed in a class distinction between the parties in a tipping situation. She said, "I, good American as I consider myself, do look down upon certain persons as my inferiors, and those persons are the ones who accept tips from me, and I expect and demand that they shall treat me as their superior." Anyone who accepted a tip from her "is not my equal. From such persons I demand, 'Yes, Ma'ams' and a certain deference. Tips and servility go together."[5]

Sometimes class and race issues were combined. In 1902, journalist John Speed recalled that when he came north for the first time,

> I had never known any but negro servants. Negroes take tips, of course; one expects that of them—it is a token of their inferiority. But to give money to

a white man was embarrassing to me. I felt defiled by his debasement and servility. Indeed, I do not now comprehend how any native-born American could consent to take a tip. Tips go with servility, and no man who is a voter in this country by birthright is in the least justified in being in service.[6]

An informal 1903 survey claimed that the average salary for black waiters was $18 to $22 per month including tips, while white waiters averaged $30 to $35 per month (see Appendix 1 for financial data). Although the whites moved on to other employment as soon as possible, blacks often worked as waiters permanently because there were few other options for them. From that survey it was clear that "restaurants invariably pay less wages to colored waiters than they pay to white ones."[7]

In 1907 Senator Tillman of South Carolina tipped black porter George Hollister 25 cents as he departed Omaha, Nebraska's Paxton Hotel. Tillman was well known for maintaining that he never "tips a nigger." Familiar with the senator's views, Hollister joked that he would have the quarter made into a watch charm. So newsworthy was the event that the *New York Times* editorialized that Tillman's previous position was "not meanness. We must assume that the Senator abstains from tipping as a matter of principle." Tipping blacks was not unusual then, and people on long journeys, said the editor, frequently were forced "to convert themselves into fountains playing quarters upon the circumambient Africans."[8]

The idea that women were poor tippers was a very old one. In 1893, one article commented that the fair sex was in general "very stingy." A decade later the *New York Times* reported that "the female sex, though it sits and shares in the receipt of tips, has a bad name among tip takers as a tip giver, and waiters elude a place which is known to be of mainly feminine patronage." Around the same time the UK publication the *Spectator* agreed that women tipped much less than men, explaining that "men yield more easily to the moral blackmail. A man is more apt to feel that the charge of a want of generosity is damaging to his sex."[9]

In media accounts of tipping, one method to demonize and stigmatize tip receivers was to present them as making a lot of money or extracting some type of revenge on the nontippers. By infusing tip receivers — who were almost all in the low-income bracket — with mythical power and earnings, one did not have to deal with the realities of an underpaid, exploited group of employees. By extrapolation, all tip receivers were well-off and powerful. One account had it that a group of waiters formed a social club in New York City in 1881 which grew to 220 members in 1884. "Three years ago they had nothing. Today they own the clubhouse, elaborately fitted up and supplied with billiard tables, a bar, and all the essentials of a well appointed club.... This clubhouse represents thousands of tips."[10]

In first-class hotels the job of head porter "was more remunerative than any other position barring possibly that of the manager, and in some instances he makes considerably more than the manager." During a divorce case, a waiter and his wife argued over the amount of alimony. He said his salary was $25 per week. His wife agreed with that number, but she insisted he also made $50 per week in tips, for a total of $75 each week. Although the reporter conceded he couldn't find any waiters who made $75 per week, he insisted there were "plenty who come pretty close to it." Concierges in prestigious European places reportedly paid, in some cases, a large premium to get the position. One Riviera concierge, in 1911, reportedly went for a three-month tour in his $5,000 car when his hotel was closed for the summer. One concierge walked out of his hotel at night to be picked up around the corner by his chauffeured limousine, and was driven home to "a villa which is the best in the neighborhood."[11]

Revenge on nontippers took many forms. One of the oldest was the story about marked baggage. A gentleman in 1893 complained bitterly about hotel servants who never helped him with his luggage. Suspecting the man was a nontipper, a friend asked him if that was the case. When the suspicion was confirmed the friend explained, "I thereupon showed him the cause of the servants' inattention, amounting sometimes even to rudeness — a little chalk mark on each bag." Advised to wipe off any such marks when leaving a hotel, the older man found his problem solved. Also used for the identification of nontippers was "the position of hotel labels" affixed to bags. Some years later, a journalist reported that a traveler who failed to tip in Europe would "find his baggage marked with little cabalistic signs, which have the same properties as red-hot coals, in that the person picking them up is certain to drop them"[12]

The most often-reported revenge was insolence or slow service. One man complained that although he received "officious politeness" on his first visit to a café, if he didn't tip, future visits produced sluggish and unwilling service. It was the same with barbers and even church ushers, causing this man to thunder, "this tipping business is an English importation and an abomination." Another man asserted that if one failed to tip in a restaurant one was almost shunned on subsequent visits. He called for "discontinuance of this abuse," complaining that a protest to the headwaiter or owner "does not help me, for they all seem to be in league together." One waiter was quote as saying that if a customer didn't tip he "will be remembered when he comes again, and will have to suffer a little"[13]

If accounts can be believed, tip receivers sometimes took revenge in a more boisterous or physical way. In 1863, a waiter in Britain chased a customer who had left the restaurant. Although the customer left a tip for the waiter, he had forgotten the chambermaid, who looked after the washroom. Berlin waiters in 1909 reportedly sometimes assailed customers in rowdy language for leaving small tips, "while in some instances they have created scenes by throwing the tips across the room, a humiliation to the tipper." Around the same time in America, the Vermont Fish and Game League held its annual dinner near Burlington. No sooner had the last course been served than waiters went around the tables with outstretched plates; "nobody escaped this indelicate attention, and the man who hesitated to give was helped to a decision by a rattling of the change already on the plate, kept up till an embarrassing amount of attention was called to his reluctance."[14]

One man gave a waiter a three-cent tip, which the waiter refused to accept. When the waiter attempted to give the tip back, the diner refused to accept it. Not willing to give up, the server pursued the diner into the street to try to return the paltry gratuity. In a different café, a patron complained he never received his change back from the waiter for a $1 bill — which he had intended to leave as a tip anyway. The headwaiter apologized, brought the correct change, claimed the waiter was new, but exchanged surreptitious winks with the waiter in question as he did all of this. One account concluded generally that the "haughty" waiters in hotels scorn "the humbler coins of the realm, and accept nothing less than half a dollar." That writer fretted that as tipping became more endemic in America its "unfortunate citizens will have to leave, and seek a cheaper country." While those who couldn't afford to tip were advised not to travel, another suggestion offered was for the nontipping traveler to "always go to a place where girls are employed," where a smile or a greeting would suffice. That didn't work on males because "a waiter cannot be subjugated.... The waiter has too many advantages."[15]

A waiter named Joseph told a story about a man who came to his restaurant regularly but never tipped. "Of course, after the first time, word was passed to every waiter in the place, and so he got the worst kind of service. But he just kept changing tables, and finally complained to the boss." All of the waiters were reprimanded by the boss. On one occasion, a waiter spilled water on the man to get him out. That waiter "didn't use good judgment though. He could just as well have crowded his table with strangers, kept him waiting, served stuff as cold as possible, and cut down on extra butter and other things," argued Joseph.[16]

Tip receivers in Italy were said to swamp travelers around 1911. Wrote one tourist,

> You may not believe it, but it is a fact that I had to brush Italians off the top and sides of that trunk before I could be sure it was mine, and as fast as I

> shooed one swarm away another came along and lit in the same place. If we
> could invent some kind of a chest that would attract and hold flies as firmly
> as a common garden trunk will attract and hold Neapolitans, the fly as a
> household pest would soon be exterminated.

The writer concluded that while the banditti may have disappeared in
Rome, "the banditti are still on the job."[17]

Most extreme of the revenge tales was from Chicago in 1918, when
Illinois State Attorney Hoyne, acting on information regarding coercion
used by waiters to obtain tips, arrested 100 waiters. Hoyne received a report
the waiters had used a certain powder in the dishes of known opponents
to the tipping system.[18]

Most of the revenge stories were perhaps exaggerated or totally false.
As reporter Elizabeth Banks said in 1905 about not tipping in hotels and
restaurants: "Of course, it is all nonsense to say that you will not receive
proper service, and will meet with discourtesy unless you give a tip. No
first-class hotel will permit that for a moment." Another journalist said
managers had pointed out to him that courteous treatment of guests was
always required from employees, whether or not the guests tipped. Any
sign of displeasure to a guest regarding the absence of a tip would result
in immediate dismissal, whether the person was a direct employee or the
hire of a contractor.[19]

As tipping became more important and pervasive, employers often
took greater advantage of their employees. By 1895 it was not unusual for
waiters abroad to receive no salary at all — just tips. At the time, the average tip in Europe was said to be 5 percent of the bill, in contrast to the
United States where 10 percent was usual, despite the fact the waiters "are
even well paid."[20]

French tip receivers in cafés and restaurants launched their own move
to abolish tips at that time. They did so because tips gave the café owners a chance to oppress their employees. By keeping a close watch, employers arrived at a fair idea of how much a waiter received on average in the
form of gratuities.

> This had gradually suggested the practice not only of paying no wages at all
> to garçons in frequented restaurants, but of compelling them to buy their posi-
> tions. Nay, in addition they are forced to turn over to their employers all that
> they receive above a certain sum, which, of course, is a sum all the while tend-
> ing to the minimum.

Large hotels and restaurants in Berlin were reported to take all their
employees' tips as part of the revenue of the house, returning to them a
percentage as commission. Not limited to Europe, the practice of waiters

paying for the privilege of working in certain fancy restaurants was reported in America by 1902.[21]

In one unnamed New York café, it was reported that "the waiters serving there pay handsomely for the privilege." French waiters paid from one to four shillings a day in restaurants for the chance to make perhaps 35 shillings a week.[22]

In America a more common way of diverting tips from employees was found in the set-up of the coat or hat checkroom, commonly found in hotels and restaurants. There was almost an unwritten rule that patrons at eating establishments had to check their hats and coats. If someone took his hat to his table "it won't be but a few minutes before the news spreads and an attendant is soon before him to exchange a check for the hat — they will even go so far as to take a hat without a word and bring back the check before one realizes that the chapeau has vanished."[23]

Patrons who tipped the employee at the checkroom usually believed the employee kept the tip, but such was not always the case. What often happened at the finer hotels and restaurants was that a contractor paid the hotel a certain amount for the privilege of running the check concession. Contractors paid modest restaurants $75 to $100 per month for the checkroom concession while in fancier places the fee was $200 to $300 per month. It was the contractor who paid the checkroom workers, not the hotel. He also kept all the tips, while paying the employees a straight, minimal salary. Employee wages amounted to some three to four dollars per week, and checkroom employees were usually minors.

A typical method of operation in 1906 was to have one employee appointed "head" who wore a leather pouch with a slot in it. All tips went into this pouch. The head kept his eye on the other workers to ensure that they turned everything in while the contractor kept his eye on the head. As far as patrons were concerned, the checkers were hotel employees. Those checkers complained they were "compelled to be polite to patrons and to smile a blessing upon every guest who presents to them a dime or a quarter, and as they don't really benefit by the tip it is hard."[24]

Around 1910, this practice was widely publicized in New York City with a resultant drop in concession profits. If an employee did not turn in five dollars a day, he was fired. Of course many tried to skim some of the money off the top; different systems were used to eliminate that practice. One method was to reward employees for spying on each other; this worked only until the workers got together to decide the rewards for spying were less than if they stuck together and skimmed. A more refined effort came into effect when the concession holders — called the tip trust — came up with the idea of uniforms with no pockets whatsoever. Commenting on the general situation, a patron who was retrieving his hat and coat from a checkroom told the employee, "I'd be glad to give you a dime for taking care of my hat and coat while I was at dinner, but I won't do it because I happen to know that you wouldn't get the money."[25]

When partners in a tip concession argued in court over the division of profits, it was agreed they supplied all the establishments where they held concessions with attendants whose uniforms had no pockets. All tips were turned over to the concession holders. Chicago Judge Theodore Brentano, who heard the case limited himself to a comment on tipping in general, which he branded as "illegal and un–American."[26]

For several years, Harry Gladstone held the check concession contract with Brooklyn, New York's Hofbrauhaus restaurant. His employees rebelled and agitated to keep their tips by launching a campaign that involved dropping the hats and coats of diners. This action led to complaints to the restaurant, which responded by taking Gladstone to court to try and have his contract revoked.[27]

Washroom concessions were also often leased out. New York's Grand Union Hotel owner Simeon Ford told a reporter he had been offered $2,500 for that concession at his hotel, with the party making the proposal agreeing to furnish his own help, soap, towels, and so on.

It was not uncommon in humor columns in the media of the 1910s to joke about buying a hat for five dollars but then paying $73 per year to store it while the owner ate at restaurants (ten cents each time, twice a day, every day of the year). A *New York Times* editorial acknowledged that checkroom employees rarely got any of the tip money, with it going instead to the hotel and the concession holder

> but to scold these invisible beneficiaries of the miserable system — miserable because it combines in about equal proportions beggary and blackmail — is a waste of time. The thing pays. Therefore it will continue just as long as the public meekly submits to thinly veiled robbery. And that, seemingly, will be forever. At any rate no movements of revolt have yet been made, except by a few brave souls who can stand the charge of 'meanness' whispered or looked by creatures whom they despise.[28]

The traveling public regularly ran into tipping situations on trains and ships. During this period, railroad porter was one occupation in which tipping constituted the chief source of the worker's income. Paradoxically, that occupation was said to have come into existence in an effort to abolish what was then a budding system of tipping in depots. Apparently, freelancers worked the stations hoping for a tip by helping passengers with their luggage. Station porters (redcaps) were hired by the New York Central Railroad in the late 1890s for just that purpose. The company took pains to inform its customers and the general public that those porters were paid by the company and "should not be tipped." Also pointed out was that

> if the public will cooperate with the company this reform will be a success, and may be expected soon to be adopted by other corporations throughout the country, and so, ultimately rid the American public of a European nuisance which everybody resents but few can individually afford to resist.

To make those employees easy to spot, they were outfitted with special uniforms, a distinctive feature of which was a red cap.[29]

If New York Central intended to eliminate tips, other railroad lines did not. They went to the other extreme by paying a smaller percentage of total earnings in wages to their porters than any other occupation. Led by the likes of the Pullman company, they hired almost exclusively blacks for porters, a group that was easier to exploit in that time. When the Railroad Commission of California investigated the Pullman firm in 1914, the latter tried to prove they paid adequate wages and did not expect their employees to exact tips. "It is hard for us to determine which should be criticized the more," said the investigators, "the attitude of the company in this regard or its suppositions that it could make this Commission believe a thing which everybody knows is not true." That commission also concluded that women traveling alone "because they are known to tip less 'generously' than men, receive the aid of the porter last or not at all."[30]

By 1915 the Pullman company stood in the public mind as the leading exponent of tipping. It then had some 6,500 porters, who received about $27.50 per month in wages. Had they not received tips, one source calculated the company would have had to pay at least $60 a month in wages. That would have cost the company $390 per year per porter, an annual payroll increase of $2,535,000. The federal Walsh Commission, appointed to investigate industrial conditions in the United States in 1915, singled out the Pullman company for probing. The company's general manager testified, "The company simply accepts conditions as it finds them. The company did not invent tipping. It was here when the company began."

All of Pullman's porters were black. Asked why the company only hired blacks from the south, the executive explained they were more suited to the work than the northern blacks and "the southern negro is more pleasing to the traveling public. He is more adapted to wait on people and serve with a smile." When he was asked whether a man could live on a porter's wage of $27.50 per month and how Pullman fixed the wage rate,

he said, "really, I don't know.... Well, I should say that tips have something to do with it. I didn't make the rates of pay."[31]

Editorializing on the Pullman testimony, the St. Louis *Republic* wrote,
"Other corporations before now have underpaid their employees ... but it
remained for the Pullman company to discover how to work the sympa-
thies of the public in such a manner as to induce that public to make up,
by gratuities, for its failure to pay its employees a living wage." By indus-
triously circulating the fact it didn't pay the porter a sufficient wage, the
company made him dependent on passenger tips.

> We were expected to pay him simply because the Pullman company didn't.
> And we paid him.... It wasn't really philanthropy to the porter, it was phil-
> anthropy extended to the Pullman company, which was glad to have the fact
> of its meanness in its relations to its colored employees — ill-informed of the
> rights of workingmen and dependent by instinct — published to the world.

Exaggerating, the newspaper concluded, "It was the Pullman company
which fastened the tipping habit on the American people and they used
the negro as the instrument to do it with."[32]

Equally underpaid were employees on ships, who were left to the mer-
cies of the traveling public. Although ship employees were permitted to
accept tips, they were not allowed to ask for them. At the end of a 1908
voyage, during which the Cunard liner *Carmania* crossed from Liverpool
to New York, a certain Mr. Parker distributed a sum of money among the
stewards but took it all back due to an annoying incident connected with
the distribution of the money, unexplained in the account. Parker complained to the line with the result that steward Walter Roche was fired.
Cunard sent a memo to other steamship companies stating that Roche was
fired for soliciting tips. The memo to the White Star Line read, "Private
and confidential: We beg to inform you that the name mentioned below
has been placed on the blacklist of this line for soliciting fees." White Star
refused Roche's application for employment. Soliciting tips was considered a serious offense. Roche later sued Cunard on the grounds of libel.
However, the case went against him when the court held that the memos
were privileged and therefore not admissible. That situation brought up
the idea of doing away with tipping on ships and adding an all-inclusive
service charge. To that suggestion a Cunard official responded, "No doubt
there are many travelers who would welcome such an inclusive charge, but
the plan is not practicable. There would still be tipping by persons urged
by the impulse of mistaken generosity or prompted by the desire to display their wealth."[33]

When the steamer *Northland* arrived in Buffalo from Chicago, 25
waiters aboard were arrested and taken before Deputy United States Mar-

shal Conkling, where they were charged with mutiny. During the voyage, the waiters had refused to serve meals because of the number of military school students on board who refused to tip them. When the waiters' demand for a wage increase was refused, they declined to work at all.[34]

Ship employees argued that tips were meager. Said one steward, "I have heard of generous tips but seldom had the gratification of receiving them." Americans "are a class who take every cent's worth of what they are entitled to and pay not a cent more than they can help." Stewards on the Atlantic crossing grumbled that many passengers tipped nothing after the five- to seven-day voyage. Inevitably, the westward trip was worse because American tourists had spent their money while abroad and economized by cutting back on stewards' tips on the homeward trip. On one trip in 1910, stewards received tips at the end of the journey ranging from one dollar to 25 cents from the passengers. They sent a delegation to management to argue that it was impossible for them to exist on their wages of $20 a month, out of which they had to pay for uniforms and laundry. A bonus was granted them to induce them to work on the next cruise.[35]

Around 1890 a tourist company published a list of recommended tips for first-class ship passengers. It read: bedroom steward $2.50; saloon steward $2.50; smoking room steward $2.50; bathroom steward $1; deck steward $1; boots 50 cents (shoeshine boy). Twenty years later the amounts were about the same, but the list had expanded: bedroom steward $2.50; saloon steward $2.50; smoking room steward $1; bathroom steward $1; deck steward $1; boots 50¢; band $1; librarian 50 cents; elevator boys $1; baggage master 50 cents. These amounts were paid at the end of the trip, $11.50 per person recommended in 1910, compared to $10 in 1890. Over that time the minimum first-class fare to cross the Atlantic had increased from $50 to $125, while a steward's wage remained in the range of $17.50 to $20 per month. One reason for a decline in the tips actually received was that whereas in the 1890 era only rich people and businessmen traveled to Europe, a generation later it was far more common for lower-income people, such as clerks and schoolteachers, to save for years to take one such trip. Those tourists usually took a cruise organized by a travel agency paying one all-inclusive price for transportation, hotels, meals, and so on, though exclusive of minor items like laundry and tips. Shoeshine boys were the only employees on the ship who were allowed to openly ask passengers for a tip (such as "remember the boots, sir"), because the companies considered shoeshining a personal service not included in the ticket price.[36]

With tip amounts down, stewards turned to other methods of making money off the passengers. One way was to report to customs officials any undeclared articles subject to duties, if they happened to see such articles in the passengers' possession. Informers got half the value of the seized goods. A second method, when a passenger was a suspected low tipper or nontipper, was for a steward to steal a favorite possession from the passenger, who would frantically offer a two- or three-dollar reward for its return. Invariably, it appeared just before the liner docked. Asked to name the worst tippers, it was reported that "all stewards agree that they dread a woman traveling alone more than any other kind of passenger, especially a school teacher."[37]

Prominently displayed on Cunard line ships was a notice asking that inattention on the part of the stewards and any demands from them for tips be reported to management "so that the matter can be dealt with." Worried that such notices were precursors to forbidding tips completely, stewards declared they would immediately stage a mass desertion of any line implementing such a policy. Given that a ban on tips did not mean a raise in wages, the stewards' anxious response was to be expected. Yet a *New York Times* editorial used the response to attack the employees, claiming that it

> shows that the class for which the abolition of the tip system would be most advantageous is not wise enough to realize that truth and prefers to go on in the bad old way. Their lack of self-respect makes the situation nearly or quite hopeless for the present. The reform must begin at the bottom, and tipping will stop if it ever does stop, not because nobody will give tips, but because everybody would indignantly refuse them.[38]

From the beginning of the custom until the present time, one of the most awkward aspects of tipping was in determining how much to bestow upon whom. A waiter grumbled in 1905 that "it is high time that the proper method of giving tips should be defined, its laws codified, its many possibilities of error guarded against.... The trouble with the American is that he doesn't know the exact amount to give, and that bothers him and causes him to curse the custom." What followed was a list of occupational groups that had to be tipped in Europe. Soon thereafter, the *New York Times* declared the painful aspect of the custom lay not in parting with the money but in calculating the proper tip and living in fear of arriving at the wrong determination: "Some years ago many rich Americans got themselves heartily disliked among other tourists in Europe by giving fabulously large tips partly to create an impression and partly to try to get attention, and so raising the tip standard for every one else." One 1912 magazine dealt with the dilemma of a first-time visitor abroad:

> When he is suddenly placed where he must act without advice, he invari-

ably, from a false pride, or a fear of looking mean, throws money away need-lessly ... There is always an air of mystery surrounding the subject — not as to fact, but as to the amount.... I have heard it said that some people make a practice of setting aside, for tips, ten per centum of their regular expenses in a hotel.[39]

If uncertainty surrounded some aspects of tipping, it was generally agreed that it got out of hand at Christmas, especially in Britain where seasonal complaints were first registered in the 1860s. One account noted, of the day after Christmas, that

every man, woman and child, on the ground of dealings with the house dur-ing the past year, shall knock at your door for a gratuity. From tradesmen such as butchers, bakers, grocers and the like, vast sums are levied as Christ-mas baksheesh by housekeepers, butlers and other servants.... Surely it behooves every one who values integrity and fair-dealing to set his face against this loathsome and corrupting form of roguery.

Thirty years later Christmas was still described as the worst time of the year due to excessive tipping; "we acknowledge the justice of the post-man's overtures, but would fain repudiate those of the lamplighter, and our gorge rises when we interview the turncock.... Can the butcher's boy reduce us to starvation, or the librarian's messenger restrict us to sermons and fifth-rate poetry, if we withhold the accustomed dole?"[40]

Famous people of the era could not be looked to for much in the way of guidance or example. When William Howard Taft was campaigning for the presidency in 1908, he was not only the standard-bearer of the Republican Party but also the "patron saint of the anti-tip crusade." He belonged to no formal group fighting to suppress the custom, "but in a quiet way he just stops paying when he has reached the amount indicated on his check." For years he had gone to the same barber, never leaving a tip. Said the barber, "Never a tip did he give. I understand that he thinks he has paid for the work when he gives the regular price, and I guess he is right." Those revelations caused the *New York Times* to editorialize that Taft's influence against the custom could be enormous if he chose to exert it, leading perhaps to the abolishing of tipping in America, "to the bet-terment of American character and citizenship." However, if tipping were indeed abolished, wages for tip receivers would have to be increased. That raise would be passed on to the consumer in the form of higher prices for haircuts, restaurant meals, hotel rooms, and so on. As that cost would not fall on those who had been generous and stingy tippers, the only losers would be nontippers.[41]

When John D. Rockefeller had lunch at a restaurant in 1908, he was served by waiter Rudolph Osterwalk, who he tipped five cents. Along with the tip Rockefeller dispensed the advice that the waiter should bank the nickel: "That's what I did with my spare cash when I was your age, and it earned money for me. Never waste your money." A few years later when Rockefeller spent one week at a hotel on the Italian lakes, his tip to each employee at week's end was 40 cents. Even the hotel owner agreed that as a tip giver the tycoon left much to be desired. When Andrew Carnegie stayed at the same hotel for three days, he left a tip of two dollars each at the end of his stay for each employee who had tended him. The employees were deeply disappointed.[42]

Ralph Waldo Emerson might have been suffering the agony of overtipping when he wrote, "Though I confess with shame that I sometimes succumb and give the dollar, yet it is a wicked dollar which by and by I shall have the manhood to withhold."[43]

Despite uncertainties surrounding tipping, many definite ideas existed as to which groups tipped the most and the least. Just before the turn of the century a waiter in France claimed that most generous tippers were "Israelitish Anglo-German financiers," followed by Russians, Englishmen, Frenchmen, and Germans; "the American is nowhere." Another waiter, working in England, found the Scots to be the least liberal tippers. Young men generally tipped more than old men. If a man dined with a female who was only an acquaintance, he left a larger tip than when he dined with a female who was his wife or sister. The most ostentatious tipper of all was a South American millionaire, although as a rule wealthy men were not always generous. Some years later in Germany, the Russians remained described as the best tippers; the Americans were still at the bottom, where they had been joined by the English. At the same time, tipping in Paris was deemed almost out of control, mainly due to the "prodigality" of American givers.[44]

In America, New York City was called, in 1908, the world city in which the largest tip was expected and the least done to earn it. On the other hand, in the same era Boston was named as a city which tipped more lavishly than did New York. The cause for this was explained by ethnic reasons: Germans and Jews predominated in New York. The former had a "genius for niggardliness" while the latter "decline to be robbed." Those two races were said to fix the standard for all of New York. Boston contained relatively few Jews and Germans; those that were not rich enough to govern the custom. However, Boston did have a lot of students and Irish Americans.

Students tipped liberally because "they don't earn the money they spend and because a student feels twenty feet tall when he has overpaid a servant." The Irish tipped lavishly because "they can't help it. It's one of the penalties of Hibernicism."[45]

Economic aspects of tipping were discussed only infrequently. Its economic extent was unknown in this early period. During the early 1910s, one estimate had it that tipping in New York City done only in first-class hotels costs residents and visitors $18 million yearly in tips; adding less classy establishments brought the total up to $25 million. A second source estimated there were 400,000 people in New York employed in tip-taking occupations, five million nationwide. With tips averaging $600,000 daily in America, the total was $220 million annually. That five million estimate was more than 10 percent of America's workforce of under 50 million employees. Yet on another page, that same writer estimated that the total given in a year in tips by the American people was between $200 and $500 million. With his estimate of $100,000 per day in New York City alone, the annual expenditure there was $36.5 million, much higher than the first estimate. Thoughts of such amounts caused estimator William Scott to complain, "If the Barbary pirates could see the ease with which a princely tribute is exacted from a docile public by the tip-takers, they would yearn to be reincarnated as waiters in America — the Land of the Fee!"[46]

In a late 1899 editorial the *New York Times* bluntly stated the economic ramifications of the tipping practice, a wretched system that was originated and perpetuated

> not by its victims, the men who give and take tips, but by those who profit by it every year to the extent of millions more than a few. The real takers of tips are the hotel and restaurant proprietors, the owners of steamships, the officers and stock-holders of railways, and a dozen other classes of employers ... every tip saves the payment of wages to an equal amount.... This throws a flood of light on the frequent assertions that the abolition of the tipping system is impossible.[47]

Around the same time another media outlet, *Gunton's Magazine*, called tipping a practice that was "offensively un-American and positively uneconomic." It was un–American because it was contrary to the "whole spirit and genius of American life and institutions," which included the true American spirit of working for wages "instead of fawning for favors." As to the latter charge, the system was uneconomic because income was made precarious and fluctuating, depending on the whims of customers and the servility of employees. Tipping never enlarged income, because as tips increased wages decreased, but tipping did "lessen the man." Tip receivers were degraded because it meant the surrender of personality which was especially offensive in America because the custom rested on no recognized principle of "equity or payment of equivalents" — it was charity, which always injured both giver and receiver. "It is a nuisance to those who pay, except they are inordinately rich and it creates in them a domineering and often despotic attitude, and it creates in those who receive it correspondingly cringing, menial demeanor," concluded the report.[48]

In his anti-tipping book, William Scott argued that employers had shifted the cost of hiring waiters onto the public, with patrons who objected to tipping having little chance of getting a "square deal" in competition with patrons who did tip, though both paid the same for their food. "The patron is required," he thought, "through fear of well-defined penalties, to pay twice." Scott also argued that tipping did not represent a sound exchange of wealth, that tippers did not receive full value for their tips. To the stock argument that the server performed extra service or gave more attention, Scott stated any such extra was "negligible." Since the price on the menu was calculated to include all costs, the tip "is clearly a gift for which no value has been returned. The waiter is paid twice for one service." Thus it was all an unsound economic transaction since the patron received nothing in return for his gift. Scott concluded, "On its economic side tipping is wrong.... Tipping is an economic waste because it is double pay for one service — or pay for no service. It causes one person to give wealth to another without a fair return in value, or without any return.... All the money given by the public on the side is unearned increment." More emotionally, Scott added, "Tipping, and the aristocratic idea it exemplifies, is what we left Europe to escape. It is a cancer in the breast of democracy."[49]

Chapter 3

"Democracy's Deadly Foe":
Tipping Responses
1880–1919

"To my mind, tipping should be classified in the eyes of the law as bribery."

—W.E. Adams

One response to the tipping situation was an attempt to establish no-tip businesses. However, the only forum in which it apparently succeeded was that of private clubs. As early as 1902 it was reported that most private clubs in the United States had such a rule. It was obeyed because "men do not enjoy tipping servants on every side." One of the clubs with a strict ban on tipping was Chicago's Illinois Athletic Club. If a member was caught tipping a waiter he was reprimanded and the waiter was fired. For a third offense, a member was suspended. Yet in 1914 the club's board of governors decided that tips for waiters were a necessity. To that end they added five cents to all food checks at the club.[1]

Around 1909 a new no-tip hotel opened in London, England. It was said to be so crowded that it was nearly impossible to get in. One reporter declared that its future success depended entirely on the mood and disposition of the public to discontinue the practice of tipping: "We have been led to believe that the frequent and vociferous denunciation of this practice by Englishmen is more or less insincere." When American Frank Finnegan traveled to London a few years later, a British friend took him to the latest rage in the city, tipless tea rooms. As they left, a skeptical Finnegan pointed to a locked box with a slot near the cashier's desk with "Depot Fund" written on it. Explained the friend, "Anyone who feels so inclined may drop a few coppers in there for the waitresses. It's divided every week, you see. It's not at all obligatory or even customary." By then

Finnegan had ceased to listen, believing "the national observance of the Open Hand was incurable."[2]

By 1913 there were some 500 eating places in London that had a "No Gratuities" policy, but still only one first-class hotel with a similar policy. That hotel was still successful, with reservations required up to one month in advance. It was the only London hotel which was full year-round. Any employee caught accepting a tip was instantly fired. Reportedly the staff was adequately paid. Management conceded that enforcing the no-tip rule was not easy and had resulted in the dismissal of a "considerable number of employees." They also admitted some difficulty in securing staff at first.

Tipless tea rooms (equivalent to U.S. lunch counters or family-style restaurants) were mostly found in three chains, with two chains having 175 outlets each, while the third had about 75 units. Menu cards and doors all had signs saying "No Gratuities." All the servers were female, and typically received a wage of $1.50 per week along with a 2½ percent commission on their billings, which added one to three dollars each week to their pay. That total wage was said to compare favorably with wages paid in similar London employment. However, the no-tip policy in London restaurants was then "confined to moderately priced establishments. The fashionable and expensive places, where men waiters are generally employed, retain the tip."[3]

American hotels experimented briefly and unsuccessfully with no-tip policies. Chicago's Parker House raised the wages of its waiters in 1905, and informed them that henceforth all their "petty graft" would go to the house. Not content with "full wages," 13 porters went on strike immediately, with their leader declaring that the men made more money under the old system. How much of a raise those employees eventually got went unreported. New York City's Hotel Breslin manager D.B. Mulligan had been on a crusade against tipping for several years, and had fired several hat check girls in succession for accepting them. He finally declared that it was impossible to abolish tips, not because he couldn't find employees who would not take them, but "because most people insisted on giving a tip to the girls, and some of them would become positively indignant when the gratuity was refused." Not wishing to offend customers, he discarded that idea convinced any method of dealing with tips had to be indirect. "I was convinced that it would be useless to forbid employees to accept tips, as many guests would insist on giving them, and a hotel manager could not presume to dictate to his patrons as to what they did with their money," explained Milligan. After concluding that tips averaged 10 percent, in 1913 he decided to give all patrons a 10 percent discount on meal checks. Notice of that 10 percent reduction was printed in red on top of every bill. Just how Mulligan thought this idea solved the tipping problem was unstated.[4]

In 1913, a *Harper's Magazine* editorial stated there was then one tipless hotel in the United States. However, the article refused to name the place due to worries that it would be flooded with business. That hotel paid its staff $60 per month, much higher than the $30 per month employees received in places that allowed tips. The *Harper's* editor thought the idea was worth emulating

> because it was in the hotels that the plague of tipping first broke out on our shores, and they have a peculiar duty to the public in being the first to attempt its cure. It is possible, of course, that the disease has now gone so far and so deep that it cannot be wholly extirpated, but we should like to have the experiment generally tried in the hope of partial amelioration.[5]

Vincent Martire opened a no-tip barber shop in New York City in 1907. He paid his barbers $17 a week with a 25 percent commission on all weekly billings over $32, which meant that a barber could make $23 a week when business was good. A barber working in a shop allowing tips drew an average salary of $12 to $13 a week. According to Martire, in those shops a shave was usually 15 cents plus a ten-cent tip and a haircut was 35 cents with a ten-cent or fifteen-cent tip; in his shop a shave was 20 cents and a haircut 35 cents. Despite Martire's calculation that a customer could save 20 to 40 percent at his tipless shop, the idea did not catch on. One year after opening, Martire dropped the ban on tips. Also dropped was the salary of barbers — to $12 a week. But, said Martire, "they are happy. The manicure girls have had their salaries scaled down but they are radiant. The brush boys are chipper, and the chiropodist will soon outsmile any of us."[6]

Around 1910 International Barbers' Union general organizer J.C. Shanley announced that a movement was underway for "tipless barbers." It was also very unsuccessful.[7]

A movement to replace tipping with a service charge was under way in the early years of the twentieth century, particularly in Europe. During a 1908 hotelkeepers convention in Rome, International Association of Hotelkeepers president Hoyer of Cologne reviewed the futile efforts made in Germany to stamp out gratuities. "It can't be eliminated, but let us try to regulate it," Hoyer told the delegates. At his suggestion the convention adopted a resolution whereby when the traveler desired it, the hotelkeeper might add a surcharge, 10 to 15 percent depending on the size of the bill. That money was to be distributed by the hotelkeeper to the employees.[8]

One American commentator dismissed this proposal as preposterous because "the very point of the tip is that it operates to transfer the 'condition of servitude,' and to convert, for the period covered by the tip, the permanent servant of the landlord into the temporary servant of the 'paying guest.'" Elaborating further, he explained that the waiter had to be prepared to go against the interest of his permanent employer in the interests of his temporary employer as, for example, in recommending something that his principal employer did not wish to sell if it was in the interest of his temporary employer to buy. Thus, of the fixed service charge, the customer "is not in the least likely to acquiesce in the ridiculous proposal that he shall hand over to a heartless and possibly corporate and incorporeal landlord the 'gratuity' for which he is thus not to receive even gratitude. That would be to deprive tipping of all its charm and poetry of personal relations."[9]

The following year, 1909, the Berlin, Germany, waiters' association put forward their own proposal to institute a fixed service charge of 10 to 12 percent on bills in lieu of tipping, because "everyone agrees that the tipping system is carried to oppressive lengths, either through the unwillingness of a part of the public to appear unaristocratic or through the shrinking of the other half from getting into unpleasant controversies with servants over a mark or two."[10]

Well-known German Silesian spa owner Bad Saizbrunn abolished tips to waiters and other employees in 1912, substituting a fixed service charge of 10 to 15 percent added to the bills and distributed among the employees. Any employee found accepting a tip was dismissed.[11]

Several Geneva, Switzerland, hotels conducted a similar experiment in 1912 when they replaced tipping by adding 10 percent to all bills. For unstated reasons, that attempt failed completely. Some of the same hotels tried again in the spring of 1913 with a slightly different plan, whereby 5 percent was added to bills as a service charge, but guests were still allowed (and expected) to tip for extraordinary services. Given the amount of confusion generated by that system, it was not surprising when it failed completely in a matter of months.[12]

There seem to have been fewer experiments with service charges instead of tips in America. One was tried at a New York restaurant in 1907, wherein the owner arranged a scale of charges to be added to the bill, 10 cents for one person, 25 cents for two, 40 cents for three, 50 cents for 4, and so on. It didn't work, according to one account, because of the motive behind the tipping system, whereby "the customer wishes to be the sole master of the amount of the tip conferred ... it is his prerogative, and he will never relinquish it."[13]

Organized drives to eliminate tipping were under way by 1904.

Formed that year in Georgia was the Anti-Tipping Society of America, whose members were required to pledge not to give a tip to anyone for 12 months, "and to meet possible resultant embarrassment each member is supplied with membership cards which he hands over to such neighbors as may be about him and endeavors to enlist them in the organization." Commercial travelers and businessmen were the principal members of this group, which claimed to have a membership of 100,000 by 1905. After this point, it was not heard from again. Traveling salesmen in Rochester, New York, announced in 1906 that they would band together to end the practice of tipping in hotels. Calling it a constant drain on their resources, the men expressed confidence that their society would be strong enough to reduce or eliminate the necessity of tipping. A second goal sought was to secure respectful attention from hotel employees.[14]

From his Syracuse, New York, headquarters, Commercial Travelers' National League (CTNL) president P.E. Dowe announced in November 1911 a campaign against tips. According to him, travelers spent $325 million yearly on hotel charges, with $50 million of that amount going in tips to hotel employees. In a letter mailed to various associations of hotel owners, Dowe issued a "final call" to the owners to abolish tipping:

> You can see that we mean business, but in consideration of the self-evident fact that your members have failed properly to gauge the sentiment against tipping we will withhold definite action a reasonable time, and if there are no signs that the hotel proprietors propose to put their help upon a self-respecting basis making them wage-earners instead of beggars for gratuities, no power on earth can prevent our carrying out our programme of reprisal.

That proposed action consisted of the CTNL threatening to compile a list of rooms and apartments for travelers in every city that did not have a tipless hotel. One editorial writer felt a simpler solution would be for each commercial traveler to raise his right hand in the presence of as many of his peers as possible and "solemnly promise himself that never, never, never will he pay another tip." [15]

At the start of 1912, Dowe called upon all CTNL members to begin the new year by not tipping. Calling hotel-owner greed the cause of the tipping system and claiming that profits from food and liquor in first-class hotels and restaurants ranged from 200 percent to 300 percent and more, Dowe fumed "Tipping has increased not only the cost of city living, but of traveling and of Bohemian life everywhere."[16]

Just a few months later CTNL vice president W.E. Adams stated that his group was thinking of building a series of no-tip hotels. If one in ten of the 450,000 commercial travelers bought 10 shares at ten dollars each, that income of $4.5 million would build 20 hotels at $200,000 each. Those hotels would be placed in 20 states to be patronized by league members and anybody else who favored a no-tip policy. "Our tips annually would be more than sufficient to finance our proposition," concluded Adams. However, it didn't happen. Two years later the CTNL had apparently abandoned any hope that its members could themselves eliminate tipping. Adams was then suggesting that the proper solution was to pass a national law ratified by the states prohibiting tipping and making it an imprisonable offense for both the giver and receiver. Said Adams, "To my mind tipping should be classified in the eyes of the law as bribery." Apparently few inroads were made, and nothing more was heard from the CTNL.[17]

Another group that announced it would fight for the elimination of tips was the Columbus, Ohio-based United Commercial Travelers of America, which announced at its 1913 annual meeting that it would press the legislatures of nearly every state to prohibit tipping. There was also the Society for the Prevention of Useless Giving, which was once addressed by New York State District Attorney Whitman, who observed,

> It is a brave thing, a womanly thing and a courteous thing for you to band together to combat an evil. And I hope you will stand pat. We are growing to tolerate a kind of petty grafting that is not right, that is un–American.... If he honestly earns the money he should have it as an earning, not as a gratuity. It is this giving of gratuities that is unlike us, it is a custom copied from a foreign country where conditions are different from ours.[18]

More general groups also agitated against the custom. At their second international conference in 1913, the Consumers' Leagues adopted a resolution condemning the tipping system and proposing means of abolishing it. Some of the planks in the resolution called for "the legal prohibition of tipping," "individual refusal to give a tip," "the legal regulation of a tipping law," and "organization of employees" against the custom.[19]

William Scott published *The Itching Palm* in 1916, a polemic against the practice. He felt the solution to the problem was the formation of a national organization, to be called the American Anti-Tipping Association, embracing both the givers and receivers of tips opposed to the practice. If this proposed organization had the same strength behind it as the temperance and suffrage movements of the day, Scott was confident that tipping would be quickly vanquished. War was to be waged on a custom, not on persons. Fair wages would have to prevail, to quell resentment of the tip takers and because "no one has a desire to deprive a waiter of an adequate compensation, but no one has a desire to give him an excessive compensation through gratuities." Another goal of his proposed group was the promotion of legislation that would involve taking up "specific instances of neglect of patrons who did not give tips." Explaining further, Scott said that if a member were neglected or insulted in a hotel after failing to tip, the organization would, after investigating, assume the task of correcting the situation though legal action, with the group enforcing the right to fair and equal service in the courts. To protect all potential complainers, Scott argued, the group should be as widespread as tipping itself, with every town and city having a branch complete with an attorney to prosecute violations. If tipping seemed deep-rooted, Scott was sure it rested on insecure foundations and "will crumble before any real attack.... The average American ... has enough inherent understanding of democracy to know that the custom is wrong."[20]

Scott thought that imported European waiters would be harder to wean from the system with their greater fondness for the custom having been nurtured in the aristocratic school, but their "opposition can be handled." Most difficult to control were the givers who liked playing the role of "Gentlemen Generous," but their pride would restrain them from "buying servility from other Americans." Scott concluded that his campaign against tipping was about much more than saving money: "Its idealism aims to reach the very pinnacle of republican society — the destiny toward which 1776 started us."[21]

None of these initiatives made so much as a small dent in the custom. As the groups and their supporters realized this fact, they began to demand that the government take some sort of action. Governments listened. Driven by agitation and lobbying by businessmen and their traveling agents, regional governments in many jurisdictions did indeed try to abolish tipping.

If workers were to abolish tipping from the bottom up then the trade union movement was key. An 1896 account argued that in the best organized industries where the laborers had the highest wages and greatest freedom, tips had disappeared. Conversely, where wages were less developed along with a sentiment of "wardship," tipping was most prevalent. Twenty years later the union was still touted as the agency to eliminate "the evil." The tip had no place where labor was recognized as honorable service:

> It is a survival of the old master and servant days when gratuities by persons to the manor born were given as a reward to servility. The tip goes always from a superior to an inferior; never from servant to master. It is not a recognition of service, for the inferior never tips the superior for the service rendered. That would be considered an insult.[22]

Generally the organized labor movement and tip recipients, as might be expected, wanted the system eradicated. Labor figures who argued to maintain the system were hard to find. One group that did was the summer resort hotel workers at the Edgemere resort in Long Island, New York, in 1915. Those workers got together to complain that tips weren't large enough or frequent enough, making it impossible for them to support themselves unless guests tipped more generously. In a written appeal given to resort guests, female employees stated,

> To the Guests of Edgemere, L.I., at a meeting held of the waitresses it was suggested that the guests be more liberal in their tips, as the girls complain they cannot support themselves and give good service, pay for daily laundry bills, and make a good appearance with a small salary. Trusting the guests of Edgemere, L.I., will be pleased to help the waitresses to live, and thanking the guests in advance, we are, sincerely, THE WAITRESSES OF EDGEMERE.[23]

Workers regularly threatened to strike, and sometimes actually did so, to protest the tipping system. Porters (today called bellboys) at most first-class hotels in New York City went on strike in 1908 to demand that all tips go to the person to whom they were given. At most hotels, all tips went to the head porter with the hotel management supporting the arrangement. The Hotel Porters' Association was organized for that fight. Said one porter, "What we kick at is being obliged to beg in a gentlemanly way for the benefit of another man's pocket." The strike brought to light the fact that those hotels had all the baggage of their patrons handled without any expense to them. In each hotel the baggage privilege was contracted to a man with an assistant, a few messengers, anywhere from six to 30 porters, and three or four wagons. The head porters were said to have gotten rich; the porters themselves received $25 per month in wages from the head porter, along with their meals at the hotel. In return, they worked 12 hours a day. The striking porters demanded that their wages remain the same and they be allowed to keep their tips. That meant the hotel would have to hire the head porter and his assistant on salaries and buy the wagons. Hotel owners refused to talk about the situation, sparking the strike. When asked how the head porter knew the amount a guest tipped, a spokesman for the porters commented:

> The minute a guest comes to a hotel the head porter sizes him up as to what kind of a tip proposition he is…. There are a whole lot of regulars that use the hotels who have an established tip reputation. There are the quarter men, the half-dollar fellers, and the greenbackers. When a porter does a job for any of these he's got to shell out to the head porter accordingly.

There were two cardinal sins that would cause a head porter to fire someone on the spot. One was to hold back any part of a tip; the second, and worse, offense was to hand over a tip in the presence of a guest. Head porters wanted guests to believe the bag-toting porters got the tips. Reportedly, several first-class hotels yielded to the striking porters' demands within a few hours.[24]

Several New York locals of the Hotel and Restaurant Employees International Alliance announced that a fight against the custom would be initiated May 1, 1909. Members of the local groups were instructed not to accept tips after that day in support of a demand for a minimum wage of $2.50 a day for waiters with no tipping allowed. It was a demand designed to make the waiters independent of tips. Leaders of the action hoped the members would follow instructions; if the campaign succeeded, it was planned to extend it to other areas. This campaign apparently failed, and nothing more was heard of it.[25]

A few years later, Boston waiters and bellboys were said to be making a concerted attempt to do way with tipping. Said one spokesman, "We think that we will be willing to take our chances with a fair wage and no tips.... I think that it's about time the hotel men were forced to pay their employees, or certain employees at least, better wages."[26]

Toward the end of 1911, the International Hotel Workers' Union was formed in New York to organize bellboys, cooks, waiters, helpers, and so on. They had a long list of grievances, including opposition to the tipping system. The union published a circular which set forth the union's demands under nine sections — the fourth demand was: "Higher wages and no necessity of depending on tips." Early in 1912, a reporter saw the circular for a second time; it was the same with one exception: demand four read "Higher wages" period. When the reporter asked union business representative J. Elster about the change, Elster looked sheepish, and quickly changed the subject. As it was the union's position on tips that had caught the public's attention more than any other demand, the reporter pressed on. "We do not want to talk about the tipping evil now," said Elster, "there has been too much said about that already." The journalist suggested that when the group announced it wanted higher wages and no tips, all that happened was that tips dropped off. Elster admitted "Yes, that was it, there was too much talking about the tip." Union executives (and brothers) president Paul Vehling and secretary Joseph Vehling had been ousted from the labor union by its members due to a number of contentious issues, "one of the chief ones was that they had caused no end of trouble by emphasizing the union's dislike of the tip." Even before their ouster, the union was backpedaling on tips. During a meeting on January 5, 1912, an organizer said,

If the wealthy classes were to stop tipping before we get a good living wage established by means of organization, it would be the end of us. After the wage is established we don't care. The tip makes of you a malicious, envious, hateful creature, but we cannot do away with it just yet.[27]

Less than two years later, officers of that union were helping to circulate petitions calling on the government to pass a no-tipping law, asserting that they wanted wages and not tips. They made it clear that such a law would make it necessary for employers to pay higher wages. Edward Blochlinger, chief organizer of the union, said his group was cooperating with both the Commercial Travelers' League and the Amalgamated Hotel Workers' Union of Great Britain in a movement to abolish tipping. Speaking of one New York restaurant that paid its waiters no wages at all, Blochlinger remarked, "The management cheerfully threw on its guests the burden of making its waiters' work remunerative."[28]

During two separate meetings of groups of hotel owners, the American Hotel Protective Association and the Hotel Men's Mutual Benefit Association of the United States and Canada, the question of tipping was raised. In both meetings a tactful decision was reached with a consensus determining the question could be solved best by hotel patrons. Hotel owners declined to take any action, or any stand on the issue.[29]

At the close of World War I, Berlin waiters threatened to strike unless they received wages high enough to subsist on without tips. They wanted to see a notice posted in restaurants reading, "Waiters in this establishment receive decent wages and do not rely on tips." Asked if they would really refuse to accept tips if their demands were met, a reporter remarked that very few waiters "remained firm." One server said, "If guests leave a coin on the table or under their plate, we shall certainly not run after them to return it, nor shall we throw it away."[30]

Sometimes labor turmoil was reported as stemming from apparently opposite reasons. New York waiter Honus Muller refused a one-dollar tip offered by a customer one evening after a meal. Muller explained he never took tips, that the company paid him well. Several days after, Waiters' Union representative M.J. Murphy paid a call on Muller at home to find out why he had refused a tip. Upon hearing the reason, Murphy reportedly blustered: "Not take a tip! Don't you know you'll break up the waiters' business and take bread from the mouths of children? If you are not discharged at once, I'll call a strike of every waiter in the blooming place."[31]

Movie ushers at the Capitol Theatre in New York City held a brief strike in 1919, after management refused to withdraw its advice to patrons to not tip them. Shortly after the film started, the ushers began to picket the inside of the cinema. When asked to leave they refused, which led to management calling the police, who arrested one of the strikers, Herman Inberg, on a charge of disorderly conduct. Theater management had called the strikers' attention to the fact that before accepting their jobs they had signed agreements that they would abide by a no-tip policy. The ushers countered they had changed their minds.[32]

High union officials were usually hostile to the custom of tipping. Journeymen Barbers' International Union of America secretary L.T. Van Fleet said, in advocating its abolition,

> I detest this tipping custom; it is base, wrong, unjust, and degrading, and the barber who willingly accepts tips simply does so by bowing in humble supplication to receive them, because he has done or intended to do work for which he cannot demand a recompense ... besides it is more manly to earn your living than to receive charity or bribes.

Many barbers opposed Van Fleet's position as they felt refusing to accept tips would result in a permanent reduction in income.[33]

American Federation of Labor president Samuel Gompers also opposed the practice. He once wrote, "While, of course, I have followed the usual custom of giving tips, yet I have maintained the principle of tipping to be unwise and that it tends to lessen the self-respect of a man who accepts a tip." While touring Europe, Gompers asked people about tipping. One reply he got was, "The system is detestable to every man and woman of the serving class possessing the least degree of self-respect. It is demoralizing to all who either give or receive tips. The real beneficiaries of the system are the employers." Gompers was not alone in wanting to see an end to the system; virtually all waiters also wanted the system eliminated "except for a small minority who in their moral make-up resemble pirates."[34]

Government involvement in tipping began in the early 1900s. It was an ambivalent involvement, with some departments recognizing the practice officially while other branches tried to formally abolish the custom. The first to recognize tipping at the government level in America seems to have been the United States Navy, which in 1907 established a schedule of allowances of tips permitted by its commissioned officers and enlisted men when they were traveling at home and abroad under orders. One media commentator lamented that move was setting a precedent:

> Tips in the old days were unheard of. They were regarded as a dispensation of largess which must be personal and not in any sense official. This is now changed. The tip is formally implanted, with whatever harm it may do to that part of the social fabric which is submitted to the gratuity.

The scale established allowed a total of 50 cents per day in United

States hotels, or $2.50 per week if it was the same hotel. Trips on trains had a scale of 50 cents per day, 25 cents for trips lasting less than five hours. For travel outside the United States, hotel tips were allowed to 75 cents per day, $3.50 per week for the same hotel. On ships, tips of $1.50 per day were permitted for trips of six days or less, a total of $10 for seven to ten day trips, with $1 per day for trips over ten days.[35]

Regulations issued by the federal Treasury Department in 1912 established a tipping allowance for hotel servants, railway porters, and steamship stewards covering traveling expenses of its officers and employees. Limits included 50 cents per day to waiters, 25 cents to a railway porter. Grumbled the *New York Times*, "Tipping gets to be more of a nuisance yearly. We may hope that it will become unbearable some day, and then it will be abolished by some means as yet unknown."[36]

Yet a year later, when United States military attaché at Rome, Italy, J.F. Reynolds, tried to claim tipping expenditures, his claim was disallowed. For each of three quarterly accounts Reynolds claimed a total of $1.93 for tips to the doorkeeper at the United States Embassy in Rome. Treasury held that gratuities to a doorkeeper were not authorized by law.[37]

Around the beginning of World War I, sentiment against tipping was rising, with the result that various state and city governments passed or tried to pass laws prohibiting the practice. As early as 1910, restaurant waiters in Washington, D.C., all of whom were black, were by the authority of Congress, to be fined if they accepted tips. Those who offered gratuities faced no penalties. A New Jersey politician unsuccessfully tried to introduce a law which would not prohibit the custom, but simply limit the size of tips. His proposal was reviled as impracticable and lacking in courage by one reporter, who commented that no laws were needed because

> by the exercise of a little moral courage in ignoring the scorn of those whom he has the best of right to consider his inferiors he can instantly and forever free himself from the tip hunter's tyranny, and though he would have some inconveniences to suffer as a result of his revolt, these would disappear as soon as all, or even a majority of those who share his dislike for tipping acquired the courage to imitate his example.[38]

That legislation was pushed forward by a Paterson, New Jersey, restaurant owner who felt tipping had advanced to the point where poor people were sometimes insulted because of their small tips. Under that proposal severe penalties were to be levied on people who tipped more than 20 cents for a meal, 5 cents for a shave, 10 cents for liquor and 5 cents for messenger and bellboy service. Under no circumstances was a tip to exceed 25 cents. Violators could be sentenced to two months in the workhouse or a

$20 fine for a first offense, escalating to six months or $50 for a repeat offense.[39]

The St. Louis city council passed a measure in 1913 making it a misdemeanor to give or receive a tip in a hotel or restaurant, with fines ranging from ten dollars to $50 for an offense. Half of that fine was to go to the informant who reported the violation of the ordinance. Federally, Senator Works introduced a bill to prohibit tips to porters and waiters on trains and steamboats engaged in interstate commerce. At the same time, the bill made it unlawful for an employer to pay such low wages that tips were necessary for employees to receive adequate compensation. That bill failed.[40]

Washington was the first state to pass an antitipping law (see Appendix 2). Its 1909 statute provided that "every employee of a public house or public-service corporation who shall solicit or receive any gratuity from any guest shall be guilty of a misdemeanor." Similar, or more comprehensive, measures were passed by Mississippi in 1912 and Arkansas in 1913. The latter bill punished only tip receivers and employers who permitted it, but not tip givers. One year later, New York State assemblyman William T. Simpson introduced a bill making the giving or receiving of tips a misdemeanor with the penalty of a fine or up to a year in jail. Tips were prohibited in hotels, inns, restaurants, saloons, barber shops, bootblack stands, dance halls, bath houses, public conveyances, common carriers on water or land, theaters, or other places of public resort or amusements. Also required was that a copy of the antitipping law be posted in a conspicuous place on the premises. Simpson's bill was not passed.[41]

Six state legislatures considered antitipping bills in their 1915 sessions with measures passed in Iowa, South Carolina, and Tennessee and defeats registered in Wisconsin, Illinois, and Nebraska. Illinois did pass a 1915 law aimed at the tip trust, which prohibited hotels and others from selling tipping privileges to concession holders. Wisconsin's governor vetoed his state's proposal on the grounds that it curtailed personal liberty. When the Wisconsin measure was making its way through the legislature, the *New York Times* commented that while the custom was "reprehensible" it "cannot be controlled by law." The acceptance of tips, gifts bestowed in recognition of service legally paid for, thought the paper, "is not compatible with the idea of upright manhood and citizenship." Iowa's law was particularly onerous in that sanctions were applied only to tip takers who were employees, while a business owner was free to accept gratuities. Georgia passed a bill in 1918 which applied only to "tips" received for the purpose, or with the intent, of influencing the action of employees in relation to their employer's business — that is, a commercial bribe. In that era, tips and commercial bribes ("payola" in the music industry) were often considered to be one and the same, which gave an idea of the emotional reaction to tipping. Technically, a tip is given *after* a service is rendered, while a commercial bribe is given *beforehand* to ensure that the service is indeed delivered.[42]

In Iowa, a barber by the name of Dunahoo was arrested, charged, and convicted after a customer gave him a 25 cent tip after a haircut. The shop contained two chairs, one staffed by Dunahoo, the other by shop owner Murphy. Had the customer chosen Murphy and tipped him it would have been legal since Murphy was a proprietor, not an employee. Dunahoo's arrangement with Murphy was that he was to receive a salary of $15 a week plus 60 percent of his billings above that amount, plus tips. When the case went to the Iowa Supreme Court, it turned on the discriminatory nature of the bill which, contrary to the United States and Iowa constitutions, denied equal protection under its laws to all citizens — separate classes were established. Dunahoo's conviction was reversed by a 4-2 margin. The majority decision said, in part, "Tipping may be an evil, but this does not justify discrimination between classes in order to put it down. In so far as the public is concerned, the evil of tipping the employer is quite as obnoxious to good morals as though it were done to the employee."[43]

By the end of the 1910s, the fever to pass antitipping laws had waned considerably. Washington's law was repealed in 1913, largely because it was ignored by all sides. Iowa's bill was declared unconstitutional in 1919 by the state Supreme Court on the ground that it was discriminatory. The remaining state acts were repealed as follows: South Carolina in 1922, Tennessee and Arkansas in 1925, and Mississippi in 1926. Although antitipping sentiment was still strong in the 1920s, those acts were repealed partly due to the fall of the Iowa measure, and partly due to the persistence of the custom, which led many to believe it was futile to try to abolish the practice. Also at work was "a certain amount of pressure brought to bear by employers in the service industries in which tipping is prevalent." Tipping, of course, kept their wage bills down. Like it or not, tipping in the 1920s was becoming an institution.[44]

William Scott's virulent antitipping book commented on the poor results of state antitipping bills. Writing before most of the laws were repealed, he tried to put a hopeful face on the situation by calling opposition to the custom "unorganized, undisciplined and inarticulate." That conclusion was incorrect, as it was organized business travelers who had banded together to create pressure that led to the laws being enacted. Even Scott admitted that Tennessee adopted its law in part due to the lobbying of traveling salesmen in that state.

Explaining why people ignored those laws, Scott thought the average citizen "feels more afraid of violating the custom than of violating the law," adding that the average waiter could do many things to annoy a non-tipper yet leave the patron with nothing to present to management in the form of a concrete complaint. What the antitipping movement needed was a spokesman and leader. If that leader stepped forth Scott predicted that the opposition "will spring into effective cooperation." To be effective, a law would have to specifically define the right of a patron to have food served or use a hotel room, with only one charge which was to be paid exclusively to the proprietor. That, said Scott, would strike an effective blow at "the universal heart of Flunkyism."[45]

Although many media accounts deplored tipping, the media generally defended the custom often rationalizing to the point where they declared that tip receivers liked the custom. An editorial in an 1886 issue of the English magazine the *Spectator* commented that it would be better if tip recipients could be paid the full value of their work and not partly paid by "more or less capricious gratuities." However, that was not practical because any wage increase would come directly from the poor in the form of higher postal rates and higher tax rates to pay for costlier rail travel, while under the tip system "the gratuities fall wholly on the well-to-do." Forbidding tips would, in any case, be difficult because both givers and receivers

> prefer it.... The servants prefer it because they feel that a dubious element in their wages which they cannot count upon with any certainty beforehand adds a definite interest to their life, and also makes them really more willing to exert themselves.

Next, the editor reversed himself by declaring that the operation of the laws of competition made it probable that the wage rate would not be raised at all, tips or no tips, because so many poor were willing to work for low wages. He concluded that

> the notion of abolishing this feeling of partial dependence and partial patronage simply by abolishing the actions by which the good will of the richer for the poorer classes is expressed, is altogether a false one. The only effect of suddenly stopping this system of gratitude would be that you would diminish the cordiality of feeling between different classes, without increasing the moral equality.[46]

Almost 20 years later, another editorial stated the system was ineradicable because people liked to tip. As a result, hotel owners took that into account when they decided on wage levels. In fact those owners made their employees "into partners, it is a system of profit-sharing.... The desire to tip servants ... is in a certain form the instinctive settlement of the question of old-age pensions."[47]

A similar argument was advanced by North American journalist Albert Caiman. He was a little more honest in saying that travelers disliked tipping, but continued to spin fiction by insisting that waiters liked the custom. Arguing that hotels, restaurants, and the like couldn't pay higher wages and eliminate tips because competition would undercut them, Caiman asserted the diner was a joint employer of both the restaurant owner and the waiter. The problem was that while the diner bought independently from the waiter, there was no set price agreement with the diner having the option of leaving no tip. Still, this was all to the good for the patron because "a customer can hardly fail to notice the difference in the attitude toward himself of a tipless clerk and a tip-earning waiter." Because of the practice, the traveler could command a much more attentive and courteous service than he would otherwise receive. Caiman opposed the fixed service charge added to a bill since it "would kill a vital part of the system ... a bad waiter would get as much as a good." It would have the negative result of the waiter becoming "a salaried servant instead of an independent proprietor selling his labor to you on the common ground of another man's hotel."[48]

Journalist Robert Sloss presented the product of a supposed interview with a waiter named Joseph in the pages of *Harper's Weekly* in 1908. Joseph was quoted as saying that the tip system was rough on the recipients but that "suppose every waiter here got a regular salary with no chance for extras. Do you suppose he'd be jumping hurdles for a lot of fussy people? ... No, sir." Joseph was also presented as claiming he could make more money from waiting tables than from any other occupation. Sloss strongly favored the custom.[49]

During World War I, America's *Outlook* magazine gave tipping an unqualified endorsement in an editorial declaring, "Most tip-giving in this country is generally a payment for personal services rendered, and as such it is to be defended both on ethical and economic grounds."[50]

Far less frequently did the media come out *against* tipping. Often they decried supposed results of tipping, such as making recipients servile, without actually condemning the custom itself. The *New York Times* once editorialized that "American workingmen should not accept gratuities. They have their citizenship, their independence, and every opportunity to rise in the world. Many a millionaire has been a railroad workman."[51]

One of the more vocal opponents was Edward Bok, publisher of the *Ladies Home Journal*. In the pages of his magazine he lashed out at tipping and its spreading influence. Bok felt the solution lay in hotel and café owners paying higher wages and absolutely forbidding tipping. However, giving no reason, he declared that the plan would never be put into effect. Given that prospect Bok opted for some sort of regulation to establish a standard tip of 10 percent: "Let us confine the nuisance, too, to public places ... if, in public, the practice has already gone too far to permit of its abolishment, then let us accept it. But let us, at least, bring it within some sort of recognized limit."[52]

Psychological aspects of tipping were also rarely mentioned. One commentator explained that when he tipped he felt a "glow of vanity when I bestow the gratuity and I avoid shame and confusion of face." When another person offered the opinion that tipping came from generous, open-hearted, noble-minded people, one cynic scoffed that, on the contrary, the tip was "a bribe, extorted under a tacit threat of inattention and impoliteness, and given from a fear, conscious or unconscious, of annoyance or delay ... it is a lack of self-respect that takes a tip, lack of moral courage that gives it."[53]

A waiter contended that a tipper was the most pleasant to serve and the best customer in every way with no thought of lowering the dignity of the server, while the nontippers "leave the table poorly satisfied with themselves, as is generally disclosed in their manner." To that thought the *New York Times* sneered that it was "so naive and therefore so amusing" it partly explained tip giving as something done for the sake of getting such approval as the waiter bestowed upon his benefactors. That waiter thought they were as happy as they made him. "Self-deception could hardly go further."[54]

A 1909 issue of *Scribner's Magazine* saw the practice in terms of conditioning in that the tip could and should be an instrument of social and moral discipline: "The withholding or diminution of it should be a punishment, as the bestowal or enlargement of it a reward."[55]

Much more frequently mentioned were the moral and ethical considerations of the tipping system, what it supposedly did to the recipient, and less frequently, what it did to the tip giver. For many, the lack of morality lay mostly with the tip receivers. One 1891 account condemned tip receivers as "arrant extortioners, whose bowings and scrapings are odious in our eyes." A few years later, another account described tips as "onerous to those who give them and humiliating to those who receive them." Calling the system an evil that should be abolished *Lippincott's Magazine* called tips "bribes, extortion, robbery, blackmail, and what-not." According to a 1911 issue of *Travel*, tipping was rapidly converting the army of serving people into "cringing mendicants or shameless bandits."[56]

A common sentiment was the idea that a moral obligation was incurred. If, for example, a porter grabbed a bag, "most men find it very difficult to realize that he is not placing them under a certain obligation, which they ought in fairness to acknowledge by means of a small fee." On the other hand, a lack of moral courage in the givers was sometimes seen as the main problem. Although a Paris theater plainly stated on its program that any attendant accepting a tip was subject to instant dismissal, a reporter noted that "not a single occupant of the stalls omitted to produce the customary franc." The conclusion was that tipping would not stop until the givers "divested themselves of the seemingly incurable habit of summoning sufficient moral courage to give an icy glance to the too insistently supplicating attendants."[57]

For some observers, the custom had negative effects on both givers and receivers, with one viewing the tip as a "vestige of feudalism." An American citizen was "degraded" by "offering it only slightly less than he would be degraded by accepting it, that it is incompatible with the institution of our 'fierce' democracy." An editorial in *Harper's Magazine* called tipping a "curse" because the giver practiced "matching our middle-class grudge with that lower-class greed.... Tipping, which is the gross and offensive caricature of mercy, inverts the effect of the heavenly attribute which it mocks; it curses him that gives and him that takes, but most it curses him that takes." No man ever received a tip without a loss of self-respect and a sense of shame. A recipient had to know the tipper believed himself robbed and plundered in his tip, therefore loathing the receiver. An English writer called heavy tips the "pauperization of manners," because men who habitually expected tips did not say "Thank you.... But if heavy tips are the ruin of good manners in the receiver, they are frequently a sign of bad breeding in the giver."[58]

One of the stranger supposed effects of tipping came from French physician Dr. Legrain, who ran an asylum for inebriates. He argued that receiving tips was one cause of alcoholism because an undue proportion of his patients were tip recipients such as waiters, valets and porters.[59]

More philosophical was H.C. Bierwirth, who thought tips were first prompted by "egotism and selfishness." People who thought too much about themselves, too little about their neighbors, and had enough money to indulge their selfishness became accustomed in some way to giving out tips. Others had to follow suit unless they wished to run the risk of being neglected. The strongest objection to tipping for Bierwirth was the effect it had on the tip receiver, causing his character all too often to become a "strange mixture of impudence and servility.... Whoever practices bribery and encourages begging must be prepared for what inevitably follows in the wake of those evils." It generated a loss of self-respect among the tipped.[60]

William Scott saw the system as possibly the destroyer of American democracy. Those estimated five million employees who derived all or part of their income from tips had a "moral malady denominated the Itching Palm." It was a modern form of "flunkyism"—defined as a willingness to be servile for a consideration. It was "democracy's deadly foe." Morally the custom was wrong, as it engendered a grafting spirit in recipients, created class distinctions in a republic and caused a loss of self-respect without which people were just "worthless dregs in the crucible of democracy." While Scott felt it might be okay for self-respect to be limited to the governing classes in a monarchy, it would not do here since "Americanism" required every citizen to possess that quality; "whatever undermines self-respect, manhood, undermines the republic." Under the idea that all men are equal some could become superior only if others grovelled in the dust; "tipping comes into a democracy to produce that relation…. It represents the root of aristocracy budding anew in the hearts of those who publicly renounced the system and all its works." Since a "gentleman" who tipped would be offended if offered a tip himself, that became a test: if a gentleman would not accept a tip was it gentlemanly to give one?[61]

To Scott, the difference was between aristocracy and democracy in that "In an aristocracy a waiter may accept a tip and be servile without violating the ideals of the system. In the American democracy to be servile is incompatible with citizenship. Every tip given in the United States is a blow at our experiment in democracy." At a somewhat lower level, Scott viewed tipping as a training school for graft, wondering if a messenger boy who thought the public owed him gratuities would develop into a man with sound morals. Would the bellboy who worked for tips grow up to be a policeman who accepted hush money from the corner barkeep? "There is a direct connection between corruption in elections and the custom of tipping. The man who lives upon tips will not see the dishonesty of selling his vote, so readily as if he discerned the immorality of gratuities."[62]

With tipping creating inequality, Scott compared that custom with slavery, stating

> the American democracy could not live in the face of a lie such as slavery presented, and it cannot live in the face of a lie such as tipping presents…. The relation of a man giving a tip and a man accepting it is as undemocratic as the relation of master and slave.

Helping to spread the practice of tipping were books on etiquette and the movies. Those books strengthened the custom since they all accepted tipping as socially acceptable. Thus, when readers turned to them they had their "Americanism poisoned at the very start." Since films and the live stage regularly featured tipping scenes they too helped spread the system. "Undoubtedly tipping is increased by moving pictures and by stage presentations. The public is made to feel that, despite the inherent wrong in the custom, it must be followed." About the only people content with the tipping system, thought Scott, were employers who profited from a no-wage or low-wage system and who disliked employees "with a degree of self-respect that makes them rebel at gratuities."[63]

Chapter 4

"Our Daily Bribe": Tipping Practices 1920-1949

"A fair tip, or one a little on the generous side, will leave a pleasant feeling and respect for you in the one who receives it. A lavish one will create a secret disrespect and add to the reputation Americans have for trying to buy their way into everything."
— Eleanor Roosevelt

During the period of 1920–1949, the tipping system remained as negatively viewed as it had been earlier. Be that as it may, attempts to ban it by law or through pressure from groups faded away to almost nothing. Hated though it was, tipping had become a pervasive part of the American social fabric; it had advanced to the status of institution. Some reactions to tipping did remain constant. One was in the media's regular attempt to portray tip receivers as wealthy; aggressive, having power over the customer, and sometimes prone to physical violence. There probably was some truth to the idea that recipients actively sought tips, because for many the wages were too low to survive on. Yet these accounts weren't entirely truthful because no business tolerated any employee who was rude, hostile, and so forth toward its customers, whether it was a tipped position or not.

A 1920 media account related that 25-year-old waitress Sophie Hodosky was in traffic court on a charge of making an illegal left turn in her $4,500 car. She explained she was able to buy such an expensive car on her wage of $12 per week because she also earned $80 per week in tips. At that time the highest paid sector of the American economy was transportation, where workers averaged $1,652 per year (retail workers averaged several hundred dollars less). Sophie claimed to make three times as much as a transportation worker, a fact unmentioned by the media. If Sophie

45

did pull in the extra $80 per week, it was more likely to have come from some type of illegal activity.[1]

The magazine *The Nation* bought the story as presented, editorializing that "one of the obvious morals that suggests itself is that the public should not give such large tips." Still, the journal admitted that there was not the slightest use in advising the American public to be intelligent in its tipping, because "if it had wished to be that, it would not have started the practice at all." Playing into the idea of tip receivers as powerful *The Nation* concluded that America had achieved "a servant class, but it is rapidly becoming, also, our ruling class."[2]

During a 1925 convention of the International Cut-Stone Contractors and Quarrymen's Association, contractor G.H. Barrett complained in a speech to the delegates that tipping had caused a shortage of stone cutting apprentices in his craft. He believed the tip giver practiced false generosity,

> actually discouraging young men from entering the trades. He will give a dollar to a bellboy for carrying a bag half of a block, five minutes work, and seriously object if a journeyman plumber charges him a dollar for an hour's work. The youth of today sees this and takes the easiest way to get the coin rather than learn a legitimate and necessary trade as his life's vocation.[3]

Another account in 1920 grumbled that penniless young men in search of an education worked as bellboys in summer hotels earning "considerably larger [sums] than they can hope to accumulate in the first years of their business life." Later that decade, an article in *American Mercury* claimed the idea that waiters were suffering menials to be "pitied and coddled by sentimental social reform was a total myth." In reality the waiter "accepts his social status without a murmur of dissent…. More, he doesn't want the public to stop insulting him by tipping him…. Tipping is too lucrative." This account did acknowledge the existence of waiters with little or no money, but declared it "does not necessarily mean that they haven't made money. It merely means that they have squandered what they made on the horses or the gals."[4]

A 1928 article in the *New York Times* told of a bankrupt financial magnate who was financially assisted by the waiter to whom he had been paying tips. The article also described a head porter of a hotel who resigned to take over the management of a hotel that he had leased for 15 years, and a headwaiter in St. Louis who went into business for himself on the strength of his tip earnings.[5]

Decades later, in 1946, *Life* magazine asserted there was one nightclub in New York where waiters reportedly took in between $100 and $200 per week in tips; the headwaiter got $300 to $600.[6]

Revenge, retaliation, and general haughtiness on the part of the tip receivers remained a popular belief. Travel writer Clara Laughlin declared in 1927 that the tipping habits of travelers in Europe were recorded on their luggage in "cabalistic chalk marks" by hotel porters. Somehow these marks identified a traveler as stingy, generous, amiable, or argumentative, with his reception at subsequent hotels being in accordance with those marks. As late as 1935 this story remained alive. James Roche, another travel writer, declared that a blue cross found on a bag was a symbol in an international code, indicating to hotel staff that the owner was a tightwad and was to be treated accordingly.[7]

Aggression by unhappy tip recipients could take many forms. An American tourist on a trip in Europe claimed she had to tip three sets of porters for handling luggage between the station and the hotel, "and getting out of a hotel is even worse." In a final fury, the traveler declared that the way American tourists were held up for tips when traveling in Europe "is quite outrageous."[8]

When a London couple returned home after a stay at a resort in the north of England, they discovered they had both forgotten to tip. To remedy that situation, money was sent immediately to the hotel. Before it arrived but after it was sent, the wife received a letter from the hotel's headwaiter, which read in part:

> Your husband left without leaving gratuities for any of the staff, which is a most disgraceful thing for a man of his standing. I feel it is my duty to forward your name to my club and association, so that every hotel in England, Ireland, Scotland and Wales will know your name and also the ungenerous way you treated the above hotel staff.[9]

In order to reduce the aggression of the tip-receiving class, several hotels came up with the idea of building "servidors" into each of their rooms. A servidor was like a narrow closet, into which a guest could put shoes and clothing for cleaning without exiting his room. Then he called a bellboy, who would remove the items by opening a narrow door in the hallway, without coming within tipping distance of the guest. When the job was finished, the bellboy would replace the items in the servidor without seeing the traveler inside the room. One purpose of the servidor was to protect hotel guests from too frequent visits from hotel employees; it was abandoned quickly as a failed experiment. One media account asserted it failed because "whenever possible the hotel employee prefers to get within tipping distance of the guest."[10]

"You are liable to open and flagrant insult not only if you do not tip at all," warned one article, "but also if you merely don't tip as lavishly as the proud modern menial thinks you should." Near the end of World War II, readers of one article were warned that when one went to a restaurant "it is a moot question exactly who is the waiter. You wait for a table. You get a table. Then you wait for the waiter. First you try being meek; then when you think you've caught the waiter's eye you venture a cajoling smile." Supposedly, this situation was due to a war-related shortage of waiters and a lack of generous tips. Here, waiters in a classy establishment were said to average $45 to $50 a week in salary and tips, while those in average restaurants totaled $35 to $40. Those figures were fairly close to the average wage paid in various industrial sectors.[11]

There were also really aggressive waiters. One was Fritz Remmele, who happened to serve patrolman Daniel Donnelly, dressed in civilian clothes, one night at New York's Adolphus restaurant. When Donnelly exited the café he left no tip. That caused Remmele to pursue him out into the street. When he caught up with the diner, Remmele asked him if he received good service. "No," replied Donnelly. One thing led to another, with the waiter becoming more vociferous to the point where Donnelly arrested Remmele on a charge of disorderly conduct. In court, Remmele complained that "I gave him six clams instead of three." Said Magistrate Louis B. Brodsky, "There should have been six clams anyway." Brodsky convicted Remmele, fining him two dollars.[12]

San Diego, California, resident Mrs. M.T. Riach took a sampan ride while on vacation near Rangoon, Burma. Giving the oarsman a small tip equivalent to a few cents caused the man to become disgruntled to the point that he asked for more. After being refused he got angry, asked again for more money, then grabbed her purse, robbed her, and threw her overboard. Mrs. Riach swam to safety.[13]

Waiters in some cases were still forced to pay for their jobs. Paris in 1925 was said to be one of the worst places for tipping with a very entrenched system where "the victim is often poorer than the man he tips." Without tying the ideas together, the point was also made that "there is a cafe on almost every street corner in Paris, yet not a waiter is paid by his employer. So too in the restaurants and the hotels. In the theatres, motion picture houses and cabarets the ushers, program-sellers and cloakroom employees receive zero francs in wages."[14]

In some of the first-class Parisian hotels and restaurants, the job of headwaiter was auctioned off to the highest bidder, with the winner holding the position until his retirement or death. The money paid to buy the post sometimes came not from the actual bidder but from financial backer who then received a share of the headwaiter's tip earnings for a set period of time. In turn, the headwaiter sold the assistant headwaiter position;

then the two sold jobs of ordinary waiters. Tips in those establishments were pooled and split; 50 percent to the headwaiter, 25 percent to the assistant head, and 25 percent to the other waiters.[15]

French tourism minister Gaton Gerard was swamped by complaints about tipping from two directions in 1930. Visitors found that on top of excessive prices, taxes, and a service charge, they were still pressured to tip. On the other side, employees were surviving, reported *Variety*, "entirely on tips, often paying for the right to work to solicit them." Gerard promised to abolish the latter practice. Six years later nothing had changed except that strikes by hotel and restaurant workers had broken out over the wages/tip system, called in one account a collaboration between employers and employees to "rob the public." In restaurants along the Champs Élysées, waiters paid ten to 12 francs a day for the privilege of working. One of those restaurants receives 250,000 francs per year from its employees. With the continuing economic depression of the 1930s, waiters found it more and more difficult to recover these costs. French premier Leon Blum tried to ease the situation with a bill to prohibit employers from charging employees for the privilege of working or to receive any part of what the customers gave them in tips. Employees were assured of a minimum wage under the bill but were forbidden to accept tips. That bill failed to pass.[16]

Buying jobs also took place in America. Reportedly, waitresses employed at the Alice Foote McDougall Coffee Shop in New York's Grand Central Station received no wages, paying management ten dollars per week for the privilege of working there. The manager claimed to have the names of 25 women on a waiting list for these jobs. These revelations came out in a court action launched by Mary Baker, who had worked there from 1927 until the end of April 1928. Baker sued to get her money back. Attorney for the five-outlet restaurant chain, Jacob Cotton, testified that the waitress jobs had been sold since the beginning of 1928. Prior to that time, workers received a salary of $1 per day. Baker stated that tips ran from about five dollars to eight dollars per day though chain executive Allan McDougall claimed that tips ran as high as $15 per day. He added that only the Grand Central outlet charged waitresses for their job, that it had only three waitresses employed there, and

> in this restaurant, unlike the other four, the waitresses have no work to do in addition to waiting on the diners. In our other restaurants the waitresses have other duties, such as polishing, cleaning, etc. These girls are paid a flat weekly salary and are permitted to keep the tips they receive.

According to McDougall, the idea that Grand Central waitresses got such high tips while having no other duties caused dissatisfaction at the other four units, which motivated the chain to charge them the ten dollar fee. "This money is put into a special fund and distributed in the form of bonuses to the other waitresses," insisted the executive. "This action resulted in equalizing to some extent the earnings of the other girls and the removal of the chief cause of the discontent among our employees." The suit was dismissed by the magistrate on the ground it was not within his jurisdiction.[17]

Several years later, in 1935, it was reported that a prominent chain of restaurants in the eastern United States required a fee from its waiters for the privilege of working there. While the chain was not named, it was not likely the above mentioned one, because all its employees were female.[18]

It was not that common for an employee to have to pay to work a tip-receiving job, but it was more common for employers to take some or all of these tips back in some way, such as in the previously mentioned checkroom concessions. An allegation was made in 1929 in the French Chamber of Deputies that establishments that added a 10 percent service charge to bills in lieu of tipping did not remit all of that back to the employees, but kept part of it for themselves. A bellhop got less under that system than he used to with regular tipping and no service charge.[19]

A decade later, this practice was so prevalent in Nevada that Governor Carville signed into law a bill that required Nevada employers who took tips given to their employees to henceforth publicly display signs to that effect.[20]

Checkroom concessions continued to operate as in the past. Hannah Stires launched an unsuccessful lawsuit in 1920 in Chicago to recover tips she had received in a restaurant checkroom but had been forced to turn over to the concession holder. Stiles and other employees in similar jobs were paid a wage of nine dollars to $15 per week and compelled to drop tips into a small iron bank camouflaged with paper. Reportedly, Harry J. Susskind paid $100,000 per year for each checking concession at a number of outlets. New York's Biltmore Hotel once refused an offer of $85,000 per year for its checking operation.[21]

Much later, in 1947, a bill was introduced in the New York State legislature by Republicans Arthur Wicks (Kingston) and William J. Butler (Buffalo) that provided for a fine of up to $1,000 and a year in jail for a firm or individual who required the return of tips. Concession holders along with hotels and restaurants successfully lobbied against the bill, claiming that both concession holders and cafés would go out of business; the former for obvious reasons, and the latter because they would lose a great deal of revenue. Another argument made by the lobbyists was that the concession fee helped in the initial financing of new places since it was paid up front. Observers believed the legislation was aimed at the Long-champs chain of restaurants, whose owner, Henry Lustig, had recently been convicted of tax fraud. Longchamps ran its own checkroom with Lustig personally pocketing tips running to several thousand dollars per week.[22]

In this period, tipping aboard ships was almost a nonstory. Much less of it took place, partly due to the Depression and World War II, and partly due to changing modes of transportation. One 1935 account claimed that air stewardesses had recently been added to the long list of tip receivers. Although forbidden on penalty of termination to accept tips, male passengers were said to have insisted, giving stewardesses from one dollar to five dollars at the end of a trip. If any tips were given to stewardesses, it was brief and episodic. More accurate was a 1939 report that stated that air travel had "remained aloof" from the gratuity system with no airplane tips necessary, not even for baggage. So long has this been true that today no one even thinks about tipping a flight attendant or ticket agent. This example is evidence that tipping can be eradicated or not even allowed to start if an industry is opposed to the system and determined to eliminate it; that was the policy of the commercial airline industry when it began. A flight attendant does similar tasks to, say, a cabin steward on a ship, yet there is no tipping for the former, but significantly higher wages. Trade unions cannot take any credit for that state of affairs. They were instrumental later in seeing that stewardesses were not arbitrarily dismissed on the basis of age or other reasons, but no-tipping had been long established by then. It was a policy implemented when those stewardesses and other personnel had little or no organized labor clout.[23]

Only the railroad remained an active arena for tipping in the transportation area in this period, as in the previous time. Although race was not overtly mentioned as often as in the past, conditions remained dismal for the mostly black porters who had to depend on the largesse of the mostly white passengers. Pullman porters organized into the Brotherhood of Sleeping Car Porters in 1925. Shortly thereafter, they sent a petition to the Interstate Commerce Commission asking for an order prohibiting tips. Said the petition, in part, "Only Negroes, many of them ex-slaves, were employed as porters. This caused the work to be looked on as menial and servile and led to the giving and taking of gratuities." In reply the Pullman company argued there was no obligation on the part of the public to tip and no right of porters to demand them; "the real purpose of the petitioners is to secure an increase in wages and changes in working conditions, and as to these subjects ... the Interstate Commerce Commission is without authority." That trade union told the Commission that the Pullman company had saved at least $150 million in salaries to its porters since 1867, due to tipping.

Within a few years of organizing, the porters' wages increased, in two stages, from $67.50 per month to $77.50, with the men averaging $58 per month in tips, out of which they had to spend $33 in job-related expenses such as shoe polish, two uniforms per year, and food in transit. From a questionnaire sent to porters, it was found that 376 men reported tips of less than $50 per month, while 245 received more than $50 per month. Five porters got less than $15 per month, with two earning over $200. "Yet each porter had approximately the same duties, spent nearly equal time on the road," remarked union organizer M.P. Webster of the unequal balance that made tipping so unsatisfactory. Webster added, "The tipping system creates social evils because of a peculiar relation between the tipper and the man tipped."[25]

In the midst of the Depression the average wage for Pullman porters was reported to total just $810 per year. They worked about 334 hours a month, 13 hours each working day, 22 cents to 25 cents per hour. Government agencies put the minimum income necessary for decent and healthful living at $1,139. The porters' union said tips had fallen off by up to 75 percent because of the Depression.[26]

Travel by rail went into decline after World War II as the airplane and private automobile industries grew. One response by railways was to try to abolish tipping. In 1946 the Cleveland based Pere Marquette Railway announced it would be a "guinea pig" in an experiment to do away with dining car tipping as "a tyranny of custom." Line president R.J. Bowman said the ban would bring no hostility from waiters because management had arranged "to compensate them for any loss." Bowman, arguing that the tipping tyranny was already too deeply rooted in rail transportation, expressed a hope that Pere Marquette's experiment would "lead to a trend that will result in much larger relief for the harassed traveler."[27]

The next year the Chesapeake & Ohio Railway (also Cleveland based) announced that it was following the lead of Pere Marquette by implementing a no-tip policy on its dining cars and coaches where porter service was provided. In advertising its new system the line asked, "Why shouldn't your rail ticket entitle you to courteous personal service — without the extra charge? The C. & O. does not believe the travelers on its railroad should have to tip — and is taking the first step toward abolishing the nuisance." None of the above bans applied to Pullman (sleeping car) porters or to the redcaps who worked the terminal stations.[28]

The no-tip policy on railways had been first put into effect in 1935 in China, when both the Nanking-Shanghai and the Shanghai-Hangchow-

Mingpo Railway administrations declared that tipping waiters on its dining cars would be prohibited. One rationale was that services rendered by them were only their duties and should be performed without thought of individual reward. Those caught accepting tips were subject to dismissal and unstated severe punishment. Waiters were told not to accept tips, no matter how insistent the passenger might become.[29]

Although tipping was well established as an institution early in this period, people still weren't sure who to tip or how much to bestow. Advice articles and guidebooks continued to find a ready market. In 1939 an issue of *Woman's Home Companion* published an article, "How much shall I tip?," for example. Two years later, the *Travel America Guide* published a scale of prices for tipping such as 10 cents to 25 cents for barbers, 20 cents for doorman, and 10–15 percent of the bill for waiters. Journalist Richard Strouse advised in 1949 that the old 10 percent standard was a casualty of the war with 12–15 percent then expected. His list of who was tipped included taxi drivers (15 percent); bartenders and baseball ushers (10–25 cents), bellhops (25 cents minimum); bus boys, butchers, and counter waiters (5–10 cents); delivery boys and doormen (25 cents); and hat-check girls (20 cents per hat). Strouse also claimed tippees included salespersons, and sometimes specialty shop girls; he stood virtually alone in this latter claim.[30]

Celebrities were sometimes mentioned. Porter Richard Pettus had been tipped by presidents; he recalled that William McKinley was a better tipper than William Henry Harrison. When the members of the Dining Car Employees Union took a 1939 vote they declared that Eleanor Roosevelt was the most generous tipper among female riders on the nation's trains. Other results were that Morton Downey was named the most liberal tipper among entertainers, James A. Farley among politicians, Grover A. Whelan among businessmen, Jack Dempsey among athletes, and Cornelius Vanderbilt, Jr., in high society. Bellboys claimed Calvin Coolidge was all right, but did not tip as well as Warren Harding.[31]

Legendary Detroit Tiger baseball player Ty Cobb was once asked by a cabby for a tip after a ride. He sneered, "Sure, don't bet on the Tigers today." A Pullman porter once attended Yankee slugger Babe Ruth on a trip into New York, at the end of which Ruth gave the man a 25 cent tip. Recalled the porter; "An' when he hands it out he sez: 'Are you comin' to the game?' 'No suh,' sez I. 'I can't affo'd no game.' Baseball players sure do keep what they got to theirselves."[32]

Terming indiscriminate tipping a vulgar American habit, Eleanor Roosevelt once warned travelers:

> a fair tip, or one a little on the generous side, will leave a pleasant feeling and respect for you in the one who receives it. A lavish one will create a

secret disrespect and add to the reputation Americans have for trying to buy their way into everything."[33]

There was again much discussion on which groups, either by nationality, geography, region, gender, or other criteria, were the best tippers. Porters on southern rail lines in the 1920s found Cubans to be the most generous. Midwestern Americans were also liberal, but New Englanders were "retentive of their money." Men were more lavish than women, and every porter knew that a female would, after a transcontinental journey, "cautiously part with a dime."[34]

Bellboys had their own elaborate rating list in the 1920s. Spanish Americans were described as fine tippers, Germans were good, the English were poor; the Scottish were very poor; Canadians were fair, Chinese were fine, Japanese were fine, the French were no good, and Americans were the "best on earth." Geographically, New York City residents were named the best tippers in the nation; Chicago good; Kansas City, Cleveland, Toledo, and Cincinnati were all good, Philadelphia was fair to poor; Boston was poor (the bellboys called a nickel or dime a "Boston quarter"); California was good; Westerners in general were good; Florida and the South in general were poor. Getting more philosophical, one bellboy remarked, "A man is never so generous as when he's on his honeymoon." Those who stayed in medium-priced rooms tipped better than those who stayed in suites. Another offered the thought that if a guest was "grouchy looking, no tip or a dime. If he's melancholy, a dime or fifteen cents. If he is cheerful, expansive and talky, a quarter or more." Talkers were especially liberal.[35]

When the Headwaiters Association held a 1935 meeting, they agreed the Japanese were the most liberal of all tippers with, in descending order, "cultured" Englishmen, "refined" Americans, French, Germans, and Russians. Mainly they were speaking of the upper classes of each country, not the average citizens. Frank Erb, headwaiter, reminisced that the best tips in history were thrown about freely at the Miami Beach Casino in 1917–1918; New York City's best era for lavish tipping was said to be from 1926 to 1928. A reporter at that meeting asked the checkroom girl at the hotel hosting the event how those headwaiters were when it came to tipping at their own social functions. "Not so good," she said.[36]

A year later, those headwaiters reaffirmed that Japanese visitors to America were, without question, the most liberal tippers of visitors to America. One Japanese journalist felt it was due to sensitivity: "They tip more than others because they fear ridicule. So do the Chinese."[37]

Another source had it that the newly rich and "shady" men consistently overtipped, but those long accustomed to wealth were unsatisfactory tippers. This discrepancy was due to the fact that service didn't impress such people the way it did the majority. Clerks tipped better than executives, and of course, men tipped better than women.[38]

A 1936 British source reiterated that females were poor tippers, remarking that when they saw the British female coming abroad "the foreign shopkeepers and hotel-keepers tremble…. The way that women generally underpay their car-drivers is the standing joke of writers; and is used by Dickens in several incidents." When those American Dining Car Employees Union members held their 1939 vote, it revealed that the average male tipped 25 cents; the average female left 15 cents.[39]

Somewhat earlier, author Frances Donovan worked as a waitress in Chicago while gathering material for a book. She observed that in her restaurant the waitresses often looked bored and indifferent when a female patron entered. They served her when it suited them because women didn't tip. Said Donovan: "The manager has a hard time to contend with this attitude." One waitress told Donovan "Our boss won't stand for anything like that. He has fired more than one girl for looking disgusted when a woman sits at her table."[40]

During World War II, a published interview from a waiter named Jimmy Nearos cited him as believing that army officers ordered expensive food but left small tips, but a "sure omen" of a good tip was an order of Scotch and soda before a meal. The best tipping party was composed of two or three New York married couples, and the worst was an out-of-town mother with grown children. Nearos agreed that men were better tippers than women, but felt that much depended on the state of the female's love life at the moment. At the New York World's Fair he found the French the best foreign tippers, followed by the English and the Dutch. Among Americans he found New Yorkers better than all out-of-towners with Midwesterners especially bad.[41]

Headwaiter Fred Sparks offered his opinion in a 1946 *Collier's* piece, in which he declared the best tipper was the middle-aged businessman who was entertaining guests of his own type. Also a good tipper was the out-of-town buyer, as was the stock broker when the market was good. Black-market operators were also among the best; among the worst were college boys, musicians, politicians, stage and film celebrities, and tourists sightseeing on a budget.[42]

The reality of tipping was much different economically than what was often presented in the media — that recipients were financially well-off. A 1925 account said the union rate for waiters in hotels was $14 per week ($40 per month for those without a union), porters $24, bellboys $25, doormen $50 to $60, and chambermaids $25 to $30. The better the chance for tips, the lower the wages were. "Six dollars a day in tips for a waiter in a hotel restaurant is considered passably good. It can go up to $10 and more very easily," stated the article. Slightly more realistic was an account in the *Saturday Evening Post*, stating that bellboys received wages of $50 to $60 per month in places without much tips, down to as low as $25 or less in big tip hotels — $16 per month at one place. From those monthly wages, bellboys were charged two dollars to three dollars for uniforms and 50 cents per day paid to the bell captain. Yet, said the account, they netted around $35 to $50 per month, with the difference coming from tips.[43]

Earlier in the 1920s the New York State Department of Labor conducted a study at a large restaurant that added a 10 percent service charge to bills in lieu of tips. Any waiter caught accepting a tip was in danger of being discharged. Those waiters were paid a wage of $12 per week and averaged $37 per week with the service charge included. The Department of Labor concluded that where tipping was eliminated, the results were more satisfactory to all concerned.[44]

An estimate made by the Motor Transit Committee of New York City had it that in 1930 taxi drivers in that city received $26 million in tips. Shortly after the war, journalist Fred Sparks declared that New York City's 1,100 licensed nightclubs did a yearly gross of $50 million with the customers handing over $8 to $10 million in tips. Sparks fueled the myth of rich recipients by claiming that some waiters made, from wages and tips, "$300 to $400 a week and to $1,000 in high season." People tipped out of the "human craving for recognition and the desire of the average man to be lifted, even momentarily, above his fellows." About the same time, Richard Strouse reported that waiters and waitresses in Manhattan were paid from $22 to $30 per week in wages.[45]

The most thorough study of the economic reality for tip recipients was in 1935, and reported by Rae Needleman in the *Monthly Labor Review*. He estimated there were over 800,000 employees in tipped occupations such as restaurant employees, hotel workers, barber and beauty shop operatives, railway porters, taxi drivers, and bootblacks. That number was high, he admitted, because the categories included all workers in those areas, not just those receiving tips. Thus the total for restaurant workers and hotel employees (333,000 and 291,000, respectively). Needleman thought the tipped percentage was around 50 percent. Annual income from tips was estimated at $130 per year per tipped employee in barber shops; $91 in barber and beauty shops; $110 in beauty parlors; $144 for Pullman porters; and $233 for workers in railroad dining rooms and railroad hotels.[46]

When the government studied workers in beauty shops in four U.S. cities (1,655 employees in 465 shops), 11 percent reported no tips in that week; 15 percent got less than one dollar; 60 percent received one dollar to under four dollars. Of the 165 men in that study, 8 percent received nothing, with the most common amount reported being one dollar to under four dollars in the week. In a New York study of hotel and restaurant workers in 1934, 105 women — 71 waitresses and 34 chambermaids — working in various establishments kept a tip diary for one week. Median tip earnings for waitresses were $7.69 that week. Of the chambermaids, nine got nothing, 11 got 25 cents to 75 cents and 14 received from one dollar to $3.35. Sixty-seven waitresses at a five-and-ten chain store's restaurants had median tip earnings for a week of $3.25. In two other New York establishments that added a 10 percent service charge to the bill in lieu of tipping, the median weekly earnings for waitresses from the extra charge were $7.97 at one place and $9.38 at the other. However, Needleman pointed out that tipping was much higher in New York than anywhere else. As a group, waitresses who received tips had a median week's earning of three dollars less than waitresses who had no tips. This survey showed the tendency was to pay lower wages to those workers receiving tips and higher wages to those who did not receive tips, such as counter servers.[47]

Several proprietors of seasonal hotels told survey takers that wages paid were based on amounts that workers would probably receive in tips during the season. Some establishments paid their workers no wages, or only a nominal wage, but guaranteed them a certain amount each week, making up any tip shortfall to that amount. Large numbers of railway station porters received no wages; in fact they were not even on the company payroll at all. Except for holidays like Christmas, they averaged around two dollars per day in tips. Bootblacks earned a wage of five dollars to six dollars per week and made about five to six dollars each week in tips.[48]

Around 1948, cab drivers in Chicago had tips amounting to about 40 percent of their earnings. A driver then worked ten hours each day, six days a week, and took home an average of $75 per week in salary and tips.[49]

Mary Anderson, former director of the Women's Bureau of the U.S. Department of Labor, pointed out in 1941 how irregular, unreliable, and undependable tips were.

> Yet it is the temper and caprice of consumers that determine to a large extent the amount of income of workers engaged in occupations where tipping is the custom ... studies show that many waitresses, for example, receive no tips at all, and others receive pitifully small and irregular amounts. Yet their wages are set at a lower rate than those of other classes of restaurant and hotel workers on the assumption that they are generously compensated by the customers.[50]

Chapter 5

"Tipping Is Forbidden, But Expected": Tipping Responses 1920–1949

"The tipping system is a relic of parasites in satin pants and servitors sleeping with the dogs on the rush-strewn kitchen floor."
— Clyde Davis

In response to tipping practices in 1920–1949, hotels and restaurants which did not allow tips continued to exist, but in very small numbers. London had one in 1927 where the penalty for any employee who accepted a tip was dismissal. Supposedly the employees were paid well with reservations in demand and hard to obtain.[1]

America's only first-class no-tip hotel was the Grace Dodge Hotel in Washington, D.C., which opened in October 1921. Its success proved that a tipless hotel could attract and hold a high class of hotel employees on wages alone. No tips were allowed in the hotel or any of the attached restaurants. For the first few years the Dodge accepted only females as guests in the hotel rooms, although both genders could use the restaurants. After three years of pressure from men who came with their families demanding admission, the hotel opened itself to both genders. Dodge Hotel director Mary Lindsley remarked in 1929, "Fifty years from now tipping in this country will be practically abolished.... This hotel is just pointing the way, it can be done." In setting its wage scale, the hotel matched the minimum wage paid by the federal government, a standard said to be "a living wage in this country." Government clerks began at $65 per month, so hotel chambermaids were paid that amount, waitresses earned $71.50, and bellboys got $75. In hotels allowing gratuities, bellboys earned wages of $25 to $35, chambermaids $35, and waitresses one dollar per day or less. When a reporter tested the Dodge's no-tip policy she related, "I personally tried to tip the hotel employees. Of twenty, just one took a tip, and he had disappeared on my second stay."[2]

Not surprisingly, hotel owners weren't happy with the concept of a no-tip hotel because wages were much higher. At a meeting of the executive committee of the Hotel Proprietors' Union in Munich, those in attendance decided that the abolition of tips had not been a success in the few places it had been tried. Most of those who had tried to abolish the practice added a 20 percent service charge to the bill. Even though notices in those establishments threatened waiters with instant dismissal if they took tips, the employees reportedly continued to look for and receive gratuities. Therefore the owners' committee decided to announce its abandonment of the no-tip system.[3]

After a Columbia University faculty member charged student waiters in the John Jay Hall grill with service discrimination against nontippers, the university used the above reasons and others to abolish tipping at that café. Said Mabel Reed, director of university restaurant management at Columbia, "The practice of tipping grew up informally in the grill, and was contrary to the custom prevailing in other university dining halls. The new agreement for its abolition has the support of the men who work in the grill." Previously student waiters were paid only a meal allowance plus tips. To make up for the loss of income under the new system, management undertook to provide unspecified outside or overtime jobs for them.[4]

One account had it that the first Longchamps restaurant opened in 1918 as the first no-tip restaurant in the United States. By 1936 it had nine outlets. All of the original company employees remained in the company's employ at the later date. Said the account, "The no-tip system increased self-respect. About 95 percent of the Longchamps men are American citizens. They are alert, clean, intelligent, courteous." However, the chain did add a 10 percent service charge to the bill. The glowing account in *Reader's Digest* claimed the basic wage for waiters was twice what employees got in equally good establishments. "Emphatic signs and folders on the tables make it plain that tips are out of order, at the checkroom as well as the tables." Only rarely did a customer try and force a tip on an employee. When that happened it was handled by a single question: "Do you want me to lose my position?"[5]

Shortly before the World's Fair was held in New York in 1939, it was announced in at least one popular magazine that no tipping was to be allowed there, with waiters, guides, shoeshiners, washroom personnel, and checkroom attendants all forbidden to accept tips. Restaurants were to add a 10 percent service charge to bills. "This will be America's largest effort to eliminate the tipping system." However, for unrecorded reasons, tipping did indeed take place at the fair.[6]

Attempts to replace tipping with a fixed percentage service charge continued to be made, primarily in continental Europe. A number of establishments in Switzerland were adding 10 percent to hotel bills in 1921. Around the same time, a number of Italian hotel keepers started a system of charging from 10–15 percent extra on the bill in lieu of tipping. Guests were warned not to tip; employees caught receiving gratuities were fired. At first the workers were not in favor of the new system, but soon they favored it in both Switzerland and Italy.[7]

Soon the experiment was being tried at many hotels in Paris, with 10 percent added on to the bill. When one American visitor went to a hotel restaurant in Paris, he didn't tip, telling the waiter he didn't have to. The waiter said to him, "That only applies to other hotel servants, not the restaurant waiters." Servants on the man's hotel floor said it did not apply to them, but to the bellboys. The porter said it didn't apply to him either, explaining, "Monsieur, the word service naturally only applies to servants."[8]

Within a few years, that method was reported to be on shaky ground in Italy. While employees, guests, and owners had initially accepted it, what happened, said a hotel man, was that "you Americans came along and persisted in giving tips as usual," even though hotel men told the Americans not to give tips. Employees "don't expect tips from Italians, but they think all Americans who come to Europe are millionaires."[9]

One of the few reported experiments in the United States with a service charge occurred when the Lexington Hotel opened in New York in 1929 with a policy of no tipping in the grill or restaurant, with a 10 percent charge added to the bill for the employees. Tipping was allowed in the hotel part of the unit. Lexington owner American Hotels Corporation announced that if the experiment was successful it would abolish tipping throughout its entire chain. It didn't happen.[10]

In some places the experiment was deemed a failure. Belgium tried the 10 percent surcharge but announced in an official report in 1936 that "it failed." That report went on to state the new system made waiters "insolent, inattentive and inclined to neglect the small services that had been coaxed out of them by a promise of extra reward."[11]

Authorities in Nanking, China legally abolished a 10 percent surcharge, which they had previously enacted to provide a better income for waiters and other service positions. Those regulations also required owners to pay their staff wages so that they wouldn't have to depend on tips. However, the owners ignored the regulations on all counts. The service charge was not returned to the help, but mostly kept by the owners with the result that most employees still hustled for tips. Wages of these employees were exceptionally low, with a majority of them receiving no regular wages, but free room and board. Said one observer, "An exorbitant tip demanded by teaboys from passengers on inland steamers is the most hated practice among all the forms of tipping in China." If anyone refused to tip "he is cursed, or sometimes even is threatened with having to pay it as a part of the regular fare."[12]

In 1944, the practice of adding a service charge was said to be not as widespread in England as on the European continent. However, *Spectator* magazine felt that the method should be made compulsory, because employees then paid income tax by having it deducted from each check — the pay-as-you-earn system. The journal fretted that under the present tipping system nobody knew how much a waiter earned or how to monitor it, making the implication that tipped employees were probably getting away with something.[13]

Groups and clubs that organized against tipping were much less prevalent in this period, mainly because the custom was indeed institutionalized. Its elimination seemed highly unlikely. One group called the Anti-Gimme League formed in Cincinnati around 1923 with a rather broad agenda. It wished to abolish tipping in all its forms, but also wanted to do away with "continual and unreasonable" demands by wives upon husbands' incomes and earnings; abolish street begging; and eliminate chronic borrowing of cigarettes, cigars, umbrellas, books, and so forth by neighbors, club members, and other acquaintances. Later that decade, two organizations, the National Housewives' League and the Associated Master Barbers, announced they would ask their members not to tip.[14]

When the Consumers' League issued a 1922 call to abolish tipping, the Hotel Men's Association refused to discuss it. They said it was up to the public; it and it alone could put an end to tipping.[15]

In 1932, a French cartoonist named Jean Charlot and a group of his friends launched their own war on tipping by giving tip receivers a pseudo-coin instead of a real one. The fake coin had the inscription "Get yourself paid by your employer" on one side and "Tipping is beggary" on the other. *Commonweal*'s editor said, "He has principles, has Jean Charlot, and character; and therefore he will not silently submit to the odium of the mere non-tipper." As for doubters who felt the hope that nontipping would become widespread was misplaced, the editor wistfully stated, "How splendid if it were wrong!" Four years later Charlot was still waging his war but with little success. "The idea caught on for a while; a score or more people adopted the Charlot tokens. But it has fallen off, because token-passers got miserable service," related one account.[16]

Government ambivalence about tips remained in evidence, although a greater effort went into recognizing and legitimizing the custom than into trying to eradicate it. Income tax department spokesman William H. Edwards announced in February 1920 that tips were taxable: "Tips are not to be regarded a gifts, but as compensation for service rendered," he said. The following year, revenue authorities in London declared that tips were subject to income tax. Recipients protested contending that tips were gifts, and thus exempt from taxation. Revenue officials based their claim partly on a 1917 Court of Appeals decision when a railroad man proved he was legally entitled to regard tips as part of his earnings. Since that time railway companies were compelled to take tips into account when compensating injured employees.[17]

A tax collector won a fight against six waiters employed at San Francisco's Solari Grill during the period 1940 to 1944, who he claimed did not report all their tips. The waiters argued they didn't get as much in tips as expected, but court evidence based on the testimony of other Solari waiters was that they all got tips of 10 percent, more or less. On that basis, the United States Tax Court decided the tax collector was right. It was an important case because it established the right of the IRS to set the amount of tips an employee received, even when there was no hard, direct evidence, and the employee insisted he had not received that much.[18]

Half-hearted banning attempts were occasionally made. A 1921 bill introduced in the Massachusetts legislature declared that anybody who gave or accepted a tip would be fined $25 or jailed for up to 30 days. Said a newspaper account,

> Of course, neither part of this law is even conceivably enforceable, for no jury would convict when the penalty was severe to a degree so obviously out of proportion to the gravity of an offense involving nothing of "moral turpitude." That certainly is not the way to stop tipping.

Six years later, another bill was introduced in that state's legislature that would have imposed a fine for giving or taking tips. Neither bill passed.[19]

British MP Holmes from Harwich introduced a private member's bill into the British House of Commons in 1936 to make illegal the practice of tipping people employed in hotels and restaurants. It was withdrawn a year later.[20]

France's Chamber of Deputies passed an anti-tipping bill in 1937 by the narrowest of margins, 267 to 265, but it died in the Senate. Had it been enacted, it would have become a misdemeanor for employers to let their workers rely wholly or partly on tips for their pay and for employees to accept or solicit tips. A suggested amendment to have the tip giver declared equally guilty was rejected. Critics of the bill argued that only "extremists" amounting to 10 percent of the employees involved favored the bill. Communists were firmly behind the bill for the sake of "decency" for workers, but they didn't believe it would ever work. During parliamentary debate Communist deputy Ramette said, "There will be nothing in the bill to stop a customer from personally 'thanking' a waiter with whom he is particularly pleased."[21]

In Italy the authorities posted signs in all government buildings in 1927 requesting visitors not to tip employees. Dictator Benito Mussolini went a step further in 1935 when he issued an order that tips must not be accepted from guests at hotels; violators were subject to a penalty of three days in jail. One year later, Hungary abolished tipping by government decree. Here the reason was said to be the lack of a Hungarian coin of suitable denomination. One coin, the pengo, was worth U.S. 29 cents while the next smallest one, the filler, was worth just one-hundredth of a pengo (U.S. 29 cents). As a filler or two seemed too stingy to leave as a tip, travelers felt obligated to tip with pengoes, which they complained added up in the course of a day. In Czechoslovakia in 1948 the tourist office asked visitors to stop giving tips in hotels, restaurants, and cafés because the custom was a "relic of feudalism."[22]

At the end of World War II, The U.S. Army issued a no-tipping order for its personnel in the European theater. It outlawed tipping in any club, bar, hotel, mess, or similar establishment operated for or by the U.S. Army in Europe. It had little effect, partly because since Americans had landed on the European continent in June 1944, and before that in North Africa, they had found that cigarettes, not coins, were the most effective reward for small and large services. A year after the original edict, officials reinforced the idea by posting signs reminding personnel that tipping was illegal, and that the ban covered the giving away of cigarettes, candy bars, or similar items. Nobody expected that order to be any more effective than the original edict.[23]

Other governmental recognition came in different forms. President Calvin Coolidge approved a new tipping scale in 1926 to be used by government employees. They could give a maximum tip of 30 cents per day to bellboys and maids at hotels; 15 cents per bag to porters at stations, and a maximum of 25 cents per day to chair or parlor car porters on trains, porters in hotels or at landings and wharfs, and stewards on steamers. A decade later the government accounting office in Washington continued to recognize the tip as a legitimate expense-account item. However, New York State employees were not allowed to put tips on their expense accounts.[24]

ot constitute wages within the meaning of the Social Security Act. That
ear they took a slight step forward when the IRS ruled that in the case
here a 10 percent service charge was added to the bill in lieu of tipping,
d where that sum was pooled and distributed among the staff, it did con-
itute wages for the unemployment and old-age provisions of the Social
curity Act.[27]

Also by 1937, 34 of the 51 state unemployment insurance laws included
s as part of wages; but some states continued to resist. A 1941 decision
the New Jersey Supreme Court reversed a decision of the State Unem-
yment Commission and ruled that tips could not be considered wages
ject to coverage under the State Unemployment Compensation Act.[28]

The state of New York did count tips a part of wages for its unem-
yment compensation, though the hearings held to set the tip amounts
re often rancorous. Barbers accepted a state estimate of their tip earn-
s, but claimed the amounts received from customers were considerably
er than the estimate. For calculation of unemployment benefits, New
k officials proposed 15 percent above base salary for barbers, 25 per-
t for manicurists, 12½ percent for taxi drivers, and 5 percent for
eshiners. Three years later the New York State Department of Labor
the scale at: restaurant waiters 7½ percent, counter waiters 5 percent
he check), hotel waiters two dollars per day, hotel busboys one dollar
day, bellhops two dollars per day, hotel doormen two dollars per day,
drivers 12½ percent, barbers 15 percent of wages, beauty parlor employ-
0 percent of wages, and manicurists 25 percent of wages.[29]

During the 1930s under Roosevelt's National Recovery Act (NRA),
t debate centered on whether earnings from tips should be included
inimum wage rates under the codes for various industries. That ques-
oomed particularly large during code hearings for the hotel, restau-
and barber industries. None of the wage codes ultimately adopted
ose industries mentioned tips as a factor in payment of wages. How-
rates set for service workers compared to nonservice employees indi-
that possible earnings from tips were in the background in setting
tes. For the hotel industry, minimum rates per week paid to non-
e workers were set at 10–15 dollars (depending on the size of the
for service workers employers merely had to guarantee those rates.
restaurant industry the weekly wage set for nonservice workers
from 12–15 dollars, but ranged from $9.50 to $10.50 for service
s. Taking tips into consideration meant that the wages paid could
er than for workers in the nontipped positions.[30]

uring discussions and hearings regarding tips and minimum wages,
as a sharp division between employers on one side, and workers

If the government was relatively quick to recognize tl
income, it was much slower to recognize it for purposes of
benefits, workers' compensation, social security benefits, al
wage. In all those cases benefits depended on an employ
higher wages resulting in greater benefits. The inclusion
crucial to recipients whose salary alone was fairly low.

Representative Hogg of Indiana introduced a bill in
to compensate a Fort Wayne, Indiana, waiter injured b
1927. Injured waiter Darold Burndig claimed loss of er
per week — $20 from wages, $15 from tips. Objecting to
was Representative Bachman of West Virginia. The '
money for tips. When waitress Ethel Powers was injur
her work, she claimed her earnings, from which comp
calculated as $20 per week — eight dollars in wages, '
won her case at a lower level. When her employer ap
rior court, the decision was reversed when it was deci
lars was earnings. Finally, in 1931 the Massachusetts Su
the original court declaring Powers's weekly earning

By 1937 there were 50 state laws and two feder
dealt with workers' compensation. Of those, 20 did r
stituted wages, while of the other 32 laws, just 12 cont
respect to tips. Seven state laws (Colorado, Kansas, N
ico, Pennsylvania, Minnesota, and Delaware) specific
the definition of wages. The other five laws (Florida, N
to a limited extent, and the two federal bills (the L
bor Workers' Compensation Act and the District (
sation Act) specifically included tips in the categ
meant that every time a tip recipient sought comp
ally had to launch a lawsuit over the tip questior
included tips in the definition of wages where tip
the wage contract, whether expressed or implied.
considered part of the wage contract, and therefo
of awarding compensation. Employers resisted
not affect them personally in the case of compe
premiums had no direct relationship to a worke
on the basis of accident rates in an industry. The
it to prevent it becoming a precedent. If tips wer
for compensation, then why not also for uner
social security benefits? In those latter cases, t'
would increase as wages increased.[26]

Until 1937, the Bureau of Internal Rever

and the public on the other. Representatives from labor and the public (with the latter including spokespeople from the National Consumers' League, the U.S. Department of Labor and various civic organizations), fought bitterly against the inclusion of tips as part of wages. Speaking for the AFL, William Green said, "Dependence on tips gives workers a great sense of insecurity." Employers argued that tipping "places control of an important amount of compensation for service in the hands of the person served," and that a customer was willing to pay a little extra if he was served promptly and cheerfully. Some countered this argument by pointing out that the trend in Europe was away from tipping and toward a service charge. Many establishments had already adopted that method with service as good as it had been before. Employers also argued that they could not bear the burden of paying NRA wages unless tips were regarded as earnings. A number of speakers from both sides stated that many service workers received only a minimal salary or no salary at all. Workers made that claim to prove that because of tipping, employers shifted the payment of wages to the public. Employers made the same assertion to prove that tips had always been considered a source of income equivalent to the wages.[31]

In hearings later in the 1930s, on whether tips should be included in fixing the minimum wage to be set for waiters, one speaker was Eleanor Roosevelt. She stated that she disliked the whole idea of tipping, regarding it as a result of an insufficient living wage: "However, if tips must be relied on for part of the income of waiters, then I think they might better be included in the bill and the total pooled and distributed among the employees on payday."[32]

When general minimum wage rates were set by the state or the federal governments during this time, tips were usually not mentioned, leaving it to the courts to determine. In 1943 the Supreme Court of California held that tips received by waitresses at a drive-in restaurant could not be credited against their compensation in determining whether the minimum wage established by the state was being met. Until then, tips paid to car-hops were their sole income. When they fell below the state minimum wage, the employer made up the difference. The U.S. Supreme Court decided in 1942 that under the federal Fair Labor Standards Act (FLSA), while employers were required to pay the established minimum wage, the employer was free, insofar as the act was concerned, to work out the compensation issue in his or her own way. That decision stemmed from the court's declaring that tips received by redcaps from passengers could be treated as wages under the FLSA. In the wake of that decision, two railroad lines served notice that redcaps had to account for all tips from passengers, with the companies guaranteeing to make up any difference between the amount of tips and the hourly wages required by law. This came to be the usual way of dealing with a general minimum wage that did not clearly specify tips. Those tips would be counted as a part of the minimum with employers agreeing to make up any shortfall.[33]

Tipping in the Communist bloc was one of many weapons used during the Cold War era after World War II. In 1936, the *New York Times* remarked on the supposed prevalence and growth of tipping in the Soviet Union, where theoretically it should not have existed at all. "The discovery that tips are not only acceptable but are subtly solicited is one of the things that most shocks foreigners who arrive ready to admire a system in which all who work honorably, no matter how humbly, are considered as equals." All occupational categories tipped in the United States and more were said to be tipped in the USSR. They were regularly tipped by Soviets, not just foreigners, although they fared worse at the hands of foreigners because those visitors assumed Soviet citizens would be insulted by the offer of a tip. Journalist Harold Denny claimed that he had only one tip refused in the course of two years in the Soviet Union. He went on to add the only place in Moscow where tipping did not take place — it even occurred in the Kremlin checkroom — was the United States Embassy, because it paid the Russian attendants adequately and treated them courteously. A worried Communist Party fretted about the issue in the pages of *Pravda*: "Is the tipping element unconquerable? Is the human dignity of petty graft-takers so sound asleep? It is incredible. It is too improbable that for the sake of a few extra kopeks or rubles the Soviet people will abandon the status of independent and proud citizens of this great country." Yet just seven months later the *Literary Digest*, an American newsmagazine, stated flatly and unequivocally: "In Russia there is no tipping."[34]

A decade later London's *Times* newspaper noted that Russians condemned tipping as a practice that maintained the old class distinctions, yet it did not stop the appearance in the Moscow guidebook for foreigners of the italicized sentence: "Tipping is forbidden, but expected."

At a 1948 meeting of a waiters' union in Prague, a deputy premier of that nation described tipping as a "bourgeois relic" and "un–Marxist." According to the account the waiters howled him down.[35]

Rationalizing the tipping system as positive continued. Usually these justifications included something to the effect that recipients liked the system. Mr. Statler, who owned the Pennsylvania Hotel, said that tips would be given and taken until the end of the world and that "the hotel guest likes the system as well as the employees do." When somebody pointed out that the Grace Dodge Hotel was proof that tips were not necessary, the rebuttal was that "even there, it seems, some of the patrons ignore all exhortations and leave coins hidden under their plates." This anecdotal evidence was used in support of Statler's assertion, yet no evidence was produced to prove it. Journalist Meyer Berger stated in 1936, with no supporting evidence, that "waiters generally seem to frown on the idea of abolishing tips."[36]

Reporter Rose Feld declared that several New York restaurants had tried the no-tipping system but that it had failed because "first, the waiters do not like it, and second, many Americans insist on maintaining their right of rewarding a person for extra service."[37]

Yet labor, both collectively and individually, was primarily in favor of eliminating tips, with strikes over the issue still breaking out at times. French waiters went on strike at every hotel, restaurant, and café in Bordeaux in 1936 in an effort to eliminate tips. The trouble arose from a wage agreement between workers and employers: employees wanted the wage increase immediately, but employers declined to implement it until a bill suppressing tips became law (it didn't). Those waiters wanted tips abolished because tipping was "too uncertain and is an affront to their professional dignity."[38]

Forty thousand Swiss hotel workers threatened to strike in 1921 if owners did not agree to abolish tipping and introduce a fixed-percentage service charge instead. Workers complained they did "not wish to be treated as beggars by the hotel guests and that they will refuse to stand at the door when guests leave for the sake of receiving tips." Hotel owners offered the weak argument that in places where a service charge had been instituted, the guests were not served as well, but still considered themselves under an obligation to tip.[39]

William Lehman, secretary-treasurer of Waiters and Waitresses Local Union 1, told a New York industrial commission in 1927 that waiters would rather have a living wage than depend on the charity of the public for tips. He referred to a city restaurant that instituted a no-tip policy and higher wages, with almost 150 men applying for the five openings. At the annual convention of the Associated Master Barbers of New York that same year, the group adopted a resolution to ask cooperation from barbers, hairdressers, and cosmeticians in urging their customers to refrain from tipping "to raise the craft to the status of a profession.... It is asserted that tipping lowers the dignity of their calling and it is unfair to the public." Their national association had already passed a similar resolution.[40]

The French Federation of Workers also waged a fight in the food industry for the passage of a bill that would systemize the distribution of tips. Under the bill, all tips no matter to whom they were given, would go into a pooled fund and then be distributed according to a specific formula.[41]

Leo Merlen, secretary-treasurer of the International Federation of hotel and restaurant workers, started a campaign in America in 1920 to abolish tips and substitute a minimum wage of $50 per week. His union declared that nine out of ten union waiters wanted to do away with tips and substitute a living wage. Samuel Gompers continued to inveigh against the custom, saying it "lessens self-respect," but admitted that he did it himself for "convenience in getting around." The International Geneva Association was a fraternal organization formed in 1877; it had 20,000 waiter members, representing 26 nations by 1920. At a Chicago meeting, five thousand members returned questionnaires. According to spokesman K. Englehardt an overwhelming majority expressed disfavor of the tipping system, with most of those wanting an alternative plan of either a straight salary or a service charge. Hotel owners argued that it was not possible to abolish tipping because "employees won't work for a salary as they will for a tip. Not only the desire for extra remuneration but the gambling instinct explains it. Every time a bellboy answers a call he goes on a gambler's errand."[42]

Based in Geneva, the Hotel and Restaurant Employees' International Association condemned tips for waiters in 1927. They regarded neither tipping nor a fixed service charge as a solution to the question of remuneration for waiters. In countries where a service charge prevailed this group declared it was less than satisfactory.[43]

When the government publication *Monthly Labor Review* published a round-up article in 1927 about opposition to tipping, it reported opposition from groups of organized labor, including Pullman porters, waiters and waitresses, chauffeurs, barbers, beauty parlor employees, and so on. All of those groups had considered the question of tipping and had apparently come out against it.

> The employer feels that the acceptance of tips by his employees relieves him of the obligation to pay full wages, and tips, thereafter have to take the place of wages. The result is a wage wholly inadequate for the maintenance of a family and to make up the deficit the employee must depend upon the generosity of the patron, an uncertain factor at best.

Unions opposed the custom because "receiving tips tends to detract from the independence of the workers and to create a servile spirit among them." Customers tipped because they felt it insured better service, or at least avoided the mediocre service which not leaving a tip might bring. Some tipped unwillingly because they felt a tip was expected, and therefore

did the "usual thing," while others left gratuities because they were aware
that tipped occupations were usually underpaid jobs and the tip was a necessary supplement to the wage. "It is safe to say that the abolition of tipping would be welcomed by the public," said the report.[44]

Illustrating public sentiment toward tipping, the review cited the following attitude, which it took from another source:

> Tipping itself is an offense to the code of American business ethics. It belongs
> in countries where begging is a recognized channel of revenue, where class
> distinctions are sharp and oppressive, and where cultivated servility is an art.
> But the custom is rooted in the United States and it will grow and thrive
> until the great army of the tipped rises in rebellion and creates and demands
> a right to straight pay.[45]

The Teamsters union opposed tips as an official policy, because it
"places the recipient in the position of a menial." Said Teamsters' president Daniel J. Tobin, "One of the substantial things accomplished by our
organization since its formation is that of discouraging the custom of tipping.... This custom, however, is gradually being eliminated amongst
union men due to the fact that our union has raised the standard of wages
and brought up this class of workers to real high-grade, independent individuals."[46]

Writing in the *Monthly Labor Review* in 1937, Rae Needleman said
that tipping in America had never been looked upon with great favor, and
when the giving of a tip became expected, the result was that "the non-
tipper began to be looked upon with scorn by the expectant tippee, the
public began to resent the practice." Needleman argued that tips began to
be actively opposed by recipients once workers in service occupations organized and entered trade unions. As early as 1896 the barbers' union
denounced the custom as humiliating and degrading. Labor argued that
workers gained nothing by tips because what they earned in tips they lost
in wages. Further, the tipping system was a cause of low wages because
the tendency was to reduce wages proportionately with the amount of gratuities received. Tips were uncertain and irregular and depended on the
whim of the customer. Additionally, labor argued that tipping was an
impediment to the organization of trade unions in tipped occupations
because the system of tips encouraged selfishness and jealousy among workers. Gratuities often served as an inducement to work long hours due to
the eagerness for extra earnings.[47]

When the Office of Price Administration (OPA) dropped its price
restrictions, shortly after the end of World War II, Hotel Trades Council
president Jay Ruben appeared before those administrators to argue for an

increase in the minimum wage. Ruben told them that tips for service employees had fallen off greatly since prices went up with the end of OPA controls. Gratuities did not rise with the increase in menu prices, but had in fact declined. Ruben felt that customers were taking out their resentment against the higher price of food on the employees.[48]

Psychological aspects of tipping continued to be discussed, with surveys showing up to gauge public attitudes. When the Consumers' League recommended abolishing tipping in hotels, it cited the position of chambermaids: "It is a pleasing appearance and manner rather than service, which brings in tips to the chambermaid." Advice given by maids to the people doing the study for the League was to "fix yourself up" and "don't be bashful" because the ones who get tips "are those who stick around and sass 'em back and make them notice you." It apparently had nothing to do with one's efficiency as a worker.[49]

The custom prompted one William Rufus Scott to launch a new magazine called the *Commercial Bribery and Tipping Review* in 1920. Calling tipping inconsistent with all notions of the dignity of labor and a laborer's personal independence, Scott declared that tipping "makes the daily income of the worker dependent upon his subservience to the passing humor of the customer. It promotes fawning and sycophancy, and kills dignity and independence." His magazine, which was dedicated to eliminating all graft, equated tipping with commercial bribery; however it only lasted a few years.[50]

Sydney, Australia's, *Morning Herald* newspaper condemned the habit in an editorial. A puzzled editor could only ponder,

> It is strange that the practice should have established itself in Australia. Elsewhere there may be a measure of justification for it; here there is none.... In Australia conditions are entirely dissimilar. Wages are fixed by law. No one receives less than a living wage.[51]

In any tipping transaction, wondered the *New York Times*, "who is the master and who is the servant? It is the recipient who dominates and the donor who has the servile psychology." One observer noted that the usual tip was not tendered as an inducement to better service because restaurant and hotel patrons "tip even though they may not intend ever to revisit the place."[52]

Waxing philosophic, the *New Statesman and Nation* declared that men could be divided into three classes of tippers — born tippers, conventional tippers, and reluctant tippers. A majority were conventional tippers, but the reluctant giver "groans over the necessity of having to give a tip at all. If he were courageous enough, he would never do so." The magazine admitted there could be a touch of vulgarity in ostentatious tipping, and that some men gave huge tips solely to impress others with the fact they had a lot of money. However, they also felt it would be a disaster if tipping were forbidden by law with a 10 percent service charge added, because customers might be "in danger of being bullied into gluttony by waiters eager to make them eat in order that they might live."[53]

When waiter Jimmy Nearos, who worked in expensive New York establishments, was profiled in *Harper's*, he declared that on the strategy of extracting tips waiters divided into two schools: the dominating and the ingratiating. Adherents of the latter method tried to win the goodwill and sympathy of the customer by treating him or her with deference while displaying alertness to carry out his or her wishes. Most waitresses, said Nearos, belong to that school. It was a method he considered flawed, claiming it to be a fact that waitresses on the same job averaged considerably lower tips than men. Nearos explained that people tipped less from goodwill than from a sense of inferiority. He felt the most important thing to do was to establish "moral dominance" over the customer. This could be done easily, because it was not difficult to make most customers believe they were tiring you and being rather boring. Explained Nearos: "The whole art lies in planting it in the customer's mind, by keeping one's distance and by subtly resisting his wishes…. This vague feeling is likely to be translated into a good tip in order to win back the good opinion of the waiter."[54]

Fortune magazine conducted a survey in 1938 to assess the attitude toward tipping versus higher wages. It asked: "Many people depend on tips as a part of their pay. Do you think it would be better to have them paid larger wages out of an additional amount added to the bills the customers pay?" Respondents in total replied as follows: yes, 65.4 percent; no, 22.2 percent; don't know, 12.7 percent. "Prosperous" respondents voted 75.1 percent yes, 19.8 percent no, 5.1 percent don't know. Respective numbers for black voters (Pullman porters) were: 53.2 percent yes, 25.1 percent no, and 21.7 percent don't know. That magazine concluded that black porters were less certain than their white patrons that tips should be abolished, but still were strongly against the system.[55]

A 1948 poll conducted by *Woman's Home Companion* asked its readers: "Do you approve of the custom of tipping?" Those women respondents declared themselves against it two to one with quite a bit of disapproval arising from feeling that tipped workers needed the money less than the givers, that is, they were paid more. Most opposed the custom because they thought it was undemocratic. Even the one-third who supported it felt that the tip should not be a foregone conclusion, but should be merited. Among suggestions received as to how to eliminate it was the idea that a national law be passed to abolish it and that "writers of etiquette books should say it has been abolished and publish it in all magazines and newspapers."[56]

Gallup poll results of April 1947 to the question "Do you believe in the practice of tipping?" yielded 49 percent who said yes. Within urban areas (over 10,000 population) 55 percent believed in it. Using the same question in Philadelphia, a newspaper conducted a poll there and found 66 percent approval. It led Leo Crespi, assistant professor of psychology at Princeton University, to undertake the first in-depth scholarly probe of tipping in America. He felt that tipping was significant in American life, citing a *Life* magazine editorial on the topic in the July 15, 1946, issue as evidence. *Life* had concluded that "tipping was a national nuisance and as such should be eliminated."[57]

Crespi surveyed 300 people, asking, "Do you approve or disapprove of the practice of tipping by and large?" His results were: approve, 68.3 percent; disapprove, 27 percent; no opinion, 4.7 percent. Responses by men and women differed significantly with the numbers for men being, respectively, 60.1 percent 34.5 percent, and 5.4 percent; for women the respective results were 76.4 percent, 19.7 percent, and 3.9 percent. Comparing a group of 99 tip receivers to 86 tip givers (matched on sex, age, and economic status), Crespi found results of 95 percent approval from receivers, 2 percent disapproval, and 3 percent no opinion compared to 69.8 percent approval, 26.7 percent disapproval, and 3.5 percent no opinion from tip givers. A second question asked was "If service workers were given fair wages for their work, do you think that tipping should be eliminated?" Results were 69.7 percent responded "yes," 26.3 percent "no," and 4 percent no opinion. There were no significant differences between males and females or between tip receivers and tip givers (for tip receivers: 56.6 percent yes, 40.4 percent no, 3 percent no opinion, tip givers: 66.3 percent yes, 31.4 percent no, and 2.3 percent no opinion). From this data, Crespi concluded that what the Gallup and other survey respondents approved of was fair wages, not the practice of tipping. He argued that *Life* was in line with popular opinion that tipping should be eliminated. Even tip receivers in his survey wanted it gone.[58]

All three of those groups (receivers, givers, and the general public) were also asked, "What in your opinion would you call the main reason for tipping most people?" From the general public it was incentive/reward, 40 percent; fear of disapproval, 34.3 percent; poor salaries, 13 percent; other reasons and no opinion, 14.7 percent. For tip receivers those numbers were, respectively, 47.5 percent, 23.2 percent, 15.2 percent, and 14.2 percent; the respective responses from tip givers were 28.4 percent, 26.7

percent, 22.1 percent, and 12.7 percent. Crespi felt that previous explanations of tipping had two proponent types — consideration of incentive/ reward, and fear of social disapproval, regardless of the original instigating motivation. When Crespi asked the general group, "Do you generally tip even when you have received poor service?" he received a "yes" response of 55.7 percent. Respondents who expressed disapproval of tipping were asked "Though you disapprove of the practice, do you tip anyhow?" The "yes" response was 83.3 percent. Both of those results supported the social pressure motive as the dominant one, thought Crespi. When asked, "Do you generally tip a shoe clerk or a salesgirl in a store?" 97 percent replied "no." Most frequently, those people said there was no social custom which made it obligatory, causing Crespi to declare "custom, meaning primarily fear of social disapproval, is today the principal reason why people tip." In error were those who believed in the incentive/reward motive and those who concluded tipping took place for ego reasons, feeling superior, showing off, and so on. "Most people tip less from wanting to and more from having to. Which is precisely what we have now verified in the dominance of social pressure and humanitarian motives over incentive-reward and ego motives."[59]

Asked "How often do you tip?" the responses were: "practically always," 67.3 percent; "often," 9 percent; "sometimes," 11.3 percent; "rarely," 2.7 percent; "practically never," 7.7 percent; and no opinion, 1 percent. Average amount tipped was 12.5 percent in a restaurant, 13.8 percent in a nightclub, and 18.4 percent in a taxi. Those results indicated "that most American urbanites tip frequently, widely, and substantially," said Crespi, who added that "tipping is an aristocratic hangover which is inconsistent with the democratic assumptions of the equality and dignity of men. But that tipping may be in fact undemocratic in its implications is no assurance that the public views the custom in such a light." To determine whether the public thought it was democratic, he asked "Do you believe it is degrading or beneath one for people to seek and receive tips?" Results were: "yes," 14 percent, "no," 82.7 percent; and no opinion, 3.3 percent, causing Crespi to conclude that tipping was not looked upon as an undemocratic practice.[60]

Because tipping was not considered undemocratic, and most people wanted it abolished, Crespi wondered why. He concluded that it was because of the social pressure motive, being pushed into actions through fear of social disapproval. When he asked respondents, "Do you or do you not feel that tipping is becoming more and more of a nuisance?" he received a "yes" response rate of only 45 percent, which was not enough for Crespi to claim his theory was validated. He then argued that his own question was too vigorously worded, missing people who felt that tipping was a nuisance but didn't say so. Such logic allowed Crespi to say, "It is safe to conclude that a substantial majority feel that tipping is a nuisance." Then he asked his three groups (general public, receivers, givers), "Would you favor laws against tipping?" Responses, respectively, were: "yes," 15 percent, 6.1 percent, 16.3 percent; "no," 81 percent, 91.9 percent, 80.2 percent; and no opinion, 4 percent, 2 percent, 3.5 percent. Then he asked, "Do you favor or oppose the practice of the management having a fixed service charge added to the bill for your tip?" Respective responses were: favor, 18 percent, 23.2 percent, 17.9 percent; oppose, 75 percent, 73.8 percent, 77.4 percent; and no opinion, 7 percent, 3 percent, 4.7 percent. Another question asked was, "Many people in restaurants, hotels, barber-shops, etc., depend upon tips for a part of their pay. Do you think it would be better to have them paid larger wages out of an additional amount added to the bills customers pay?" Responses for the three groups were, respectively: "yes," 57.3 percent, 53.5 percent, 60.5 percent; "no," 33.7 percent, 37.4 percent, 31.4 percent; and no opinion, 9 percent, 9.1 percent, 8.1 percent.[61]

These results caused Crespi to conclude that people did not like laws in general, and the main objection to the fixed service charge idea seemed to be curtailment of personal choice, with that option seen more as a fixed tip than a service charge. Crespi did admit that if he ended the question with the phrase "instead of a tip" rather than "for your tip" the results might have been different. Still, he felt the majority of receivers and givers were ready to eliminate tips by accepting higher prices. To implement this change would require persuading management to take the step. That could be done best by obtaining the customer's refusal to tip while simultaneously publicizing the customer's willingness to pay higher prices. During that phase it would have to be made clear that in not tipping one was not a "piker but a conscientious objector." Crespi advocated forming a group to carry out his ideas, the "initiation of an anti-tipping league with a card left in lieu of a tip." His suggested card would be headed "FAIR WAGES —NOT TIPS!" It would then read,

> Public opinion polls show that the majority of the American people want tipping eliminated and service workers to get fair wages for their work. The only way to achieve this is by our refusing to tip. It's up to you to go to your employer and say we are willing to pay higher prices if necessary, but no more tips. (signed) National Anti-Tipping League.

Note that the onus here is all placed on the tip receivers.[62]

Finally, to measure tip receivers' attitude to nontipping he asked,

"What do you generally think, feel, or do when someone you have served does not tip you?" Fifty-three percent responded "nothing" or words to that effect; 23.4 percent said something equivalent to "thinks he's cheap;" 14.3 percent "cussed mentally," 7.1 percent held that it was "okay if he hasn't got it;" and 2.2 percent gave other responses. From this Crespi decided "tolerant" responses added up to about 60 percent. A second question put to receivers was "Suppose a person you had served gave you no tip with the explanation that he disapproved of tipping, what would your reaction be?" Tolerant responses to that question rose to over 80 percent, said Crespi. These results also negated media images of hostile servers taking some sort of revenge or aggressive action against nontippers. Even the intolerant responses by those surveyed were limited to thinking negative thoughts.[63]

Moral and ethical effects of the tipping system remained in the news in this period; they were all negative. In fact, one who had received tips in a job could be supposedly ruined for life as an employee, even for work in a nontipped position. Personnel executive H.A. Haring sternly warned his readers in a trade journal in 1921 that to reduce labor turnover it would be unwise to employ men from certain occupations. First category to be avoided were tip takers such as former waiters, bellboys, porters, and so on (the other two classes of labor to avoid hiring were railroad crews and coal miners). A tip receiver's whole character was undermined by gratuities; "once under the spell of the gratuity system, a man will never be satisfied with his stipulated compensation." That was true even when the wage of the new job was greater than the previous total of wages and tips. As an example, Haring told of a promising former porter employed in a school building for $20 more per month than his total income had been as a porter. Things were fine for a while with the man being steady and his character above average. Then he went downhill. When he was asked why, the man replied, "This ain't no job for a man. No one's given me an extra dollar all this year." The quickness and alertness often attributed to those in tipped jobs were, thought Haring, more illusion than real. Of men who had worked in tipped employment, Haring concluded that

> such men are poorly fitted to become employees of an industrial plant with its monotony of work. They weary of regular duties and they are unhappy if working within confined areas ... in their heart they are pondering and plotting not for more work to do nor for newer work, for the work's sake. They are scheming to get more money for the same work in the form of extra pay.[64]

Another objection Haring raised to former tip takers was his belief they had been educated in petty thievery by stealing towels, soap, table linen and so forth. "It is probably sufficient to recognize that such employees are specially liable to be well laden as they pass the factory door at the end of the day's work," he warned. As a final consideration, Haring pointed out those brought up under the tipping system

> will, as a class, be cringing in nature, not at all afflicted with a tendency to talk back. They will probably be all too ready to acquiesce in any suggestion or instruction, and forthwith prove to be fickle in performance, with probably, a tendency to deceitfulness. Experience, too, will show that they are not possessed of red blood. As a whole they lack stamina and are not aggressive or courageous. Drinking, too, is quite common, with a habit of taking rather larger drinks.[65]

Speaking in 1940 before the annual meeting of the American Association for Labor Legislation, Mary Anderson, director of the United States Women's Bureau, described tipping as "unwholesome and undemocratic," urging its abolition. Also speaking was University of Chicago assistant professor of economics Mary Barnett Gilson, who said that the custom "corrupts the character" of the tipper and added that

> we should consistently refuse to recognize it as a part of wages.... The tipped with whom I have talked, and I have talked with many, tell me they object to being tipped because of the implication of servility and inferiority as much as because of the insecurity of a living dependent upon tips.

The tipper's character was corrupted because "it gives him a sense of superiority and prestige derived from undemocratic origins." [66]

That same year hotel manager H.A. MacLennan said his 20 years of experience in the hotel industry made him very critical of the gratuity system because it "gives the receiver an entirely warped attitude toward life in general." Many disliked the habit, with half the complaints in a hotel linked to tipping. Guests didn't like it because of the uneasiness it generated; owners didn't like it because of the "greediness" it produced in employees. "There seems to be no halfway between inferiority and superiority complexes," he thought. On a poor day, the tip taker squandered money because it was not worth saving, while on a big-tip day, he or she squandered it in celebration.[67]

Clyde Davis, writing in a 1946 issue of the *Atlantic Monthly*, declared that "no man tips his equal." Whenever an American citizen tipped another American citizen he was tacitly proclaiming "I am a noble lord generously scattering largess to subhuman serfs." Although the receiver was politically and legally the giver's equal, by accepting the tip the recipient was tacitly "pulling his forelock, fawning and murmuring gratitude." Davis wondered why unions had not made a stand to retrieve the human dignity of their members. He concluded: "The tipping system is a relic of parasites in satin pants and servitors sleeping with the dogs on the rush-strewn kitchen floor."[68]

Chapter 6

"Public Nuisance Number One": Tipping Practices 1950–1969

"We found that our patrons were ill at ease not leaving a tip, and equally ill at ease if they slipped a coin under a saucer. Either way the diner often felt he was on the spot."
— C & O Railway

"Tipping, sucker, is paying for the privilege of paying."
— Stuart Wood

The period 1950 to 1969 was marked with more intensive government efforts to collect taxes on tips. Gratuities had been taxable for a long time, but there were great difficulties in trying to enforce those rules due to the nature of tip income. There were also more psychological investigations into tipping. There were more guides to tipping published to advise readers who to tip and how much. Those articles reinforced and legitimized the practice even more. It was partly a reflection of the affluent post-war America with more and more people being confronted by tipping situations.

Some things did not change, however. Media reports continued to portray waiters and other tip recipients as rich, aggressive, or in a dominant position compared to the tippers. Journalist Peter White reported in 1956 that one headwaiter earned $36,784 in tips in one year, more (by $1,784) than the salary of the chief justice of the United States. A few waiters were said to gross twice that amount in tips annually. Even in a modest New York restaurant chain waitresses were guaranteed $100 per week while, wrote White, in an average place a seasoned waiter was paid $32 per week in salary but moved it by tips to $175, $9,000 per year, as much as the governor of North Dakota and as much as some Ivy League university professors.[1]

Writing in *Coronet*, Mort Weisinger called the undeclared state of conflict between waiters and their customers the oldest cold war in the country. The average waiter, he declared, "will ignore you, insult you and intimidate you — and there is nothing you can do about it." If the average man was a lion in his own kitchen, then "he is invariably a Caspar Milquetoast when it comes to dealing with this bullying type of waiter." If a diner left 10 percent for the "poor service" he inevitably received, one of those "meal saboteurs ... will scowl, mutter and stormtroop away in a rage." A tip of 10–15 percent could cause the server to show his contempt by grabbing the money without a word or sign of acknowledgment while a fat tip of 15 percent merited only a slight nod of thanks. Only when the tip hit 20 percent or more would the waiter have the courtesy to thank the giver audibly. Weisinger wondered why waiters made dining out a tragedy instead of a treat. Were they lazy or just plain ornery? Or was it because they resented the public feeling they had to grovel for tips? The reason, he thought, is "lack of training, no school for waiters."[2]

Even more vitriolic was Stuart Wood in a 1956 article in *American Mercury*, where he stated that tipping had degenerated into "nothing short of impudent gangsterism, a sort of 'protection racket' scourge." Like the Chicago hoodlums of the 1920s who came around selling protection, "today's shark-toothed waiter operates in much the same vein." Perhaps, thought Wood, the waiter didn't realize that the "long-fostering gimmevirus has morally reduced him to the status of a surly beggar cadging as cadge can, left and right." A waiter's base pay might be "amusingly negligible" but their potential tip taking was "practically ceilingless." Tipping was "Public Nuisance Number One" and, concluded Wood, "Tipping, sucker, is paying for the privilege of paying."[3]

Less subtle were servers who reportedly used verbal attacks on their hapless customers. In a restaurant in China (probably before the 1949 Communist takeover) after a waiter received a tip he went to the balcony, where he announced the amount to everybody. Thus if a diner left a big tip he exited the café to a buzz of approval. Dock worker Peter Masterson once told a passenger where to place his car for loading on the Cunard liner *Queen Mary*. That traveler told Masterson that the porter who eventually came to unload his luggage would not be tipped. This was not Masterson's job, but he nevertheless yelled at the passenger several times, "You'll be sorry." After the traveler complained, Masterson was suspended from his job for three months for having sought gratuities from passengers under conditions amounting "to intimidation." This decision was upheld in the courts.[4]

When three women dining at Manhattan's Trattoria restaurant paid their $11 bill but left no tip, their waiter allegedly verbally abused them for not tipping. He was dismissed from his job immediately. More than 300 employees at that restaurant and several others walked off the job in protest and sympathy in a short-lived strike. The union went to bat for the fired waiter but only to the extent that they claimed he was entitled to 48 hours notice before being dismissed.[5]

There were also some physical retaliations. In the mid–1960s, John Patton declared in the *Saturday Evening Post* that "dozens of my friends have told me of the dented fenders, soup burns, lost luggage and other revenge they have suffered for holding back tips they did not feel were deserved." As for hotel owners, who were the strongest supporters of the custom, Patton could only sneer, "This is a pathetic case of self-delusion. Who can deny that customers are driven away by the insolence that tipping often breeds?" Noting that most tippers were afraid to punish even extremely bad service by withholding a tip, the *Wall Street Journal* warned its readers of how disgruntled tip receivers might get revenge on ocean liners. A couple might find they were unable to fit their keys into their luggage because the locks had been jammed or the luggage could fall apart two weeks later because it has been weakened by invisible razor slashes at critical points.[6]

When 45 state governors participated in an eight-day cruise to the Caribbean area as part of a governors' convention, they received a welcoming brochure from Virgin Islands governor Ralph Paiewonsky, a convention host, advising the executives of what was expected of them. Stating a standard tipping agreement has been agreed to with the cruise company, American Export Isbrandtsen Line, each passenger was to pay $3.50 per day, which would cover everything on board the ship. The only item not covered was baggage handling by longshoremen upon embarking and disembarking. Advised the brochure, "it would be wise to tip these persons separately."[7]

The checkroom concession rip-off continued into this era. Complaints had long been made about the high cost of hats, a certain amount to buy one, much more to annually "store" it at restaurant checkrooms. A Philadelphia businessman Harry Wright calculated in 1950 that in one year he paid $24.75 in checkroom tips for checking a ten-dollar hat. Around the same time, James B. Lee, president of Lee Hats, began to sell a soft-roll hat that could be folded like a handkerchief and tucked into one's pocket. It proved to be a strong seller in urban areas, mostly because men could fold it and put it into their pockets before entering a restaurant, thus avoiding the checkroom.[8]

As in the past, tips continued to go to the concession holders, not the employees. Virtually all of the big concession owners paid their help $40 for a six-day week (in the early 1950s) with no overtime, although one day could be ten hours long. For unionized checkroom workers, the starting salary was $41 for a 40-hour week, with overtime benefits. Of New York's 2,245 hat-check girls, only 400 were unionized, and most concession holders would not hire a union member. One man who had the check concession in a large restaurant would stand around watching on Saturday nights. If a man retrieving his hat did not reach for his wallet fast enough he chanted: "Take care of the girls! Take care of the girls!" In 1954 the Waldorf-Astoria check holder hired assistants to monitor the employees at unexpected times, in order to make sure they didn't keep any tips. If checkroom receipts dropped with no obvious cause like the weather or holidays, the concession owner checked with the establishment's management as to any possible drop in business. If told that business was normal, the concession holder would send an assistant to work that checkroom for a few days. Likely it meant somebody would be fired. Long-time checkroom worker Blanche Holland said the workers still deceived the owner when they could, although details were not provided. When hats faded in popularity, almost disappearing as an article of dress in the 1950s, checkrooms become much less important. In summer, and year-round in some climates, men often had nothing to check but their hats if anything at all.[9]

The no-tipping policy instituted in 1947 by the C & O Railway lasted just three years. On the tables in the dining cars were cards that informed the passengers: "You are our guest—please do not tip." Yet in 1950 the tipping ban was lifted with its failure blamed on the public. The railroad explained: "We found that our patrons were ill at ease not leaving a tip, and equally ill at ease if they slipped a coin under a saucer. Either way the diner often felt he was on the spot." Commenting on the experiment, a labor official remarked that the plan could have been successful if the entire railroad industry had got behind it "so people traveling on this particular line wouldn't feel they were defying convention. Experience has shown that although the public gripes about tipping, too many people lack the courage to participate in an experiment that breaks with custom." A different account blamed the waiters for that failed experiment; a business journalist told his readers he was on a C & O train one day reading the "don't tip" card on his table, when the server told him, "You ain't supposed to pay no attention to that." The journalist didn't; soon thereafter the C & O abolished its no-tipping policy.[10]

Shipboard tipping was in the media a little more as ocean cruises became a bit more fashionable and popular in the 1950s and 1960s. According to an official with the New York State Department of Labor, in the mid–1950s waiters on American passenger ships averaged only $2.51 per day in tips, headwaiters $3.36, and night stewards just 93 cents per day.[11]

Around 1960 the Holland-America line banned tipping on its European cruises, then later on its cross-channel trips for its western European service. Next the ban was extended to its North Pacific Coast trips, and finally to its trans-Atlantic service in 1968, making the company entirely tip-free. Holland claimed that crew members were fully compensated for any loss of income, that its policy was developed with the cooperation of labor unions, and that the reaction of passengers had been very favorable. Crew members agreed to accept no tips, even if they were offered. Reportedly, Holland strictly enforced its no-tip policy. Joining in was the Cunard line, which first banned tipping in 1968 on its fly-cruise holidays from Gibraltar to Mediterranean ports. Seven percent was added to the fare, to be passed on to the crew. If successful, they hinted at extending the ban to all their sailings. Explaining why they were taking such action, a Cunard spokesman said, "We find that the question of how much to tip is quite a problem to some of our cruise passengers." However, less than six months later — still in 1968 — Cunard announced it was abolishing its no-tip experiment. They reverted to a reinstatement of tips and a fare cut.

> It isn't that we don't think it right to abolish tipping, or that the staff don't like it. It's just that a very considerable number of our passengers insist on going on tipping anyway, although they know from the brochure that the service charge has been included in the fare.[12]

The uncertainty that underlaid tipping was one of the reasons the growth in tipping guides took place, along with an increasingly affluent population. *Time* magazine declared in 1953 that France "is one long landscape of outstretched, tip-extracting hands — the doorman, the waiter, the wine steward, the cabby, the deliveryman, the barber, the...." A tip had to be made, on top of the 15 percent service charge added to the tab at most establishments. And how was it to be figured?[13]

Around the mid–1950s *Travel* magazine advised that in city hotels in America bellboys should be tipped 25 cents minimum per bag, nothing to the doorman unless he did something special, 25 cents per person to the chambermaid for a hotel stay of two nights or more, 15–20 percent of the bill in restaurants, 50 cents in beauty shops to the person who cut and set the hair, and 25–50 cents to the manicurist. *Holiday* magazine counseled its readers that a 15 percent tip in a restaurant was customary. If the restaurant check included a service charge it was not necessary to tip, unless the service was especially good, in which case the waiter would "appreciate a little extra"— 5 percent. Washroom attendants and theater ushers were always tipped, while barbers expected 10 percent. Hairdressers and taxi drivers each expected 15 percent. A woman's magazine with three million readers told them that in the case of a $5.75 bill in a beauty shop, the hair stylist should be tipped 50 cents, the person who washed the hair 25 cents, 50 cents to the woman who set the hair, and 25 cents to the manicurist. Much pricier advice for beauty shop tipping came from the *New York Times*, which declared that the operator who cut the hair should be tipped one dollar, three dollars to the person who did a permanent, two to three dollars to the woman who did a tinting and dyeing job, while the person who gave a facial and the one who washed the hair should each receive 15 percent of the bill.[14]

Advice guides tended to get bigger and more comprehensive in the late 1950s, reflecting increased domestic and international travel. An affluent America was taking advantage of very favorable exchange rates with most European nations. *Changing Times* published a comprehensive guide for domestic travelers with suggestions for tipping amounts in expensive restaurants, average restaurants, lunch counters, hotels, bars, ships, airports, trains, beauty shops, shoeshines, and to cab drivers, deliverymen, and parking attendants. *Good Housekeeping* published its own guide in June 1957. It was reprinted verbatim in *Travel* magazine ten months later. Tipping advice was given for seven European nations by categories, which included barbers, bellhops, chambermaids, coatroom attendants, doormen, hairdressers, station porters, taxi drivers, theater ushers, restaurant waiters, nightclub waiters, and washroom attendants. *Holiday* declared that in British hotels with a service charge, the extra fee didn't cover the waiter, who should be tipped 10–15 percent. Even when a service charge did cover all personnel, employees expected extra tips if they gave that ubiquitous but never defined "special attention." In the absence of a service charge, the tip in British city hotels should be 15 percent with 10 percent sufficient in country inns and small-town hotels. That percentage was to be divided among the bellboy, waiter, hall porter, and chambermaid.[15]

Good Housekeeping published a guide to Christmas time tipping in 1950. Many more would follow in various sources over the coming years. The *Good Housekeeping* guide dealt with apartment superintendents, doormen and elevator operators, mailmen, delivery people, garbagemen, policemen, gardeners, school bus drivers, and so on.[16]

The American Automobile Association, the American Hotel Association, and other agencies all offered tip recommendations, summarized in *Coronet* in 1961. These recommendations dealt with people such as wait-ers, taxi drivers, bellboys, porters, doormen, hat check girls, bartenders, sports ushers, barbers, chambermaids, beauticians, shoeshine boys, furni-ture movers, cabin stewards on liners, deck stewards, dining room stew-ards, washroom attendants, mailmen, garbagemen, apartment building superintendents at Christmas, golf caddies, and parking lot attendants.[17]

Mademoiselle published its own advice later that decade for the "intel-ligent woman traveler." In an ever-expanding list, this guide explained whom to tip and how much in the following areas and occupations: planes, ships, trains, charter buses, hired cars, hotels, restaurants, taxis, ushers, gas station attendants, hairdressers, barbers, guides, tour conductors, tour dri-vers, and house servants. In Holland, Britain, France, and Switzerland, readers were advised to discreetly tip house servants (butler and maid) while vacationing as weekend house guests. Going even further was the *New York Times*, which published a very large two-page spread detailing who and how much to tip in 35 different countries and regions (a region contained several nations). Going further still was an entire book on how, where, and how much to tip; *All About Tipping* by Jean Sprain was a 50-cent paperback released in 1965.[18]

Celebrity tippers weren't mentioned much in this period. According to one report, the Duchess of Windsor never tipped the washroom atten-dant at the El Morocco nightclub. When that item became public, the reporter professed amazement at the number of his readers who wrote to him in praise of her "firm stand." During the 1955 spring baseball train-ing season in St. Petersburg, Florida, New York Yankees manager Casey Stengel posted a notice informing his baseball players: "Tipping: 25 cents for breakfast, 50 cents for dinner, $1 per week for room maid." Appar-ently this was done because the Yankee players had been tipping only a dime.[19]

Much discussion still centered around who tipped the most and the least, based on geography, gender, occupation, and so forth. Around 1950 it was said that tipping in Europe was out of hand because of lavish tips left by American tourists. It embarrassed native citizens who were getting used to, and respecting, the no-tipping rule in many establishments that had added a service charge to the bills in lieu of tipping. Americans reg-ularly ignored it and tipped anyway. While Americans abroad had the dubious reputation of leaving the biggest tip when away from home — a distinction belonging to Americans back to pre–World War II days — by 1952 it was reported that wealthy Egyptians and the rich from South Amer-ica had claimed that spot. European travel officials who attended a 1952 Naples meeting of the International Union of Official Travel Organizations agreed, off the record, that people from those two groups were then the heaviest spenders and biggest tippers when abroad.[20]

Most European waiters in the early 1950s had no weekly wage at all, subsisting entirely on tips, compared to America where most waiters received a weekly salary — albeit often minuscule. Those European waiters said the best tippers were waiters and former waiters, followed by clergymen and gamblers.[21]

According to reporter Peter White, waiters rated a guest as a poor tip prospect if he wore a "cheap tie, smoked a pipe, studied the menu closely, ordered rye and ginger ale and finished every bit of food on his plate." Hope for a better tip were raised by a scotch-and-water drinker who paid little attention to the menu. People with expense accounts didn't always tip well. A man tipped liberally if he was with someone else's wife; however, with his own wife he was "budget-conscious. If he leaves a big tip anyway, she may grab some of it back."[22]

In a 1957 story in *Newsweek* southerners were said to tip 15 percent in their cities for meals, with 12 percent being average in the midwest, and 15 percent on the west coast. New York City remained the most expensive city in which to tip, with a New York cabby rated as one of the rudest of all tippees. Said writer Robert Ruark, "If they don't say thank you for the tip, I don't close the door when I get out." A Tennessee businessman stated, "I tip in New York because I'm shy. I don't want to create a disturbance. I don't tip taxi drivers or bartenders at home, but up there they expect it." Although a Detroit executive tipped cabbies 15 cents at home he gave 25 cents in New York. A manufacturer from Chicago felt the minimum tip in New York was 20 percent, more than at home. Tippees in New York said the most generous tippers were salaried men, especially in the liquor, tobacco, and advertising businesses; out-of-town buyers; and stockbrokers. Among the notoriously poor tippers, or stiffs, were doctors, dentists, college boys, actors, politicians, musicians, company presidents, and expensively dressed people. Proportionate to their income, the most generous tippers were waitresses and taxi drivers. Women in general had a "stingy reputation." Wondering why this should be, a New York hotel executive theorized that "a woman can't do percentages. She can figure out 10 percent in her head, but certainly not 15 percent. And so she leaves only 10 percent."[23]

During the early 1960s the staff at Chicago's Palmer House asserted that a guest wearing crepe-rubber soles or a golf hat was a stiff. On the other hand, if his shoes were well-polished and he carried an attaché case, he was a "live one." Among the best tippers were furniture men, restauranteurs, clothiers, and Shriners; among the worst were doctors, politicians, traveling salesmen, and Lions Club members. Also among the poor tippers were people with lots of luggage, and Cadillac owners. No one was held in lower esteem at the Palmer House than the "sanitation specialist," the hotel guest who hid in the bathroom when the bellboy arrived with the suitcases. Ironically, said a Detroit restaurateur, a well-known stiff sometimes got better service than a liberal tipper because he was considered a challenge, with waitresses doing everything to see if his wallet could be loosened.[24]

Well-known writer Gay Talese reported on the tipping situation in New York City in 1964 by noting that next to "well-bred" ladies and major league baseball players the worst tippers were tourists at that year's World's Fair. Instead of their usual one to two dollar tip on a five-dollar tab, hairdressers said they were getting only quarters from some female tourists. Good tippers, stated waiters, were gamblers, jockeys, politicians, and other waiters, with everyone else, especially women and ball players, being stiffs.[25]

As before, the economic reality of tipping was rarely mentioned; when it was, it was usually not in the mainstream media. What they presented was anecdotal evidence of high tipping amounts. Calling New York City the capital of tipping, *Newsweek* magazine cited an unnamed out-of-town executive who estimated that a trip to that city cost him at least $20 each day in tips alone, in 1957: redcap 50 cents; bellhop 50 cents; five taxis $1.25; lunch waiter two dollars; four doormen one dollar; three hatcheck girls 75 cents; two bartenders $1.25; dinner waiter serving 4, $7; captain $5; sommelier $1; cigarette girl 25 cents; a total of $20.60. According to the magazine, the average waiter earned four fifths of his income from tips, bartenders and taxi drivers earned about half their total income from tips, and captains and doormen got two-thirds of their income from gratuities. Gone were the days of the easy tips of the 1920s, declared the magazine (apparently seeing no contradiction with the numbers it had just cited), "when employees paid for the privilege of working in a club known for high rollers."[26]

Reporter Craig Claiborne stated in 1962 that in a first-class dining room in Manhattan a waiter was paid a salary of about $40 for a 40-hour week, but his tips could total $250 each month or more. Journalist M.J. Arlen cited the same $40 salary for a Manhattan waiter, but noted that in most states there was no minimum wage for waiters. In Arkansas, for example, the going rate was 16 cents per hour and, said Arlen, "restaurant owners never pay above the minimum." A bellboy working in a first-class New York hotel could earn $2,000 annually in tips, added Arlen.[27]

According to an estimate made in 1964 by the U.S. Department of Commerce, Americans handed out around $750 million in tips annually, with about $450 million going to restaurant employees. A second source put the amount of tips dispensed in the United States at roughly $594 million yearly, with waiters taking $400 million, taxi drivers $139 million, barbers $48 million, and porters $7 million. For the year 1960 the Department of Commerce estimated that Americans would spend some $2 billion on foreign travel, much of it in Europe. Of that sum, 60 percent would go to hotels, restaurants, cafés, and places of entertainment. Assuming a tip rate of 10 percent, then $120 million would be dispensed as gratuities.[28]

For 1961 the federal Bureau of Labor Statistics (BLS) conducted a survey of 6,650 bellhops working in hotels employing 50 or more people, in 24 major metro centers. Of that total, 2,632 reported tips of under one dollar an hour; 756 reported tips of one dollar to under $1.25 an hour; 2,556 reported tips of $1.25 or more an hour; for 706 data were not available. For the under-one dollar group, the breakdown was: one cent to less than 25 cents, 326; 25 cents to under 50 cents, 780; 50 cents to under 75 cents, 648; 75 cents to under one dollar, 878. There were 1,167 bellhops whose paid wages came to less than 40 cents an hour — of that number 288 (25 percent) received tips of less than 75 cents an hour, 432 (37 percent) received between 75 cents to one dollar and 433 (37 percent) earned over one dollar an hour in tips. A total of 298 bellhops had a wage and tip income of less than one dollar an hour. Also surveyed by the BLS were 15,809 servers, within the same parameters as the bellhops. Reported hourly tip earnings broke down as follows: one cent to 24 cents, 21; 25 cents to 49 cents, 487; 50 cents to 74 cents, 1,640; 75 cents to 99 cents, 2,103; one dollar to $1.24, 2,122; $1.25 and over, 8,240; not available, 1,196. Of the 1,037 servers with less than 40 cents an hour in paid wages, 31 percent received less than 75 cents an hour in tips; 42 percent made between 75 cents and 99 cents, while 27 percent received over one dollar an hour in tips. There were 6,954 servers with earnings of at least 80 cents an hour in wages and at least 75 cents an hour in tips, 48 percent of the total employees for whom the BLS collected data. Even the BLS admitted their sample was not representative as it sampled only from large establishments located in major cities. Writing in a business journal John Henderson commented, "It must be concluded, on the basis of the evidence presented, that the paid and tipped income of the unsampled employees in the industry is considerably lower than that of employees working in large city hotels." Low-wage areas were also low-tip areas. Regions with the highest average hourly wages were also the areas with the highest percentage of employees receiving tips in excess of one dollar an hour. In large establishments (sales of $1 million annually or more), 70 percent of servers and 64 percent of bellhops had tips in excess of one dollar an hour; for those employed in establishments with annual sales of under $1 million, the respective percentages were 47 and 38. Only 17 percent of the nonsupervisory employees in those establishments surveyed by the BLS received tips; the other 83 percent were almost entirely dependent on wages. Low wages for the nontipped were at least partly a function of low paid wages received by tipped employees. Noted Henderson, "that is, the fact that some employees receive tips influences the level of paid wages for all workers."[29]

George Stelluto reported in a 1962 issue of the *Monthly Labor Review* that employer payments to servers averaged less than one dollar an hour except in five metro areas: Minneapolis–St. Paul, Los Angeles, San Francisco, Portland, and New York City. In New York, waiters were paid an average of $1.02 an hour, waitresses were paid 92 cents. Averages below 50 cents an hour were frequently recorded among the southern cities with waiters paid 20 cents in Atlanta, 27 cents in Memphis, 37 cents in Baltimore, 44 cents in Dallas and Houston, while in Miami waiters were paid 49 cents an hour, and waitresses were paid 41 cents. Tips averaged the highest in the northeast and the west; they were lowest in the south. In metro areas (over 750,000 people) employers paid wages averaging 86 cents an hour with 5 percent of those employees receiving no tips, 9 percent from one cent to 49 cents, 12 percent 50 cents–74 cents, 15 percent 75 cents–99 cents, 19 percent one dollar to $1.24, 40 percent received tips of $1.25 an hour or over. Two years later, Stelluto reported that servers received on average employer-paid wages of 81 cents an hour, with a range of 54 cents in the south to $1.20 in the west. Forty percent of those workers received wages of less than 75 cents an hour, 66 percent got less than one dollar and 90 percent received an employer-paid wage of less than $1.25 an hour.[30]

Chapter 7

"The Average Person Is Inherently a Tipper": Tipping Responses 1950-1969

"Accept tipping. Think of the good it does. You make the tip employee
happy, although he may be too naturally discreet to show it."
— M.J. Arlen

Establishments with a no-tip policy that did not substitute an added
service charge were rare in America. One was the restaurant chain Chock
Full o' Nuts, which had 25 outlets in New York City alone in the 1950s.
The policy was implemented when the down-scale company opened its
first outlet in 1926. Maintained for 40 years, the no-tip policy was finally
abandoned in 1967. Explained company founder and chairman William
Black,

> I lay awake nights before I consented to this about-face in our long stand-
> ing no-tipping policy. In spite of the fact that we pay as much as, or more
> than anyone in our industry, I didn't like the way many of our customers were
> being treated. I hope that tipping will bring on a smile, a "please" and "thank
> you," which are so essential to the enjoyment of a meal.

Black added that the wages of employees were not to be reduced.[1]
One place where tipping was definitely out of line was the White
House. As people collected their coats after a Supreme Court dinner held
at the White House in 1958, several unidentified guests left 25 cents each
on the coatroom counter. A White House social assistant pointed out that
"anyone who comes here regularly knows that it just isn't done." Describing
the incident as very embarrassing, the official suggested that "apparently a

guest was unfamiliar with the fact that the White House is considered a residence and not the same as a hotel or restaurant."[2]

Service charges added to a bill in Europe continued to expand. Britain had lagged in that regard, but more establishments changed to that method when the Labour government brought the Catering Wages Act into effect in 1948; this act established a minimum wage for service employees, thus ending their complete dependence on tips for income. When this change in policy was implemented, it led to a cessation in tipping only when management made it clear that the surcharge was in lieu of tips. Art Buchwald noted that most employees in European restaurants and hotels who had direct contact with patrons received no wages, depending entirely on tips. Most establishments on the European continent added 15 percent as a service charge. Confirming the tendency of Americans abroad, Buchwald remarked on the Continental service charge method:

> The system is a good one, but Americans, who by nature are kind souls, have an inferiority complex when traveling abroad ... he louses up the system completely by tipping as he would in the United States. This has become such a typical practice that now hotel employees expect Americans to tip extra and above the 15%, and even show disappointment if no further gratuities are offered.

Holland's Amstel Hotel gave its waiters the choice of trying for a regular tip from a guest or having a straight 15 percent service charge added to the bill with the proviso the waiter would refuse any extra offered. A journalist commented, "almost none of the waiters gamble; they settle for the 15 percent." The system of pooling tips was also a popular European method of dealing with the issue, particularly in France. All tips in an establishment were pooled, then divided up among the staff according to a predetermined formula.[3]

One of the reasons Americans may have continued to tip when abroad in places with a service charge, was the rarity of such a system in the United States. One place where this system was used was with the banquet waiters at the Waldorf-Astoria hotel, where the hotel added a 15 percent charge for those special functions. A group of banquet waiters sued the hotel charging that while 15 percent was added to bills, only 10 percent was returned to the waiters. After years of legal wrangling, the case was thrown out when the court decided that the waiters knew that other, higher-level, nonservice employees were receiving a part of the 15 percent.[4]

Longchamps restaurant chain once tried to abolish tipping by substituting a service charge, but reverted to the old system when they decided their customers were paying the service charge but still leaving a tip. The

Pittsburgh Athletic Association was a private club with a no-tip policy (common in U.S. private clubs), with a 10 percent service charge substituted. This club found many of its members tipped anyway. Explained one member: "It's a no-tip club ostensibly, but you don't get very good service if you don't add a tip."[5]

Until the early 1960s, Mackinac, Michigan's seasonal resort the Grand Hotel operated in a standard fashion with employees receiving a minuscule salary, their income dependent mostly on tips. The hotel had been paying bellhops and cocktail waitresses $15 each month, waiters and maids $60 each month, and dishwashers $150 per month. To those wages were added free room, meals, uniforms, and "high tips." During the Michigan legislative sessions of 1962, 1963, and 1964, when the issues of minimum wages and maximum hours were debated, Grand Hotel general manager R.D. Musser traveled regularly to Lansing to lobby against such provisions extending to service workers. When the Michigan legislature passed a minimum wage law that applied to service workers, the Grand considered itself forced to investigate a system that would permit them to obtain what they called proper credit for employee meals and lodging, formerly provided free, and employees' "large tips." The resort began operating on a no-tip basis in 1965 for the first time, although they weren't completely sold on the idea. With the state minimum wage set at $1.25 an hour, employers were allowed a maximum credit of 25 percent of that wage for items such as room and board, tips, and anything else provided as an extra — resulting in a minimum wage of 94 cents an hour for, say, a waiter. When the Grand Hotel changed its policy, it added a 15 percent service charge to bills while guaranteeing its service workers $1.25 per hour by contract. At first, the Grand operated paid no salary at all but used a piecework payment system (still guaranteeing the $1.25 per hour). With wide swings in room occupancy rates, the Grand found the system did not work to its liking during slow weeks. After two weeks the Grand reverted to a different system, giving all employees a base salary and reduced piecework payments. Thus a dining room waiter was paid a salary of $200 per month, a $125 per month season-end bonus, and 35 cents per breakfast served, 50 cents per lunch, and 65 cents for each dinner. Chambermaids got $225 per month salary, $100 per month bonus, and 30 cents per bed serviced; bellhops got a salary of $75 per month, $100 per month bonus, and 60 cents for each room checked in, checked out, or changed, and 10 percent of room service checks served. Cocktail waitresses received a $75 per month salary, a $75 per month season-end bonus, along with 10 percent of each tab they served. All those employees were docked four dollars each day for their room and board. Although they didn't have to live in the Grand, there were few other options. The bonus amounts were withheld and paid only at the season's end, and only if the employee stayed until the end. The season ran from late May until late September.[6]

Clubs formed during this period to battle the system, as in the past. Compared to previous groups, these were very mild-mannered, which may explain why the American club continues to exist, decades after its formation. Robert Farrington lived in the Boston suburb of Wayland, Massachusetts. In 1959 he was 33 years old, a 15-year employee at the Boston office of the advertising agency Batten, Barton, Durstine & Osborn. He was also a firm opponent of perfunctory tipping for what he considered mediocre service. Wanting to do something about it, he took out a newspaper ad calling on like-minded readers to join the budding organization Tippers Anonymous (TA), of which Farrington was founder and president. For one dollar members received wallet-size forms enabling them to hand a written complaint or compliment to a waiter. Farrington spent $300 of his own money to print those forms for TA. They were to be left, with an appropriate tip, to inform the server that he had just served a TA member and that he was not opposed to tipping, but that he felt "its meaning has been lost in the hurried pace of the modern world." He hoped waiters, porters, and so on, would pass their good ratings on to their employers. Poor ratings were intended to serve as a reminder as to how service employees could improve their incomes. Recalling a poor rating Farrington himself bestowed on a waiter, the TA leader admitted, "I got out so fast I didn't wait for a reaction." Waiters randomly sampled by a reporter at a few restaurants revealed little enthusiasm for the TA approach. One of those queried retorted, "That's a good system for people who can't talk." Two years later TA claimed to have a total of 800 members.[7]

Another U.S. group that surfaced briefly was NOTIP (Nationwide Operation To Instill Pride), which organized in the New York area in 1967. Its members left cards with service personnel instead of tips, which explained that tipping was unacceptable and that the recipient should receive a proper wage. NOTIP disappeared quickly.

Maurice Ellman, a 28-year-old British lawyer, launched his Anti-Tipping Campaign, in London at a Fleet Street restaurant in April 1966 when he left no tip but a card which read,

> Thank you. I do appreciate your service, but I have not left a tip. I believe that tipping is a patronizing habit, and that you should receive a proper wage without having to rely on charity. Please pass this on to your employer or union. Published by the Anti-Tipping Campaign, 25 Westminster Mansions, Gt. Smith St., S.W.1.

Having renounced all tipping himself, Ellman believed a service charge should be added. Tipping, he said, was socially divisive. He claimed to have received 100 letters pledging support for his campaign. Those supporters came from all walks of life, including tip receivers. Believing his group must proceed by trying to influence public opinion, Ellman asserted that legislation was not the answer.[9]

By early 1967 it was reported that waiters, hairdressers, and taxi drivers supported the campaign, though Ellman admitted in the group's first progress report that it had not made any progress toward abolishing tips. "It is scandalous that some employers should rely on the public to make up ridiculously low wages. Some people think they are doing a waiter a good turn by giving him half-a-crown, but the result of this is just to depress his wages," he remarked. Ellman was optimistic that tip abolishment would come. Surveys carried out independently, including one by the Manchester Consumer Group, indicated that the public was 70 percent in favor of eliminating tips, if wages were improved. Taxi drivers pledged support because they found it difficult to get mortgages; lenders, unlike the British tax department, did not recognize tips as income.[10]

On the occasion of the group's first anniversary, reporter Mark Donald published a negative article about them in the *New York Times*. He described it as "a movement that is going nowhere and has achieved absolutely nothing in its year of existence." Ellman claimed to have 100 members. When asked how many he had to start with, Ellman explained, "Well, we had a hundred people who were interested. Since then, they have actually joined." Discussing the original card handed out to service people, Ellman was quoted as saying "This was a direct frontal assault on the tipping system because we handed over no money. It proved too rough a ride for many people, including myself." His worst experience came when he handed a card to a waiter, who glared in disbelief, then he put the card in his mouth and slowly tore it to shreds in his teeth. "He was very upset. I think he was swearing in Greek," added Ellman. As a result of that and other similar experiences the campaign abandoned its hard line, explained Donald, handing out new cards designed to accompany a tip. They said: "Thank you, I have left a tip although I disapprove of tipping. You should receive an adequate wage without having to rely on tips. If you agree, please pass this on to your employer or union." These new cards proved much more popular. Symbolically, noted Donald, "They are colored yellow." Said one anti-tipper, "There are some convictions it is terribly difficult to have the courage of." Donald concluded his article by declaring: "The plain argument against Mr. Ellman's campaign is that tipping works. It works in capitalist societies because it gets things done. It works in controlled economies for exactly the same reason."[11]

One month later the *New York Times* published a letter to the editor from an angry Ellman, who claimed that Donald's article was full of errors. Declaring that he had never met Donald, Ellman denied making any of the statements Donald attributed to him. As to the group's membership number, Ellman stated it had gone from one member to more than 100 with nearly 400 supporters worldwide in the first year. The new, soft-line cards were not in use because Ellman found that the originals gave too rough a ride. Instead, because the principle was to obtain proper wages for tippees, the campaign got in touch with supportive trade unions for advice. One such union pointed out that it would be equally effective and easier on its members financially if the groups produced a card to be given with a tip. That, explained Ellman, was the reason the cards were changed. They had the added advantage of winning the sympathy of even more of those who received tips. Even after this persuasive letter to the editor, Ellman's group was not heard from again.[12]

During this period the U.S. federal authorities began to vigorously pursue those evading income taxes on tips. Early in 1956, Hans Paul, a headwaiter at the Waldorf-Astoria hotel from 1943 to 1952, was indicted for income tax evasion. According to Assistant U.S. Attorney David Jaffe, the Waldorf collected $1 million annually from a service charge for its banquet division waiters, and put the money in a common pool with two-thirds divided among the waiters and one-third to those in higher positions such as Paul. The indictment was thought to be the first in metropolitan New York for tax evasion based on a failure to report tips. As a result of that investigation, the Internal Revenue Service broadened the scope of its investigation to cover all the hotels in the area. According to a government spokesman, the investigation revealed that waiters "in the main" had been reporting only 10–25 percent of their tips, and the government was being defrauded out of millions of tax dollars each year. Paul's indictment covered the years 1949 to 1952, during which his base salary was $3,000 or less annually. For 1949, Paul reported a net income of $13,650 while the government said it was $39,784; for 1950, $14,483 versus $24,357; for 1951, $16,196 versus $29,220; for 1952, $11,243 versus $29,316. Only about 5 percent of the money was collected by Paul personally, the other 95 percent came to him contractually, through the pooling of the service charge and division formula. Jaffe explained that Paul came to the attention of the IRS a couple of years earlier when he made investments of over $10,000 in Wall Street stocks. If convicted, Paul faced a maximum of five years and a $10,000 fine on each of the four counts.[13]

Later in 1956, in an apparent plea bargain, Paul pled guilty to evading $4,992 in 1951 income taxes, for which he was sentenced to four months' imprisonment and fined $7,500. By then, Paul's successor as headwaiter at the Waldorf-Astoria, Arthur Hagedorn, had been indicted for evading income tax in 1952 and 1953. The state alleged that he paid $9,110 in taxes for those two years when in fact he actually owed $20,981. The hotel cooperated in both investigations. Hagedorn later pled guilty to the charges. *Time* magazine covered the story of the two men under the title "The Real Rich."[14]

Still later in 1956, indictments on tax evasion were issued against two headwaiters from the Statler Hotel and against 13 captain-waiters at the Waldorf. All were charged with failing to report tips. The Statler men, Malachia Cesario and Ramon San Martion, pled guilty to failing to report tips totaling $19,632 and evading payment of $4,296 in taxes from 1952 to 1954. They were given a one-year suspended sentence, fined $1,500 each, placed on probation for two years, and of course, had to pay the taxes due plus penalties.[15]

A few years later, Fred Stauber, the captain of waiters at the Pierre Hotel in New York, was sentenced to 60 days in jail for income tax evasion. He was convicted of evading $2,750 in taxes on undeclared tips of $12,000 received form 1952 to 1954. In 1960 Ronald Egleston, former headwaiter at the Copacabana night club was sentenced to 60 days in jail for failing to report $44,000 in tips for 1953 through 1955. He pled guilty.[16]

To catch Egleston the government used net worth evidence to present to the grand jury. Investigation showed that Egleston created a $21,000 account in 1955 in a Mississippi bank. That same year he also bought a $124,000 warehouse in New Orleans with a cash payment of $40,000 down.[17]

This kind of activity was not limited to America. According to the British tax department, the Inland Revenue, in 1959 waiters at a London restaurant, Talk of the Town, substantially understated the amount of tips they received under the pooling system. Three waiters were charged with conspiring together to cheat and defraud Inland Revenue on behalf of all 30 waiters who benefitted. Over eight months Inland Revenue alleged it has been defrauded of £ 3,664. Said prosecutor A. Alexander, "It is quite clear that not only did the whole of the staff benefit but they knew all about it."[18]

What made it easier to catch the American underreporters was the fact that a paper trail existed; they were all involved in banquet service where a service charge was added and then split among the staff. It meant the hotels had fairly complete records, very unusual in the case of tips. Such stories in the media, while true, were very exceptional. They played into the image of all tip recipients as being if not outright rich, then at least very well-off. If that were true, then there was no need to concern oneself over a server's salary, or over a two-tiered minimum wage system with a lower minimum for service workers. It allowed one to overlook the inconsistency, arbitrariness, randomness, and capriciousness involved in tip income. An extremely tiny proportion of tip recipients were in the position of a Hans Paul. And in those cases it wasn't really tipping, but a mandatory service charge split many ways, though of course a few guests would have insisted on tipping. A man in Paul's position would have almost never served guests personally. The high tips contained very little that was actually handed personally by a diner to Paul or others in a similar position.

Government involvement shifted more to integrating tips into the system but always at some disadvantage to tip receivers. While the government was quick to make tips taxable, it was much slower to integrate tip income into the Social Security system. A two-tier minimum wage system developed in some jurisdictions, with tip receivers being paid at a lower rate. Attempts to ban tipping by legislative fiat had nearly disappeared; if they surfaced at all they were laughed at or ignored. A bill was introduced in the Mississippi legislature in 1951 to restore the law prohibiting tips, but it was viewed merely as an indignant legislator's outburst, not to be taken seriously. Argentine leader Juan Perón signed a 1948 decree abolishing tipping in that nation's hotels, bars, restaurants, and so on. It was replaced by a service charge of 22 percent added to all bills, to be distributed among service workers. Peron intended to eliminate that "humiliating habit of giving charity to honest and decent workers." For the first two weeks it was reported that nobody tipped but the service deteriorated to such an extent that everyone started to give a small additional tip. The decree was still in effect in 1966, but reportedly everyone tipped 10 percent, making a total of 32 percent on top of the bill. In the mid 1960s some U.S. Senators decided that the free haircuts, shaves, and shoe shines they received in the Senate barber shop should be free of tips. They installed a no-tipping rule; it was quickly thrown out by a bipartisan majority.[19]

When the state of New York conducted 1954 hearings on proposed minimum wage laws, industrial commissioner of New York Edward Corsi stated: "Tipping is unworthy of labor in the twentieth century. It makes a servant out of the worker. It is a disgraceful thing that the worker has to depend on tips for a living." At hearings on the minimum wage two years later, Western New York Restaurant Association counsel Edward Kavinoky told the panel that a rise in tipping made it unnecessary to raise the minimum hourly wage of service employees in the restaurant industry, arguing that industry tips had a "built-in escalator tied to the general economy." In 1967, when the state of New York raised its minimum wage from one dollar to $1.50 an hour, they allowed employers to charge 35 cents an hour in tips against that wage, meaning tip recipients could be legally paid only $1.15 an hour by their employers.[20]

Nowhere was the fight more protracted than in getting tips covered as income for benefits under Social Security, a program started in the 1930s. At a 1950 hearing, Imogene Wright told the panel that servers collectively received $2 billion each year in tips. She calculated that number by assuming there were three million servers in America's 522,000 public eating places. She then assumed that they averaged $2.75 per day in tips and worked about 280 days each year, $8.25 million daily, $2.310 billion yearly. Wright favored abolishing tipping and replacing it with a service charge of 10 or 15 percent.[21]

Hearings were held on the same topic in 1956. One who testified then was Vernon Herndon, manager of Chicago's Palmer House and speaker for the American Hotel Association. He told the panel that he didn't think tipping could be abolished nor should it be extended to Social Security taxes because the employer just didn't want to know how much his employees got from tips. Pointing out that some establishments had tried to abolish tipping, Herndon claimed that they had abandoned the effort because patrons sought speedier service or special attention. If tips were included in Social Security taxes, "it would create the worst possible employer-employee relationship if management were required to wring from an unwilling employee a statement as to his tip income." As those hearings took place, the *New York Times* editorialized on the custom in general terms, that there was a time in America when the "honest American toiler" would accept tips from no one. "But that time is past. The vain, the exacting and the merely scared among us would invent tipping tomorrow even if it had never been heard of before. Within limits it isn't too bad ... it can coexist with good nature and goodwill."[22]

Still the fight dragged on. In 1960 five unions formed a coalition to lobby Congress that tips should be counted as wages in determining Social Security benefits. Unions estimated that 1.5 million workers would benefit from such a move. Their basic argument was that it was not fair to consider tips as earnings for income tax purposes without adopting a similar measure for Social Security taxes and pensions. With tips not counted as income for Social Security, some workers got credit for only one-third of their income. In addition, the IRS insisted on a full accounting of tips for income tax purposes and had conducted a special drive in that period to trap those shortchanging the government. Trade unions in a coalition for tip credit were the Hotel and Restaurant Employees International Union, the Barbers, Hairdressers and Cosmetologists International Union, the National Maritime Union, and the Seafarers International Union. AFL/ CIO president George Meany was also pushing for tip credit.[23]

Lobbying by unions continued into the 1960s. At that time, a married waiter earning $4,800 per year — assuming half from tips — paid a Social Security tax on only $2,400. That translated into a retirement benefit at 65 of $84 per month for himself and $42 for his wife. If tips were included in the premium paid by both employee and employer, that benefit would be $127 per month for himself and $63.50 for his spouse. If that same hypothetical waiter was unemployed in Michigan, he would receive a benefit of $47 per week for 26 weeks, as against $32 when tips were not given credit. Employers fought tip credit for the obvious reason they had to pay their share of premiums on it. Employees were also reportedly against tip credit because they would have to also pay more income tax. Of course, they already had to pay income taxes, but with tip credit under the Social Security system, a more definite and comprehensive paper trail of tip amounts would be established. However, the IRS crackdown on evaders and the increasing use by patrons of credit cards (also establishing a paper trail) made tip tracking easier. Thus tip receivers felt that because they would have to pay full income tax, they also wanted to receive Social Security benefits. At least, that is how business reporter John Henderson interpreted the reasons that unions were fighting for tip credit in the 1960s.[24]

All the lobbying paid off when a tipped income provision was passed easily, with other amendments to the Social Security Act, in July 1964 in the House of Representatives by a vote of 388 to 8. However, strong opposition to that provision caused it to be killed in the Senate Finance Committee. Led by J. Willard Marriott (founder and owner of the Marriott chain), restaurant and lodging industry spokesmen were able to convince enough members of the committee to stop the tipped income provision from ever reaching the floor for debate. Ranking committee members Senators Robert Byrd of Virginia, Russell Long of Louisiana, and George Smathers of Florida all strongly opposed further legislation over hotels and motels. Employers opposed the measure because it added to their costs but not output, and that necessary bookkeeping would be cumbersome and difficult. The tipped income provision was thus allowed to die in committee. In testifying before Congress on the advisability of applying minimum wages to the lodging industry, American Hotel and Motel Association spokesmen claimed that "many of the employees of a hotel earn tips equivalent to $1.25 an hour, or more ... we have always insisted that the average employee who receives tips does pretty well, provided that he is alert, clean and courteous."[25]

Finally, a tip income provision to the Social Security Act did pass both the House of Representatives and the Senate in 1965, taking effect at the start of 1966. The IRS decided employees would be required to make monthly reports to their employers on the amount of tips they received.[26]

With tip income leaving little or no paper trail through the mid-1960s, state governments were forced to somewhat arbitrarily declare what percentage tip was left for tax purposes and so on. In the mid–1960s the state of New York used a figure of 7½ percent for tax purposes, while federal tax collectors assumed the number was 15 percent of the bill. Servers argued that was high, saying 7½–8 percent was more realistic, while the New York City Hotel Association declared that 15 percent was the generally accepted figure. Waiters acknowledged incomes of about $4,000 per year, half from tips and half from salaries of $40 or so per week. Restaurant industry spokesmen argued that servers in some of the higher-priced places cleared up to $200 per week in salaries and tips.[27]

Soviet Union media outlets devoted some space to the issue as well. *Izvestia*, a government newspaper, launched a drive against tipping in 1954, calling the practice one that "humiliates the honor of men" and was a "survivor of capitalism." The campaign opened with a letter from a Leningrad citizen who reported that tipping was widespread in that city, particularly in restaurants, baths, lunchrooms, and checkrooms. According to a Soviet dictionary, tipping was defined as a "prerevolutionary custom," and people who gave tips were as much to blame as those who took them. Measures were being taken to improve service to the public without tips, assured the newspaper. Several years later *Pravda* published an account claiming that waiters, salesgirls, and bathhouse attendants in Moscow all expected tips. Any self-respecting city dweller offered a tip while "the stingy are denounced as country hicks." *Trud*, the Soviet trade union paper published a half-page denunciation of the practice in 1959, declaring that hands held out for gratuities "must be slapped down."[28]

Pravda told of barbers who "scalped" nontippers to show them up as cheapskates, while *Izvestia* reported barbers who tried to increase the bill, adding cologne and so forth, because the tip would be higher on larger tabs. *Soviet Culture* told of a checkroom attendant who boasted that on a good night his tips could go as high as U.S. $20. Restaurant employees, said the magazine *Literature and Life*, "must be made to realize that they forfeit their human dignity by accepting tips, which are an insult to those who give and those who take." Asked if there was even one waiter in Moscow who would turn down a tip, Nikolai Fedorovich Zavyalov, head of the Moscow Restaurant Trust, sighed, "Not one." He said a recent experiment of adding a 4 percent service charge had failed to stop tipping.

Doormen were considered the most controversial of all tip receivers as they expected at least two rubles — 20 cents. *Literature and Life* suggested that doormen be abolished.[29]

Despite media agitation against tipping in Russia, the practice was reported to be still flourishing in the late 1960s. Reportedly, in Stalin's era checkrooms and restaurants all had signs reading: "Don't tip. Don't insult your fellow men." They were all gone at the end of the 1960s, as *Newsweek* reported the custom was "back with a vengeance" from one end of the Soviet Union to the other. When Moscow's *Literary Gazette* gave a semi-official blessing to the custom, it provoked a counterattack from Marxists in the next issue in the form of an article that denounced tipping as insulting, corrupt, and uncommunistic.[30]

Rationales for tipping by the upper class continued to stress such fictions as the receivers liking the system. *Newsweek* reported in 1957 that "most tippees prefer the system to a fixed higher wage"; no supporting data were offered for that contention. Journalist M.J. Arlen offered the following advice: "Accept tipping. Think of the good it does. You make the tip employee happy, although he may be too naturally discreet to show it. You make the tip employee's employer happy."[31]

Business writer John Henderson offered the thought in 1965 that an employee who received 75 percent or more of his income from tips was not an employee in the usual sense, but simply a private entrepreneur doing business on somebody else's property. As an example he cited towel boys in Miami Beach, who in 1963 typically were paid less than 15 cents an hour in wages by the hotels employing them. Henderson concluded,

> Obviously, the employer derives more benefits from the tipping system than does the tipped employee, since he is able to offer a consistent level of services at low labor costs to himself, while the consumer's direct payment for those services fluctuates at the employee's expense.[32]

Continuing that theme was a 1968 article in the *Cornell Hotel and Restaurant Administration Quarterly* that noted first that federal minimum wage laws permitted hotels and restaurants to pay 50 percent of the going wage to tipped workers who received the other 50 percent in equivalent benefits through a combination of gratuities, meals, and uniforms. The article went on to state that waiters in busy metropolitan dining rooms could take in $100 to $200 weekly in tips. Combined with the fact that most establishments operated at a profit margin of 10 percent of sales volume, then the 15 percent gratuity on sales volume "means that service workers collect more from customers than does management or ownership. When full-time employees are laid off during dull periods, they qualify for unemployment compensation, placing an added burden on management." A matter to ponder, felt the magazine, was whether hotels and restaurants were subsidizing their guests by not adding a service charge to their price structure — or whether the guests were subsidizing the employees. Not discussed was whether the employees were subsidizing the establishments. With the rosy picture painted of tipping it was not surprising when the article concluded that "the system has always been unpopular with the American public but supported by gratuity workers, for whom it supplemented low wages in the past."[33]

Organized labor's response to the issue was sometimes effective (as in the decades-long battle to include tip credit in Social Security) sometimes led to strikes, and sometimes was weak and ambivalent. When the Netherlands adopted the practice of adding a service charge in place of tipping — 20 percent at luxury places, 15 to 10 percent at less expensive places — the change came about as a result of two years of negotiations between the Federation of Hotel, Restaurant and Cafe Organizations, and the waiters' union. Waiters in the Netherlands had pressed for that change for an even longer period.[34]

While the Waldorf-Astoria had many of its banquets held with an added service charge in lieu of tipping, some other hotel banquets still went ahead without a service charge, just regular tipping. In May 1962 some 1,400 people were attending a $75-per-plate dinner sponsored by the Jewish Chronic Diseases Hospital of Brooklyn. Diners had started to eat the first course at 7:15 PM when the waiters abruptly vanished. It was a strike with the waiters complaining to hotel management that they would have to depend on diner goodwill for tips. They had been trying for many years to have all catered banquets covered under a service charge agreement. Passing the plate for tips, they complained, made them "beggars." One of them commented that waiters were sometimes "insulted" by diners who already felt they had given enough donations by paying for their tickets. Half an hour after the strike began it was announced the dinner would continue — but without the food. At 8:45 PM the waiters ended the short strike with an agreement that the dinner committee would take care of the tips. When the banquet started each table had a card saying, "On this occasion your committee has not taken care of gratuities." After the walk-out ended, new cards were distributed reading, "On this occasion your committee has taken care of gratuities to your waiters." Settlement was said to have been based on a straight 12 percent of the cost of the dinner, exclusive of the donation to the hospital. In this case waiters received $18 for a table of ten, while in the past when relying solely on diners to contribute tips they sometimes received only four to six dollars for a table of ten.[35]

In Britain the General Post Office issued a ruling that postmen could receive, but not ask for, Christmas boxes or tips. That initiative came from the postal workers' union. In the early 1950s, the two major unions in Britain that accepted waiters as members did not advocate the elimination of tips as a matter of immediate policy. Said one trade union official, "we would like to do away with the necessity of tipping but can see the folly of trying to abolish it immediately."[36]

In the Chicago area in 1960 unions signed a new two-year pact with 43 major restaurants, calling for pay raises for waitresses, bartenders, and kitchen staff, but not for waiters because reportedly their tips had increased so much over the past several years. Increases in menu prices along with the growing use of credit cards were said to be behind that phenomenon.[37]

When the state of New York held hearings in 1966 into proposed changes in the minimum wage law, hotel owners argued that the changes could increase costs to hotels, resulting in the closing of many of them. At the time the minimum wage was $1.25, with service personnel having to be paid only 90 cents an hour (the remaining 35 cents supposedly came from tips). Proposed changes would move the minimum wage to $1.50 an hour, and $1.05 for tipped employees. At those hearings, union locals in the Catskills area that represented plumbers, carpenters, electrical workers, and other nonservice employees testified that they opposed higher wages for waiters, bellboys, chambermaids, and so on. Those unions supported the owners' contention about establishments being forced to close and worried about the effect these closings would have on their members. Catskill hotel owners called the wage proposals a disaster because competitors in Pennsylvania, New Jersey, and Florida paid a basic wage of about 55 cents an hour, plus tips. Additionally, the owners argued their workers made far in excess of 45 cents an hour in tips. Those unionized carpenters made $5.26 an hour.[38]

Surveys conducted on the issue of tipping produced mixed results. When pollster Elmo Roper conducted a national survey in 1953 on the subject, 65.1 percent of those queried said they were opposed to tipping, 22.2 percent were in favor, and 12.7 percent were undecided. One public opinion study polled people who had declared that they disapproved of tipping in principle, and asked if they tipped regardless. Eighty-three percent said yes. A Gallup poll revealed that while 80 percent of the people in large cities tipped, they were divided on the merits of the system. In general, 45 percent of business and professional people, 59 percent of white-collar workers, 52 percent of manual laborers, and 32 percent of farmers believed in the system.[39]

Six eastern resort hotels received 1,766 replies to 3,000 questionnaires they sent to guests at their hotels to sample opinions on tipping. One question asked was: "I prefer the present system of voluntary tipping," to which they received 68.6 percent "yes" responses, and 31.4 percent "no." Asked whether a leaflet in the guest room indicating suggested minimums for tipping would be helpful, 84.5 percent replied "yes," 15.5 percent "no." Also asked was, "I prefer a service charge of 15% added to my bill which includes payment for services of the following: doormen, waitresses and others in the dining rooms, maids, housemen and housekeeping personnel." The "yes" response was 53.8 percent, and the "no" was 46.2 percent. The American Hotel and Motel Association reported that in its frequent surveys of hotel guests, a no-tipping policy was consistently listed as the improvement in service the guests wanted the most.[40]

Psychological motivations were probed more than ever before. Somewhat simplistic was the view of Herbert Slokman of the Illinois Restaurant Association who stated: "The average person is inherently a tipper. It gives him a chance to be a big shot." One tipper admitted he tipped 8 to 10 percent when dining by himself or with male friends, but when on a date he left 15 percent.[41]

American psychiatrist Gregory Zilboorg said in 1957 that tipping had nothing to do with service.

> There is a long, silent tradition that humans are either master or slave. The moderate tipper caters to frugality, but he thinks "Don't spoil the slaves." The lavish tipper says money means nothing and believes all men are beggars.... In her traditional protected role, woman is not man's equal, but a plaything who does not consider it her business to tip.[42]

Fear and guilt were often mentioned as motivating forces behind the custom. Craig Claiborne announced it would be a blessed day if the public could be persuaded to quietly denounce poor service and tip honestly according to conscience; but "apparently there are few things in life more forbidding to a guest in a restaurant than a waiter's scorn or, worse, his silence if the gratuity is less than that to which he is accustomed." Claiborne felt the greatest share of blame "falls to the public, which accepts poor table service without protest, and which rewards both good and bad table service equally."[43]

Psychologist Ernest Dichter, president of the Institute for Motivational Research, called tipping an anachronism in a modern society that placed emphasis on equality. "It is embarrassing to have another person wait on you. The need to pay, psychologically, for the guilt involved in the unequal relationship is so strong that very few are able to ignore it. It is a custom fraught with psychological problems, whichever way you look at

it." Reporter Hans Koningsberger told readers in 1960 that when psychologists were asked to explain tipping, they replied that man has always
felt slightly guilty and afraid of being envied when having a good time so
he propitiated the people who served him. Not only did he buy off their
jealousy but he also atoned for acting superior or perhaps even being rude
to those servants.

> Fear is his motive — fear of envy, fear of not being accepted in his role of
> temporary master. And, on the other side of the fence, the less pride a waiter
> feels in his profession, the bigger a tip he expects to be paid for his "humil-
> iation." American waiters are a case in point.[44]

Of course, owners were motivating in a different direction. Edward C.
Sterling, president of the Mansion Hotels Corporation, prepared and
handed out a pamphlet primer for his hotel personnel. It said, in part: "Giving superior and thoughtful service is the only honest way to succeed. We
want you to increase your tips.... We're looking for happy customers, happy
employees and happy stockholders." If, in fact, the system made everyone
unhappy, as it appeared to do, there was only one way to end it. An
unnamed leading New York hotel man declared in 1956, "If the hotel people got together now we could end this tipping nonsense in three or four
years."[45]

Other psychological interpretations from the early 1960s were more
sinister. One unnamed psychiatrist divided tippers into seven types: first
were masochistic undertippers seeking punishment. Paranoid undertippers had a persecution syndrome that could be triggered cheaply by tipping. Xenophobic undertippers operated on the theory that all foreigners
(anyone who had to be tipped) were trying to cheat them. Xenomaniac
overtippers, conversely, found all foreigners utterly delightful. Exhibi-
tionists were self-explanatory. Obsessive overtippers had to play it safe
(these were the people who made trans-Atlantic phone calls to their apartment superintendent to make sure the bathtub taps had been turned off).
Finally, reaction-formation overtippers were actually suppressing the
impulse to undertip.[46]

In a 1964 issue of the *Saturday Evening Post* John Patton explained
that psychologists related that tipping was involved in the quest for social
status, that "we lather palms to impress our friends and to prove that we
have the savoir-faire associated with the higher rungs on the social lad-
der." Some of us, said those analysts "have deep-rooted inferiority complexes that drive us to try to buy the respect of those who serve us, or to
pay generously for the privilege of displaying our superiority over somebody
else who is in a demeaning position." Patton, a management engineer,

added his own thoughts about tipping by declaring: "I'm fed up with it. I'm sick and tired of the tip seekers — of the glint of greed in their eyes and the word 'gimme' on their lips. I resent the intimidation, and I also resent being robbed."[47]

Robert Karen turned his summer job as a taxi driver in La Jolla, California, in 1961 into a psychological study, based on 351 observations. He found the tip percentage to be an inverse function of fare size, at least up to a certain point. The largest percentage tip was given for the smaller fares while the smallest percentage tips were given for the larger fares. Transient passengers tipped far more often than did Karen's regular passengers. Most cab riders were tippers but both tippers and nontippers were consistent in that they always tipped or never tipped. Karen also found that men tipped far more often than did women. The widely used 10 percent rule did not apply to Karen's data, because tippers gave a higher percentage, up to 40 percent on the smaller fares. Karen speculated that tippers desired to make a "good show," at least for the lower fares. Among his other conclusions he found that tipping frequency did not vary according to the number of passengers nor were tipping frequency and fare size related. "It is surprising that the variable of special service did not evoke a significant increase in tipping frequency," he added.[48]

Chapter 8

"Surliness Prevails in the Tipped Professions": Tipping Practices 1970-1995

"I think there's an unwritten rule that tipping is mandatory, but it's made to seem as though it's a courtesy."
—Jeannine Braden

During the time 1970 to 1995, guides to tipping became even more pervasive. Tips were more institutionalized in the economic system at all levels. Still, a two-tiered wage system was allowed to exist in many areas. More intensive efforts were made by the government to try and ensure that all tips were reported and all taxes paid. Lastly, psychological studies of the custom turned into a flood.

The idea that service people grew rich on tips was a notion that refused to die. Journalist Paul Camp said in 1986 that he asked a waitress in a New York hotel bar how much she made in tips. Her reply was $250 per night, $300 to $400 on a good night. Camp calculated that out to an income of $60,000 per year. Several years later a different reporter declared that in New York a waiter was paid the minimum wage in salary but also made "well over $200 a night in tips." In 1987, discussions were held on a minimum wage increase, which included a proposal to freeze the tip credit where it was (meaning a small raise for service personnel). A restaurant industry trade publication grumbled that the proposal would force an owner to give a wage increase to a captain, then making $32,000 per year for a 40-hour week, and to a waiter, then said to be making $24,000 per year for a 40-hour week. Ella Brennan, owner of Commander's Palace in New Orleans, made this prediction. Brennan asserted the minimum wage

111

increase proposed would increase her payroll costs, which would lead to higher prices, and "give waiters bigger tips." Said Brennan to her industry readers: "We need your help in amending the proposed minimum wage law to allow a 100 percent tip credit and to prevent forced raises to people already making much more than the minimum wage."[1]

Aggressive tippees also remained a prominent feature of the accounts, from surly to physical to murderous. Columnist Colman McCarthy told his audience in 1982 that he was a nontipper and had been so for several years. He explained,

> I've been cursed by waiters and threatened by cab drivers. But that was the reason I stopped tipping in the first place. Those waiters and cabbies who ill-treat the public do so whether they are tipped lavishly or are, as they phrase it, "stiffed." Surliness prevails in the tipped professions. As it understandably must. Economic hardship exists, but the cause is not stiffs.

Anger should be directed at the employers, he concluded.[2]

In the late 1980s Kennedy International Airport introduced baggage carts that could be rented for one dollar. Since then, of course, they have appeared at virtually every airport. The company with the concession at New York's Kennedy International was Smarte Carte Inc. Shortly after the introduction of the carts, the number of porters decreased from 89 to 64. A popular story had it that a traveler pulling a rented cart asked one of the remaining porters for directions. "Your cart says it's smart," replied the porter. "Why not ask it?"[3]

When cab driver George Lewis picked up a fare he was unhappy with a five-dollar bill for a $4.50 fare. Complaining about the tip, Lewis followed the passenger into a building, where he then slipped on the floor and injured himself to the extent that he was unable to work for a time. His application for workmen's compensation was denied, a decision upheld by the Court of Appeals. The court held that Lewis' act of leaving his taxi constituted an abandonment of his employment, which meant his injuries did not arise out of his employment (a necessary condition to be eligible for compensation payments). Later that decade, Sanford Evans phoned for a cab only to have the dispatcher call back to cancel it. When Evans arranged for a second cab, the driver asked if he got the cab over the "Gold Line." Evans learned that the Gold Line was a special telephone number reserved for big tippers who routinely tipped four to five dollars over the fee to assure themselves of taxis in times when they were hard to find. Evans phoned the company, Scull's Angels, to enroll in the Gold Line but was refused until his tipping reputation became known. Company manager Pete Photos confirmed that "the Gold Line is for good customers. We put in a little more effort for them." He insisted it was a tip and not an extra fee, which would have been illegal. Asked how many people were on the Gold Line, Photos replied: "Fifteen or 20. We don't have that many generous people."[4]

After two customers ran up a tab of about $50 at the Dragon House restaurant in Norwalk, Connecticut, they left a tip of two or three dollars. So angered was the waiter that he reportedly pursued them into the street, where he attacked and stabbed them. In a senseless and brutal murder in Montreal in 1995, an elderly couple were bludgeoned to death by three teens. Frank Toope, a 75-year-old retired minister, and his 70-year-old wife Jocelyn were murdered. A 15-year-old accused of the crime knew the Toopes, because he had delivered their newspapers until two months before the April killings. The teen said he didn't like the Toopes much because they never tipped him, not even at Christmas. They were cheap, he added.[5]

Although the tip trust of the early days was long gone there were still reports of employers trying to claim tips meant for the employees. New York State's Department of Labor announced in 1985 that a Manhattan restaurant, Tandoor India, had been ordered to repay $181,227 withheld in tips collected over the period 1983 to 1985 plus $24,000 in interest. Additionally the company was fined $27,000. Tandoor's argument that it had an agreement with its waiters, waitresses, hostesses, bartenders, and captains that a portion of their tips would go to the restaurant was not accepted.[6]

Tipping aboard ships remained fraught with peril. Most did not have a no-tip policy. A psychologist who took a Caribbean cruise in the early 1970s computed that 61.5 percent of the conversation among passengers during the final 36 hours of the voyage was devoted to how much they should tip the stewards. Nobody seemed to be able to offer definite advice so some puzzled passengers asked the cruise director. Even his response was vague. Shipping lines themselves were also said to often be unwilling to be specific.[7]

Holland America's no-tip policy remained in place, but not without problems. At the end of a 1973 cruise, a dispute arose when ship's officers advised passengers not to tip. However, that angered the crew, who staged a walkout a few days later, causing cancellation of a 14-day Caribbean cruise aboard the firm's *Statendam* liner. The crew was composed of 416 people, almost all Dutch and Indonesian; following the labor dispute the company announced "those who took part in the work stoppage are being repatriated."[8]

Several years later Holland America officials admitted that while it had a no-tip policy, "this hardly means that gratuities are not accepted or expected." Tipping on ocean liners varied only slightly according to the price of the cabin although passengers in the higher priced cabins tended to be a little more generous on a percentage basis. Until 1987 Holland America's official policy was "no tipping allowed;" however, in 1987 the official policy was changed to "no tipping required." Company spokesman Rich Skinner said that the change was made because passengers resented the old policy. Basically abandoning a no-tip policy, the company suggested tipping levels of three dollars per day per person for cabin stewards, and $2.50 per day per person for each waiter, the same amounts as suggested by other shipping lines.[9]

The longer tipping remained institutionalized, the greater the proliferation of advice articles in the popular press counselling who to tip and how much. Some articles were broad, aimed at everyone, some specialized in specific areas or on certain tippers. *Fortune* published a 1971 guide for corporate "nomads," with advice given for cabbies, bellhops, chambermaids, waiters, and so on, in 13 foreign countries. Eleven of those nations imposed a service charge on all bills; *Fortune* nevertheless advised tipping extra, to the extent of 2 to 5 percent in three of them (Italy, Lebanon, and Brazil), and 10 percent extra in Argentina. Fourteen years later, *Fortune* repeated the exercise with a similar article. This time it noted, with some envy, that the recently oil-rich Arabs then dominated the "big tipper sweepstakes."[10]

Travel/Holiday published a 1989 article on shipboard tipping, while the *New York Times* reminded its readers in 1975 that in New York the 10 percent rule was then long dead with 15 percent being the "magic number."[11]

A guide devoted solely to tipping in beauty parlors appeared in a 1982 issue of *Glamour* magazine, with advice on tipping the stylist, stylist's assistant, shampooer, make-up artist, esthetician, waxer, and manicurist. Thirteen years later *Glamour* featured a longer, more complicated version of the same article. Tipping guidelines were given for each service: haircut, color or perm, shampoo, styling for special events, manicure or pedicure, facial, massage, brow tweezing or waxing, and body waxing. Tipping standards were then given for each service according to whether the salon was upscale, mid range or low-price. Most undertipped people in salons, reported *Glamour*, were manicurists and assistants. The latter did not receive, as many people thought, a portion of the stylists' tips. Advice was also given for what to do in embarrassing situations such as tipping with the wrong bill, being short of cash, and hating your haircut but being too afraid not to tip. Regarding whether or not big tippers got better service, Leslie Westphal, manager of the Horst Salon in Minneapolis, offered a popular sentiment by saying: "Bigger tippers don't get better haircuts, but they do get squeezed in on a busy Saturday afternoon. Or a stylist may come in early or stay late for them." *Glamour's* survey of employees indicated that 90 percent of their clients tipped. Said Santa Monica salon owner Jeannine Braden, "I think there's an unwritten rule that tipping is mandatory, but it's made to seem as though it's a courtesy." Minneapolis stylist Russell Sherman commented, "a stylist will try to do a perfect job on a good tipper — he'll work harder to get her scheduled, stay late for her, give her freebies and spend more time with her." Lastly, *Glamour* provided its readers with a list of tipping dos and don'ts such as, don't leave a tip at the workstation and don't give coins. If the reader was still confused about who or how to tip, she was advised to ask the salon receptionist.[12]

There were also guides concerned solely with Christmas tipping. Such articles, to mention just a few, appeared in the *New York Times* (1981, 1982, and 1989), and in *Kiplinger's Personal Finance Magazine* (1994). Just whom to tip during the holidays could be difficult to determine, thought reporter Ken Sheets, because modern life had spawned service providers — such as aerobics instructors — whom Emily Post had never dreamed of. Noting that it was illegal for letter carriers to accept cash tips, the recommendation was to send a letter of appreciation to your letter carrier's supervisor. Differentiation was made between the extra money given at Christmas to someone regularly tipped throughout the year (such as a hair stylist or barber): it was still called a tip; the money you gave to somebody you didn't tip throughout the year (such as sanitation workers) was called a gift. Hilka Klinkenberg, of Etiquette International, an etiquette and business-protocol consulting firm, said of holiday tipping: "It's highway robbery, quite frankly, but one does have to be practical about these things." Basically, added John Schein, president of Tippers International, a tip during the holidays was down payment on better service in the coming year.[13]

More comprehensive guides addressed the question of tipping at Christmas and the rest of the year. Such articles included one by Sylvia Porter in a 1981 issue of the *Ladies Home Journal* and one in *New York* magazine in 1989. Even more wide-ranging were articles on tipping around the world. *Travel/Holiday* published one in 1979 with recommendations given for 31 nations; the only country listed as having no tipping needed anywhere was China. Among the others, the country with the lowest percentage standard given was the Soviet Union, where 5 percent was the recommendation. Another world guide, for the United States and 23 other countries, could be found in a 1990 issue of the magazine *Changing Times*.[14]

Among celebrity examples was former U.S. Secretary of State Edmund S. Muskie, who was actually a "distinguished" nontipper. At the Congressional Golf Club, Muskie's philosophy was not appreciated by the caddies. One remarked: "Every time he came here, the caddies ran the other way."[15]

In 1991, *Sports Illustrated* asked clubhouse men who served visiting major league baseball teams to name the most generous tippers. Heading that list were George Brett of the Kansas City Royals and Dave Smith of the Chicago Cubs who were both said to tip $100 per day, well above the norm of $25 per day. Rounding out the top 10 were Tony Gwynn (San Diego Padres), Jack Clark (Boston Red Sox), Kevin Mitchell (San Francisco Giants), Orel Hershiser (Los Angeles Dodgers), Fred McGriff (San Diego Padres), Danny Jackson (Chicago Cubs), Roger McDowell (Philadelphia Phillies), and Tony La Russa (Oakland Athletics). A comment on La Russa was that he was "easily the best among managers and better than most players. But then, when he first became the [Chicago] White Sox manager, he asked me how much other managers were tipping and said he wanted to be the best."[16]

Regarding the best tippers, *New York Times* reported in 1974 that Europeans complained that one casualty of the 1973 U.S. currency crisis was "the once-liberal American tip." The Japanese tourist was then the big tipper. One French waiter wondered if the Japanese might not understand French money but a bartender corrected him by saying, "No. They understand. They are generous because they are rich. You saw them last summer — they were the new Americans."[17]

Bartender magazine surveyed 200 New Jersey bartenders to determine who were the best tippers. Publication editor Ray Foley (himself a bartender for 20 years) declared, that it was basically the people who depended on tips for their living — such as waiters and beauticians — who were good tippers at bars. The survey indicated the "Magnificent Seven" (the best tippers) were bartenders, waiters, tavern owners, regular customers, small business owners, beauticians, and blue collar workers. The "Seven Stiffs" (the worst tippers) were doctors, lawyers, bankers, 18–22 year olds, women, educators, and musicians.[18]

A decade later Foley conducted another survey on the same issue. This time the "Magnificent Seven" actually numbered nine; bartenders, waiters, waitresses, hairstylists, "wise guys," regular customers, small business owners, liquor salesmen, and chief executives. Doctors headed the worst list, followed by teachers, accountants, lawyers, and women over 40. Physicians always led the list of bad tippers, so Foley called up some doctors to see what made them so stingy. He explained that they told him it was because when they were interning they never had any extra money for tips, and they just kept it up as a habit. Foley conceded that younger businesswomen tipped adequately, but women over 40 often ate and drank in groups: "they not only split the tip, they split the check, which is a six-hour process. They come with their own calculators." Lounge lizards also made the worst list: "Guys with open collars and polyester suits. They don't have it. They're spending it on one drink that they keep all night." Computer fanatics were another out group, explained Foley: "The nerds. They don't go out a lot. It just doesn't interest them and they just don't know." While not quite on the stiff list, foreign visitors rated an honorable mention primarily because most of Europe had an added service charge, making spontaneous tipping the exception rather than the rule. Many assumed a service charge was added to their American bills. Among athletes pro golfers were the best tippers, with professional tennis players being the worst. Discussing cities, Foley claimed that Chicago was the best, followed by New York, with the worst tipping city being Atlantic City, New Jersey, "because they busload 90-year-old people with quarters." Las Vegas and Reno, Nevada, were only slightly better than Atlantic City.[19]

When the Canadian Restaurant and Foodservices Association surveyed Canadians, they found Quebecers to be the best tippers. Respondents indicated they tipped from zero to 40 percent, with the most popular amount being a 10 to 15 percent tip (given by 37 percent and 36 percent of respondents nationally). Over half the Quebecers said they tipped 15 percent while 44 percent of Ontario residents tipped 15 percent; 33 percent of Quebecers declared that they tipped 10 percent.[20]

The image of women as lousy tippers remained alive. Journalist Bill Granger reported on "Melissa" the bartender who railed about tips from females. Said Granger: "Melissa is not alone in her low opinion of womankind as tippers. Anyone who works in the trade knows instinctively that women either don't tip or are lousy tippers." If a taxi driver saw two people signaling for a cab, one male, one female, he would invariably pick up the man since the chances of getting stiffed were less. Concluded Granger, "I can't figure it out; Melissa can't. We both just know that's the way it really is."[21]

Mentioned less often was the fact that women made up a disproportionate share of the servers in downscale eateries, where prices were cheaper, and of course tips were lower. Kellye McKinna filed a 1990 lawsuit in Los Angeles for just such a reason, charging two posh establishments, Citrus Restaurant and Ma Maison Sofitel Hotel and Restaurant, with discrimination. McKinna had worked for eight months at a relatively downscale Maison restaurant. Her repeated requests to be transferred to the posh Ma Maison Restaurant were consistently denied. She claimed it was because the company had a policy whereby female servers were prohibited from that formal dining room. Her application to the Citrus was rejected, also because she was a woman, she alleged. Speaking of the higher tips servers made in more upscale establishments, McKinna said, "It is absolutely unfair that women of equal experience and ability have been completely frozen out of almost all of the most expensive restaurants at dinner." Maison spokesman Michael Carcieri acknowledged that no waitresses worked the lucrative evening shift, but made no other comment. Citrus executive Jean-Jacques Retourne denied that there was a policy against employing women, noting it then had one such employee serving on the evening shift "and it has nothing to do with the lawsuit." Retourne explained that the city's finest restaurants had traditionally hired male servers exclusively "for the single fact that women never came around asking for jobs." McKinna's attorney Gloria Allred remarked: "We believe that many restaurants have hired only men because they think it adds prestige and importance to the restaurant to only employ men at night. Such practices serve only to perpetuate the false notion that women are of no value."[22]

Once again economic reality was a long way removed from the media image of the rich tip recipient. In a large study undertaken in 1970 and published in the *Monthly Labor Review* in 1971, data was assembled from some 333,000 service workers in the restaurant, bar, and hotel industries. All the data on tips was derived from information provided by the employers. The study was nationwide, covering establishments with gross annual receipts over $250,000. At the time, the minimum wage was $1.45, moving to $1.60 on February 1, 1971. With the tip credit then at 50 percent, the effective minimum wage for tipped personnel was 72½ cents per hour. From the study it was found that table servers in restaurants averaged $1.14 an hour in wages and $1.80 in tips. In full-course and other types of restaurants, waiters received $1.14 an hour in wages and $1.93 in tips, while waitresses received $1.16 in salary and $1.36 in tips. Counter waiters and waitresses got $1.50 per hour in restaurant wages and 44 cents in tips; in hotels, they earned $1.28 an hour in wages and $1.07 in tips. Waitresses outnumbered waiters by 4½ to 1 but averaged less in wages and tips. Men worked in establishments having higher-priced meals. Bellhops in hotels averaged $1.18 an hour in wages and $1.23 in tips, while hotel chambermaids earned $1.67 in salary but only 5 cents per hour in tips.[23]

A study four years later in the same publication indicated bellhops received 40 percent or more of their earnings from tips, with servers earning tips that made up 50–70 percent of their total average hourly earnings. For bellhops, higher wages meant lower tip averages. The opposite was true for table servers in full-course restaurants, where average tips increased as wages reached their highest levels. In expensive New York

City, where so many "rich" tip recipients supposedly were employed, table servers in full-course restaurants earned $3.49 an hour (tips were 55 percent of that total) while hotel room clerks (not tipped) were paid $3.88 an hour. Bellhops in that city made $3.13 an hour (45 percent tips). In Washington, D.C., those servers received $3.68 an hour (68 percent tips), compared to $2.88 for room clerks and $3.05 for bellhops (53 percent tips). In Detroit servers earned $3.07 (49 percent tips), desk clerks $2.65, and bellhops $2.60 an hour (34 percent tips). Table servers in Los Angeles–Long Beach received $2.75 (40 percent tips) compared to $2.72 for room clerks, while bellhops got $2.22 an hour (31 percent tips).[24]

Five years later, *Monthly Labor Review* reported 1978 data indicating that table servers in full-course restaurants received a total of $4.59 in New York City ($2.45 in tips); in Washington it was $5.15 ($3.33 in tips); in Detroit it was $3.89 an hour ($1.42 in tips); and in Los Angeles–Long Beach it was $5.49 ($2.99 in tips). Dallas–Fort Worth table servers received $3.27 ($1.83 in tips), while in Cincinnati it was $3.28 an hour ($1.79 in tips). When bellhops were studied in 1983, half received a total hourly income in the range of $2.88 to $3.52 an hour.[25]

Speaking of the economics of being a tip recipient, researcher Suellen Butler remarked in 1980 that "nearly one and a half million Americans make a living 'waiting tables.' Ninety percent are women who work for a dollar and a half an hour and rely on tips for at least two-thirds of their income." That was perhaps a slight exaggeration but was generally a valid assessment of the financial reality of working for tips.[26]

Just how much money was received by Americans annually in tips was unknown. Reported tip income jumped 127 percent, or $1.2 billion, just two years after the changes made by Congress in 1982 with regard to the reporting of gratuities.[27]

A 1990 report stated that wages received nationally by waiters and waitresses averaged $2.25 an hour. For such restaurant employees, the average annual income was less than $7,000 after deductions, with no benefits such as health insurance and retirement plans. Most European full-service restaurants had a 12–15 percent service charge added to the bill, instead of a tip; in America only a small minority of establishments had such a charge. Employees generally favored such a plan since it would obviously help servers move toward a decent standard of living. Restaurant owners generally opposed the fixed service charge because it would increase their costs; in public they tended to use other rationales such as arguing that servers would no longer have an incentive to give customers quality service if tips were predetermined.[28]

Chapter 9

"Let Your Tip Do the Talking": Tipping Responses 1970–1995

"I'm a coward when it comes to tipping ... I'd like to put an end to all tipping but I don't dare start the movement all by myself."
— Andy Rooney

No-tip establishments remained few and far between in America. Although the Chock Full o' Nuts restaurant chain — then with 73 outlets in metro New York — dropped its 40-year no-tip policy in 1967, that policy was reinstated in 1974. The reasons behind the reinstatement were somewhat mysterious. One store manager said, "I don't know why the change was adopted. The letter didn't say. I wish they'd tell me — all my customers are asking." Restaurant founder William Black was not available for comment, but his wife explained that he had been concerned about the rising cost of food, which caused the cost of meals to rise at his eateries. Black felt he could reduce those costs a little by eliminating tipping, she explained. Employees were to be reimbursed for their income losses. The letter announcing the new reinstated no-tip policy said that tips averaged $37 per week, so wages, averaging $2.50 an hour, were increased 93 cents an hour to a total of $3.43 per hour. Additionally, employees were to receive a 7 percent bonus on all sales above their normal volume level; this policy was supposed to give them an incentive for selling more and for serving customers speedily in order to handle more during a day's operation.[1]

San Francisco's 30-room Inn at Union Square hotel instituted a no-tip policy late in 1995. It was done, explained general manager Brooks Bayly, after a guest answered the "What could we improve?" question on a comment card with "eliminate the tips." To compensate employees for financial losses, the hotel claimed it raised the wages by the average of past tips; bellhops' wages were moved to $8.50 an hour from six dollars, while the salary of housekeepers was raised to $6.80 from six dollars an hour. Signs posted at the hotel warned quests: "The Inn at Union Square staff does not accept gratuities." The hotel also informed guests of its no-tip policy when they made reservations and checked in, and on hotel litera- ture and rate cards. In the case of those guests who tried to tip anyway, management trained the employees to say "Thank you very much but the Inn at Union Square is now a non-tipping hotel" or "No, having you as our guest is our pleasure." Bayly commented that it was awkward at times to stop tipping because "it's a macho thing." There was said to be only one other no-tip hotel in America, the 54-room Alexis Hotel in Seattle, which established its policy in 1982. That hotel's rationale was that the policy would increase the place's European ambience, since there was no tipping in European hotels. To compensate employees the Alexis raised the hourly rate of its bellhops, but not the salary of the housekeepers.[2]

Establishments with a fixed service charge in lieu of tipping also made little headway in America, although they were the norm in many parts of the world, especially Europe. Even there some patrons still tipped spon- taneously. Writing in the *Times* of London in 1981 regarding the service charge, Bernard Levin confessed: "I am afraid that I for one still feel con- strained, though most uneasily, to distribute largesse none the less, and I have never yet had it refused."[3]

On the other hand, Europeans were regarded as a problem in Amer- ica when they were here as tourists precisely because they tipped very lit- tle or not at all, believing a service charge was included in the bill. Accord- ing to Sheldon Tannen, one of the owners of New York's 21 Club, it was not unusual for a group of European businessmen or tourists to spend hundreds of dollars for dinner then leave a tip of a token dollar or two on the table, assuming service was included. At Windows on the World restaurant in the World Trade Center in New York, co-owner Tom Mar- gittai complained along the same lines, stating that "Europeans are our biggest problem. They don't know how to tip." In the late 1980s, restau- rants in America were said to be engaged in some discussions about adding a service charge, especially those establishments catering to tourists from abroad because many came from nations with service charges where it was "customary to leave only 3% to 5% extra, if service was exceptional."[4]

Only a small percentage of commercial hotels or restaurants levied a fixed service charge, but some top resorts did. In 1986, the Breakers in Palm Beach, Florida, added a ten-dollar charge for a single room and $14 for a double; the Greenbrier in White Sulphur Springs, West Virginia, tacked on seven dollars per day per person. One restaurant that tried a service charge was the Quilted Giraffe, which moved to that system in 1985. Three years later it was still in place with owner Barry Wine commenting, "The customers uniformly like it." However, most owners did not. National Restaurant Association treasurer Mike Hurst spoke for many when he said: "You're dealing with a public custom. Americans are used to using the tip to reward good service or punish bad service. You just don't take that right away from the people." Out of the roughly 100,000 establishments where tipping would be expected, in America in 1983 it was estimated that no more than 5,000 of them used the service charge.[5]

Discussion on the topic reached a higher level in 1988 because Congress expanded the employers' share of Social Security taxes to cover all tips. One owner who switched to a service charge said he paid his waiters $11.25 an hour under that system, compared to $2.01 an hour salary under the tip system. His servers who had worked for him under both systems were said to all prefer the service-charge system because they were receiving a steadier income. They also had an easier time obtaining loans and credit. At that time restaurant owners could pay employees $2.01 an hour with the remaining $1.34, 40 percent of the $3.35 minimum wage, coming from tips. Peter Berlinski, who edited the trade journal *Restaurant Business*, complained in his magazine that because of new taxes and more recordkeeping,

> I believe the time has come to replace the voluntary tip with a mandatory service charge.... The custom of giving a voluntary gratuity to service people in restaurants is unique in America. For decades the mandatory service charge system has been common in Europe.[6]

That same year the magazine surveyed 375 restaurant owners on the question of a service charge — only 1 percent of them had such a charge in place. Those that did were upscale establishments adding 15–20 percent to the bill. Twenty-three percent of all respondents and 32 percent of upscale respondents indicated that they were not opposed to a fixed service charge, but just 8 percent of the total respondents and 17 percent of the upscale said they planned to implement one. Forty-two percent of all respondents and 54 percent of the upscale would consider adopting a fixed charge, if the majority of operators in their market did so. Of those opposed to a service charge, 28 percent indicated they would consider adopting it if the majority of establishments did so; 86 percent of those not opposed to a service charge said they would go along if others did. Concluded *Restaurant Business*: "In general, something like half of the poll respondents view the service-charge concept favorably — they just don't want to be the first ones on the bandwagon." When the Gallup polling organization conducted a telephone survey of 1,007 adults in August 1987, they found that 54 percent of their respondents disliked service charges in expensive restaurants. In the late 1990s the situation remains the same: only a small proportion of establishments have a fixed service charge as everyone apparently waits for the others to form a majority.[7]

In the area of clubs formed against tipping there was one additional entry, to complement the still existing Tippers Anonymous (TA). Founded in Oshkosh, Wisconsin, in 1972 by traveling salesman John Schein, Tippers International (TI) claimed to have 2,700 members in the United States and Canada two years later. "We're tired of being sheep," explained Schein. TI provided members with a "painless, positive and dignified way of conveying their dissatisfaction to waiters, managers and owners alike." If a member found the food or service to be poor in an establishment, he or she left no tip but a card that read: "This card ... is left to notify you and your facility that we were dissatisfied with (check one or more) Prices ... Quality ... Cleanliness ... Courtesy ... Atmosphere ... and we will forward (this information) to T.I. headquarters." For an annual fee of ten dollars, members received a supply of those cards, plus a supply of commendation cards that were to be left with a tip, literature on tipping tactics, and a newsletter listing restaurants in America that TI members recommended as "giving customers their money's worth." Members also used the organization's headquarters as a clearinghouse for their restaurant horror stories. TI cards and letterhead were adorned with a tiny silhouetted figure representing the group's mascot, Robby Tipper. Robby was shown wearing a tuxedo with outstretched arms, welcoming members to the group. When someone suggested the symbol could be taken to represent a waiter throwing up his arms in despair when he received a TI card and no tip, Schein was not amused. Asked to comment on the club, a spokesman for Local 6 of the New York Hotel Trades Council said: "That's Oshkosh. What else do they have to do in Oshkosh?"[8]

With regard to his philosophy Schein explained: "I think tipping is a way of life but I think we have to control it a bit." TI's card system, he reasoned, provided patrons with a "diplomatic, dignified and effective means of letting people know when you're satisfied with their service and when you're not." Members' complaints about poor service were sent to TI headquarters and then forwarded to the offending establishments as well because Schein worried that the owners rarely got the benefit of the constructive criticism on the complaint cards. "Waiters and waitresses surreptitiously pocket the telltale complaints even faster than they snap up tips." Slogans of the group included "What you receive is what you leave," and "Let your tip do the talking."[9]

By 1975 TI claimed 5,000 members. Hard times did not keep people from tipping, observed Schein; "No matter what the economy's like, people are still going to tip." TI had extended its scope to offer its members discounts or preferred rates from companies such as Hertz, Best Western and Howard Johnson Motor Lodges. The club still received member complaints at its headquarters and passed them on to the establishments because, said Schein this time: "People don't want to become personally involved. They'd rather have us do it for them."[10]

In 1995 TI, still led by Schein, claimed it had 35,000 members including individuals, organizations, and corporations, united to help create better communication between customer, service, and management personnel. It still handed out condemnation and commendation cards (one card then served both functions through checked boxes) and referred member complaints it received back to offending establishments. TI sold a 60-page booklet *Guide for Tipping* and a full-length 253-page book *The Art of Tipping Customs and Controversies.* Both covered tipping situations in a host of situations in the United States and 42 other countries. The full-length offering was also meant for tippees who could "use this book as a training guide to improve their job performance." Also offered was something called a "tipping computer," a pocket-sized item with a couple of independently turning discs. A user set the percentage of tip he wished to leave against the cost of the service and read off the appropriate tip.[11]

Tippers Anonymous reported its 1995 membership as 15,250 individuals. It limited itself to supplying its members with rating cards that were left with the server and the appropriate tip. Ratings were limited to excellent, good, fair, or poor. Robert Farrington continued to head that group more than 35 years after its formation. In literature mailed out to prospective members Farrington wrote

> I'm sure you will be one more enthusiastic member who will work hard toward rewarding or chastising waiters and waitresses for the service they render. Furthermore I am sure that never again will you automatically tip at the end of a meal because everybody does it.

Farrington refused to tell people how much they should tip but did state that he personally followed these rules: 20–25 percent for excellent service — "you won't get this very often" — 15 percent for good, 10 percent for fair, and 5 percent for poor service. "I always leave something so that they will know that I didn't forget the tip. I simply tipped for what the service was worth," explained Farrington.[12]

Tax evasion became harder to accomplish by tipped personnel, particularly as the use of credit cards became the norm, especially in upscale eateries where cash was rarely used to pay for food. Eight waiters at the Palm Restaurant in Washington, D.C., received three- and four-month prison sentences in 1989 for failing to report nearly $145,000 in tips to the Internal Revenue Service. Those charges were filed after an audit at the Palm for 1982 to 1985. That compared total tip income reported by the restaurant to the IRS with the individual tax returns of the waiters. Income reported by the waiters ranged from $7,000 to $52,000 per year, while the IRS assessed the actual figures ranged from $27,000 to $67,000. Tips from meals paid in cash were not included in the audit. Each of the eight waiters pled guilty to one count in a plea bargain. In addition to the prison time, the men had to pay back taxes, interest, and penalties. Six of the eight continued to work at the Palm and did so through their jail sentences; they were required to report to prison at night and on their days off.[13]

More downscale operations were also hit by IRS audits. In the late 1970s hundreds of young waitresses in Washington, D.C., were served tax bills accusing them of deliberately underreporting tips they had received as waitresses for Marriott Corporation restaurants. A typical case was 20-year-old University of Maryland student Terri Todd, who in 1976 reported $1,601 in tips. Using charge slips, Marriott payroll records and restaurant bills the IRS computed her earnings at $2,030. She was ordered by the IRS to pay them $230 more in taxes, interest, and fines. Stating that unreported tip income was a serious national problem, IRS spokesman Robert Kobel said, "Of course, it's been taken for granted that underreporting was a common practice among waiters and waitresses. And we're taking steps to alleviate it." Debbie Maul reported less than $1,000 in tips in 1976 but the IRS computed it to be $1,500, ordering her to pay them $128 more. The Marriott investigation was said to be one of several tip probes conducted around the nation. Marriott was required to submit its records or they would have been served a subpoena. Employees accused the company of turning in its waitresses; some of them, like Todd, blamed Marriott for not explaining how to report tips accurately. Company officials rejected allegations that their employees had been encouraged to underreport their tips. Such a move would have reduced a company's costs because they wouldn't have to pay the employer's share of such items as Social Security taxes on unreported tips.[14]

In the wake of a four-month IRS probe of 28 San Francisco–area restaurants in 1992, over 500 servers and other tipped employees suffered stiff penalties for failing to report and pay taxes on gratuities. According to the IRS, those workers received tips amounting to about 15 percent of gross sales but only reported an 8 percent tip rate. Since the 1982 tax reform, restaurants claiming an aggregate tip rate of less than 8 percent were required to submit detailed tip reports for each employee. To avoid the extra paperwork many employees simply reported an 8 percent rate, leaving any excess unreported. Said IRS spokesman Larry Wright, "Virtually all of the employees we audited reported half or less than half of the amount of tip income they received." Most of the restaurants involved were fined for failing to file Form 8027, an annual return showing the aggregate tip rate and gross sales along with credit card receipts and the tip rate on those transactions.[15]

Agitation in the Congress over the minimum wage, and how much of it did not have to be paid to tip recipients (the tip credit) was prominent again in the 1970s. Representative Mario Biaggi (D-NY) and Senator Richard Schweiker (R-PA) hinted in 1974 that they would propose legislation guaranteeing a full minimum wage to waiters and waitresses. Under the laws at the time, it was assumed that a tipped employee received tips equal to 50 percent of the minimum wage. Thus the employer only had to pay 50 percent of the minimum wage. Argued Biaggi: "I do not believe that assumption is fair or correct. In any case it is no excuse for the employer to be let out of his obligation to pay—fair and full minimum wage."[16]

When the minimum wage was raised in 1977 both the House and the Senate approved a raise to $2.65 an hour, up from $2.30. The House rejected a proposal to eliminate the tip credit, while the Senate voted 81 to seven to decrease the tip credit from 50 percent to 30 percent, in phases over four years. House and Senate colleagues compromised on the tip credit by agreeing that it would be reduced to 45 percent of the minimum wage by 1979 and 40 percent by 1980.[17]

Among the many industry lobbyists fighting any reduction in the tip credit was Joe R. Lee, president of Red Lobster Inns of America. In an ad he placed in the *Washington Post* in 1977 directed at members of Congress, Lee warned that "waiters, waitresses and other workers where tipping is the American way may earn less money than they do now," if the tip credit was reduced. His reasoning was that meals would cost more, customers would get less service, establishments would close, there would be less jobs in the industry, and so on. Claiming he was not against an increase in the minimum wage, but just a decrease in the tip credit, Lee stated,

> Tipped workers ... earn an above average income. In fact, because of this American tradition of individual incentives working for them, most waiters

and waitresses now earn in excess of $5.00 per hour (in some cases much more).... Don't upset a system that works beautifully for everybody.... Under our present system, "everybody wins."[18]

In 1980 the minimum wage stood at $3.10 an hour with a tip credit of 40 percent, bringing it down to a minimum of $1.86 an hour in salary which had to be paid by an employer to tipped personnel. All of this was worrisome to the editor of the trade journal *Restaurant Business* who feared the future of the tip credit was cloudy. According to him, organized labor scored a significant Congressional victory in getting the credit stepped down to that 40 percent level. Labor interests were anxious to reduce it still further because union dues were based on a member's stated cash intake; when wages rose, so did union dues. Labor groups argued further, said the editor, on how could anyone allow a "poor girl" who only made $3.10 an hour to have her employer take away half of that. "Uneducated consumers and members of Congress are extremely vulnerable to that argument, especially when it is coupled with labor's observation that only the restaurant industry gets such a benefit, and why should that be allowed?" asked the editor. Admitting that many service people cried poverty, he then asserted that "It is a proven fact that many of them do very well in financial terms. This is often difficult for people outside the industry to accept." The only way to save the tip credit was through a "vigorous educational program" conducted by the entire restaurant industry. Said Clyde Griffith, National Restaurant Association counsel, about that campaign, "It will be attacked from all sides but the restaurant industry won't lose it if we get to the proper people." One place where the tip credit had disappeared was in California, when the state legislature abolished it in 1976, after many previous attempts to kill the credit had failed. Specifying only the fixed service charge as an alternative the editor concluded "should those [Washington lobbying] efforts fail and tip credit is abolished, every restaurant owner should have a contingency plan ready to go into effect."[19]

Believing tip income to be unreported to a high degree, the government moved in 1982 to remedy that situation. In a Congressional hearing IRS commissioner Roscoe Egger said that lost taxes on unreported tips cost the United States $2.3 billion each year, while the National Restaurant Association estimated $89.2 billion would be forked over at bars and restaurants in 1982. An official in the Treasury Department's Office of Tax Analysis stated that only 16 percent of tips were reported. That rate of tax dodging was said to be exceeded only by such criminals as drug dealers and prostitutes. Originally the proposal in the Senate Finance Committee to tighten tax collection on tips was fought so vigorously by the union representing waiters and other tip recipients that the effort temporarily paid off for the Hotel and Restaurant Employees International Union; the proposal was killed. However, Bob Dole (R-KS), chairman of the Senate Finance Committee, inserted instead a measure to limit the deduction for business meals to half the cost, as an alternative revenue raiser. Restaurant owners and workers joined forces to fight that proposal on the grounds that it would lead to a loss of jobs. That intense lobbying led the Senate to drop the plan. Instead, a compromise was reached in which the proposal to tighten tax collection on tips was restored and became law.[20]

Under the old rules, written reports of tips in a particular month had to be given by workers to their employers by the tenth of the following month. Reported tips were subjected to income tax withholding and the employees' Social Security tax. If a service charge was imposed and distributed to the employees, it was not considered a reportable tip but part of the server's regular wage. In that case, the employer was responsible for withholding income tax and Social Security from the employee's regular paycheck, and for the employer's share of the federal Social Security tax and the unemployment tax. When a tippee received less than the minimum wage, in accordance with the tip credit provision, the owner was responsible for paying the employer's share of Social Security taxes on tips to the extent needed to bring the total compensation up to the minimum wage, whether those tips were reported or not.[21]

Under the new rules, everything remained the same as long as tips reported by workers to their employer totaled 8 percent or more of the gross sales of the establishment. However, if reported tips fell short of the 8 percent threshold, the employer had to report that to the IRS. For example, a restaurant had gross sales of $500,000 in a three-month period and the employees reported tips of $25,000 to the restaurant. Since 8 percent of the gross was $40,000, that shortfall of $15,000 had to be allocated among the employees by restaurant management based on some formula yet to be devised. As to why the 8 percent figure was selected, IRS spokesman Rod Young explained: "Eight percent is quite a conservative amount. If we are talking about an average of 15 percent tipping, then it's not unreasonable to expect 8 percent information reporting." Government officials hoped the new rules would boost tip reporting compliance from 16 percent to 70 percent, a figure still regarded as low. Employers did not have to withhold income tax or Social Security taxes on any tips that they were forced to allocate under the new rules. Neither owners nor employees were happy with the new rules because it meant more paperwork, more tension, and more taxes to be paid by both sides. For restaurant owners, the choice was between accepting the new rules or losing the time-honored tax deduction for business lunches. Explained restaurant association counsel Robert Palmer: "Our judgment was that tip reporting will mean a sizable burden across the industry, but elimination of the business meal deduction might have spelled the death of many restaurants. Tip reporting is the lesser of two evils."[22]

Under those new rules all tips received by an employee were considered as wages and subject to all the statutory employer payroll taxes levied under the Federal Insurance Contributions Fund (FICA); under the old rules only those tips reported by an employee were subject to those taxes. However, the problem was how to get the tips reported. To that end the government arbitrarily set a minimum of 8 percent that it deemed an employee received. Unintentionally, that 8 percent also became the maximum, because it was in the economic interest of all parties (except the government) to do so. Operators had to pay 7.51 percent in payroll taxes on the reported tips; they didn't like to do it on 8 percent, they wanted to do it even less on a higher rate, say a 15 percent rate that prevailed in their establishments. It was extra costs on a deemed 8 percent for all tipped employees — there had been no prior minimum, no real standards, only occasional audits on individuals, or areas in the past. The owners worried that the tip standard would increase or perhaps workers would report actual amounts, always believed to be higher. It set the industry off on a serious discussion of adding a service charge. However, all of the service charge turned over to employees would be subject to deductions, any such charge would be certainly beyond the 8 percent level. Under those conditions, owners' costs would increase but workers would find that all their income was reported to the government and taxed. One of the major reasons that the tipping system remains institutionalized is the economic incentive for the owners — the only ones who could abolish it. When tipped employees can evade taxation on part of their earnings, it amounts to extra money — a pay raise, in a sense. If it was all reported, owners feared workers would either push for higher wages or leave the industry altogether. Owners had, and still have, powerful reasons to help tipped employees, directly or indirectly, to continue to receive tips and to report as little of them as possible to the government. All the public hype about tipping being needed to produce good service, and so forth, was just that: hype. The industry didn't believe it itself. As Alfred Demaria discussed the service charge controversy in the trade journal *Restaurant Business*, he revealed that "many operators, in fact, have never believed that the tipping system induces better dining room service." Teamwork and a positive attitude were fostered by "higher hourly wages and the certainty of income." Admitting that most diners claimed they wanted the opportunity to reward good service and penalize poor service, most tips averaged 15 percent — regardless of service quality, said Demaria. He concluded "it would be difficult to establish that tipping practices in America today have a material effect on overall service."[23] Over the following year or so there was much grumbling from both sides about the complexity of the new regulations, the administrative cost and that tips were being allocated to some tippees who in fact had not received 8 percent in tips. Relenting slightly, the government changed the rules to allow a reduction in the rate from 8 percent to as low as 5 percent — but no lower — if and only if the establishment could show that the lower rate actually prevailed.[24]

Rules for tip allocation varied, with the allocation initially being allowed on the basis of hours worked. In 1986 that method was restricted to establishments with 25 or fewer employees. Larger businesses had to allocate on the basis of receipt records. By 1988 the IRS allowed an individual establishment to have its threshold lowered to as low as 2 percent of the gross, after intense lobbying for relief from the food service industry. Complaints continued to pour forth, with owners particularly incensed at having to pay Social Security and unemployment taxes because, they argued, they didn't pay the tips to their workers so why should they have to pay taxes on them. One owner whined that the rules "are affecting my bottom line." Conveniently forgotten was the fact that tippees received very little in the way of base salary from the owners — less than many other workers thanks to the tip credit — resulting in lower payroll costs to start with. Lobbying by the owners continued as they demanded legislation to allow them to count tips as a full credit against the minimum wage — in other words, a tip credit of 100 percent instead of 40 percent.[25]

Apparently the new rules weren't too effective because in the early 1990s the IRS tried a different method. It was a pilot project started in Phoenix in 1991 and was still being pushed in 1994. Under the program the IRS wanted to get employers to calculate and report employees' tip income, as opposed to the current system whereby the individual recipients did the reporting. The allocation of tips under the 8 percent rule was, of course, an exception. If a restaurant signed on to the plan, or "Tip Rate Determination Agreement," and persuaded at least 75 percent of its employees to cooperate by reporting their tips on a government tip-to-sales formula, the IRS said it would not expose the establishment to a tip income audit. "If an establishment doesn't sign the agreement," explained IRS executive Marshall Washburn, "it will be more exposed to an audit because there would be a greater likelihood of noncompliance." Any such audit could leave a business owing a lot of back taxes including Social Security, Medicare tax, unemployment tax, income tax, and some state taxes.[26]

That plan was not particularly successful because it was seen too much as the government holding a gun to the head of the restaurant business. A new plan introduced by the IRS, called TRAC (Tip Reporting Alternative Commitment), was intended to persuade businesses in a gentler way to set up tip reporting measures and train their staff on policy. Threats in the past to perform audits on businesses deemed uncooperative had the industry up in arms, forcing a change in IRS direction. Businesses who signed on to TRAC were promised that no audits (such reprieves were not quite absolute) would be performed on them — a subtle difference. The IRS estimated staff at large restaurants were reporting perhaps half of their tips.[27]

California's elimination of a two-tiered wage structure, based on a tip credit, lasted only until 1988 when that state put into effect a minimum wage of $4.25, replacing the $3.35 an hour in effect since 1981. An employee who made at least $60 per month in tips could be paid a minimum of $3.50 an hour. The difference of 75 cents translated into $130 per month.[28]

Focus on communist countries' tipping practices in this period switched from the Soviet Union to China. Soon after taking power in 1949, the Communist authorities banned the custom on the ideological ground that workers should "serve the people wholeheartedly" without the thought of monetary gain. After the Cultural Revolution (1966–1976) and Mao's death (1976), many workers were demoralized and cynical, reportedly often expressing their deep dissatisfaction by sullen and inefficient service. Leader Deng Xiaoping attempted to rectify that and other economic problems by permitting the gradual introduction of some capitalist concepts. Waiters, taxi drivers, and porters had supposedly long argued that tipping would encourage more prompt and cheerful service. Nevertheless tipping remained officially banned, though some workers ignored the prohibition. In southern Guangdong province, bordering on Hong Kong, employees in foreign-owned hotels in the late 1980s had been discreetly accepting tips for two or three years. The Great Wall Sheraton hotel fired two porters for using pressure tactics to extract tips from foreign guests. Some international visitors noticed that cab drivers awarded themselves de facto tips by keeping the change from fares, declaring they had no small bills or coins with which to make change.[29]

The *People's Daily* newspaper published a 1987 commentary suggesting that tipping might be a way to raise standards of service in the travel industry. Yet one month later the national radio news declared that Chinese hotel staff and other tourism employees caught accepting tips would be punished. On that radio newscast, tourism authorities were quoted as saying that tipping was strictly forbidden, with offenders subject to prosecution or dismissal. Tour operators from abroad complained that some employees had begun to demand tips from foreign travelers.[30]

At the end of the 1980s, tipping was still formally banned in China. Workers who received tips were supposed to turn them over to the management. However, authorities had unofficially begun to permit the practice, at least selectively. On the counter of the Tianjin-Orchid Fast Food restaurant near Beijing was the sign "I ♥ Tips." Said manager Peter Chik, "as for tipping itself, I don't think it's a bad thing and it would be accepted by the Chinese people." After reading the sign "I ♥ Tips," some of the restaurant's 5,000 daily patrons asked what tips were. At the beginning, when customers (mainly foreign) left tips the waitresses didn't have the courage to accept them, insisting on returning them to the customers. Only a few Chinese patrons left tips and when they did they were for smaller amounts than was left by foreigners. The largest tip left by a Chinese was 5 yuan ($1.35) while the highest tip left by a foreigner was 50 yuan ($13.50). Waitresses received an average salary of 7 yuan ($1.90) per day. One was Miss Wang who commented, "I enjoy my work here, but it's a pity that I have not yet received any tips since I began working. I do want to get some tips, but we can't ask the customers for them." When the restaurant opened, the issue of allowing tips was debated back and forth in the newspapers. Sheraton hotels in China still had a policy forbidding tips, it was the only nation of the many in which they operated that such a policy was in place. That same policy prevailed at other hotels, whether locally owned or joint ventures. Still, some tips in those establishments did change hands. One housekeeper, employed in a large joint-venture hotel in Beijing, commented, "I usually get tips at least once a month, and several months ago, a customer from the United States gave me 100 yuan ($27) as a tip"—nearly half her monthly salary. Several employees said that they preferred to work in the restaurants or housekeeping department of their hotels because "that provides you with more chances to get tips."[31]

A 1978 survey showed that half of all Americans considered tipping a fair way to compensate workers, with younger people being more inclined to believe in tipping. When asked "Would you like to see an automatic service charge replace tipping?" 69 percent of the respondents said no, 19 percent said yes, 5 percent didn't approve of either, and 7 percent had no opinion. Older people favored the idea of a service charge more than other groups. Ten years later, *Time* conducted a survey on the issue of a service charge. It found that 77 percent of their respondents said they opposed a system under which restaurants would add a mandatory service charge of 15–18 percent to their bills; 19 percent were in favor.[32]

One of the odder survey results was obtained by the Gallup organization from a 1987 poll conducted for the National Restaurant Association. Gallup found that while 46 percent of those surveyed thought employees who received tips should pay taxes on those gratuities, 39 percent disagreed. Among 18- to 24-year-old respondents, 61 percent didn't think recipients should pay tax on tips.[33]

In an effort to gauge the extent of tip underreporting, the IRS hired University of Illinois researchers to study the tipping habits of 13,000 American households in 1986. They found that people ate least often in Italian cuisine restaurants (2½ percent of the time), but left the highest tip there —15.8 percent. Other tip averages included 14.1 percent at seafood places, 14.8 percent at Mexican restaurants, 15 percent at Chinese eateries, and 15.2 percent at establishments featuring a general menu (accounting for 58 percent of the meals). Between 1983 and 1986 the average tip overall rose from 14.6 percent to 15.1 percent. However, the range was large as diners left tips of over 18 percent 30 percent of the time, while 9 percent of the time tips left were under 10 percent. Highest tip rates were found in the northeast with the lowest being in the interior states. Even the lowest rates, the IRS learned, were well above the 8 percent government standard.[34]

Consumer Reports Travel Letter published an article on tipping in October 1995 that was partly a guide on who to tip and how much, and partly a survey of the custom. Virtually all the respondents tipped airport curbside baggage handlers; cabin stewards and waiters on cruises; hotel doormen, porters, and room-service waiters, restaurant and coffeeshop waiters; cab drivers; and parking valets. The rate of not tipping for those occupations ranged from 2 to 7 percent. Only 54 percent of respondents tipped hotel housekeepers, airport shuttle bus or van drivers were tipped 62 percent of the time, and fast-food servers were tipped 18 percent of the time. Fifteen percent remained the nominal standard in this survey. Americans in Europe continued to tip abroad even though service charges were included in most bills. As well, around half of them gave a standard American tip of 10–15 percent, instead of the small change usually left by Europeans (when they left anything). A majority of the magazine's respondents agreed with the statement, "I enjoy tipping to reward good personal service." Yet two-thirds of those surveyed also agreed with statements expressing dissatisfaction with conventional American tipping practice, such as, "too many employees expect tips for doing nothing," service "should be included in basic prices for all travel services (tour, hotel, restaurant, cruise)," and "tipping should be reserved for unusual service." Four in 10 went so far as to agree with the statement, "I dislike the whole system of tipping." Confusion about tipping still prevailed in 1995, as a little over half of the respondents agreed that "I often face situations in which I don't know whether to tip or not."[35]

Psychological assessments and opinions ranging from anecdotal evidence to full-scale scholarly investigations about tipping increased dramatically in this period. Tom Margittai, co-owner of Windows on the World restaurant, explained that one big problem was the overtipper.

> Every house like ours has three, four, five people who wildly overtip. Men who will run up a $500 bill and leave $250 in tips. A restaurant is not overly fond of these people. They rent the help. The crew adores them, of course, but they create dissension in the dining room. What table do they get, who will serve them; there is a ripple of tension and envy through the whole staff when they come in. There is a lot of ambivalence about these people. They get more attention but not necessarily more respect.[36]

Emily Post advised people that if they patronized luxurious restaurants and wore expensive clothes with valuable accessories, or if they were critical and difficult to please, then greater compensation was expected than if your appearance "were simpler and your demands less exacting." If one received "rotten" service Ann Landers advised the customer to not tip at all: "The notion that a small tip will 'give them a message' is absurd. You are throwing away your money."[37]

Contradicting Ann Landers was reporter Wallace Immen who wondered how much to tip if service was poor, then answered his own question that the best way to make your point was to leave a small tip instead of no tip. If one left no tip it could be interpreted that the person forgot, but a small tip clearly indicated that the patron was disappointed. Ann Landers weighed in again on tipping with a 1989 column about a dinner party that left a tip of two dollars on a $173 tab. That produced several letters complaining about tipping in general. Two of three letters wanted a service charge added in lieu of tipping. The other letter, dredging up the "tip recipients are rich" image, argued that a waitress could make $200 per night in tips, while other low-wage workers didn't make anywhere near that. The letter writer thundered,

> What's so special about waitresses that they can demand a 15–20% bonus for service? Why do they think they are working any harder than a typist or telephone operator who put in the same hours.... It's time somebody put an end to the perpetual whining and the implication that waitresses are entitled to a "secret bonus" for simply doing their job.[38]

Media figure Andy Rooney admitted in 1981 that he left the same tip for good service as he did for bad service. Occasionally, when he found the service to be really terrible he would reduce the tip to "the socially acceptable minimum, but never below that. I'm a coward when it comes to tipping ... I'd like to put an end to all tipping but I don't dare start the movement all by myself."[39]

Noting the class difference, journalist Emily Card, writing in *Ms* magazine, commented that today's tipped service worker on a temporary basis replaced the private servant, who in bygone days accompanied the master everywhere to look after his needs. When a porter carried a patron's bag in a hotel, the patron tipped, but if for some reason a management person carried it, it would be considered rude to offer a tip, thought Card. Similarly, a beauty shop stylist was tipped, but not if the stylist was also the owner. Judith Martin ("Miss Manners") called for tipping to be abolished and replaced by a comprehensive salary policy. Tulane University professor of social psychology Frederick Koening declared that tipping service workers encouraged "a lack of responsibility on the part of the employer. This is contrary to the principles of the American labor movement, where a person's salary is related to his worth as an employee."[40]

Columnist Alexander Cockburn called tipping a paradox: formal yet informal, public yet private, commercial yet intimate, voluntary but in reality very close to compulsory. He felt that as the service economy exploded decade by decade it would affect the tipping process by leading to an increase in the number of services with which people had to tip.[41]

Writing in the *New Republic*, Zachary Citron stated that Americans spent some $11.2 billion in 1987 on gratuities. "There's something absurd, even downright unhealthy, about restaurant tipping in late–20th century America," he thought. Discussing the government's 8 percent standard for tip reporting, Citron argued that the unintended result was to provide owners with a financial incentive to collude with tippees to underreport tips. He concluded: "Let's face it: as anyone who's ever stiffed a waiter or waitress can tell you, tipping is about power.... But aren't we bigger than that? Do we really want the moral burden of consigning a whole class of Americans to a life of tax evasion?"[42]

An article in *Restaurant Business* by James Degen in 1981 observed that over the preceding two years personal and business dining had both declined, with fewer patrons meaning less tips, resulting in dissatisfaction among the servers. This in turn led to "less enthusiasm, productivity, or possible resignation." Not only were there fewer diners, but they tipped a smaller percentage, according to Degen. Whereas a $50 tab might have led to a $10 tip a few years earlier, it now produced one in the five to eight dollar range. Facing pressure to reduce expenses, one response by corporations was to lower the tip. One solution was to increase base salaries or fringe benefits. However, Degen dismissed this because "these compensation elements form the base of security level of waiter/waitress compensation, not motivation." Other options mentioned by Degen included putting servers on some type of bonus system dispensed over a certain dollar amount, and so forth.[43]

Also needing motivation, in some cases, were the tippers. In 1994 the Nevada Casino Dealers' Association paid for a series of billboards lining the highway into Las Vegas to remind visitors to tip the dealer. Those signs read: "Casino dealers' income depends on your generosity. Thank you and good luck." Most dealers, like so many other tip recipients, earned only a minimum wage, depending on tips to bring their income up to a reasonable level. Since the late 1970s, dealers' tip income had fallen 33 percent for unknown reasons. Some thought it was related to Las Vegas casinos developing more nongambling attractions to draw in more tourists, who didn't tip the way gamblers did or supplanting some gambling tourists themselves.[44]

Columnist John Berendt complained in a 1994 issue of *Esquire,*

> I happen to think tipping is one step removed from bribery and that it is a degrading and outdated custom that imposes a master-servant relationship on the tipper and the tipped. There's no escaping it, however. If tipping was ever voluntary in this country, it's not anymore.

However, he added that tip earners did not need any sympathy because they had ways of getting around the system. The only ways mentioned by Berendt were to favor big tippers at the expense of everyone else, and to underreport tips to the IRS. That agency, said Berendt, declared that only 50 percent of the annual total of $6 billion in tips was reported. He said that clearly something needed to be done about the custom but he couldn't think of what that should be. Fixed service charges were dismissed by him because only 1 percent of American restaurants had adopted them with the remainder in no obvious hurry to sign on. This reluctance was because Americans liked to tip; they felt it gave them the upper hand and led to better service. Noting that almost all European restaurants had a service charge, Berendt saw no deterioration in service and no upset European patrons demanding their right to tip be returned to them. Calling for a full-scale assault against the custom, he saw no absolute solution in sight. Tippers Anonymous was mentioned as a group that championed the rights of tippers, but he termed their approach as peculiarly timid. Berendt called their method of handing out report cards as "hardly a manifesto, let alone a declaration of war."[45]

Michael Kinsley, in a 1993 *Time* column, suggested abolishing tipping.

Noting that in most fields of endeavor the economy had found plenty of ways to create incentives for good performance he wrote: "The real function of tipping is to make a business relationship seem more like a feudal one. Our goal in America should be exactly the opposite, and yet we are far behind Europe in replacing tips with standard service charges."[46]

Scholarly papers on the custom studied every aspect of tipping imaginable. Psychologists Stephen Feeman and Bibb Latane believed that the presence of others diffused responsibility, leading individuals to feel less personal responsibility to act. To see how that related to tipping, they conducted a study in 1973 at a Columbus, Ohio, restaurant, where 11 waiters kept detailed records on all meals served to tables of from one to six people, a total of 396 groups of diners. Researchers studied the amount tipped by those groups as a function of the number of people eating together, the size of the tab, and whether or not alcohol was ordered with the meal. Overall tips averaged 15 percent, an expected amount. Individuals dining alone tipped 19 percent; groups of two, 15.5 percent; groups of three, 14.1 percent; groups of four, 13.9 percent; groups of five, 12.9 percent; groups of 6, 13.5 percent. The average group contained 2.67 people, was billed $6.96 per person, and tipped one dollar per person. Overall, groups of four to six people tipped an average of 13.5 percent per person. Tables where drinks were ordered tipped 15.3 percent versus the 14.6 percent from nondrinking tables. At tables where bills were higher than average, the percentage of tip left did not change. There was also no difference between tips left by groups of women, groups of men, or mixed groups. Researchers concluded that the data supported the diffusion of responsibility idea, commenting that

> With respect to tipping, we suggest that diffusion of responsibility may also operate in nonemergency settings: to the extent that many people contribute to a check, the responsibility of each to the waiter may be psychologically divided among the people present. Thus ... people who dine in groups should leave smaller tips than people who dine alone.

Americans were said to have spent some $30 billion in eating establishments in 1973, meaning something like $3 billion, or more, in tips. One reporter commented that given the result of this study, it might be worth the extra time it took for waiters to always write out separate checks for their diners.[47]

In her experiment, Jayne Stillman studied the effect on tips when a waitress wore a flower in her hair. It was done in an unnamed midwestern city with six waitresses in a restaurant whose clientele was mainly businesspeople and where the average tab was $10.20. Those servers were asked to wear the same jewelry, perfume, make-up, and hairstyle for the four nights over which the study took place, but to wear a rose or a daisy in their hair on two of those nights. Overall diners tipped an average of 26 cents extra when the waitresses wore a flower. Although men tipped more than women, the flower had a greater effect on women patrons who increased their tips an average of 39 cents versus a fifteen-cent increase from male diners. Stillman speculated that women were simply more likely to notice the difference and respond to it.[48]

Around the same time, researcher Joanne May of Loyola University studied the effect of waitresses' attractiveness on tipping behavior. She found that attractive waitresses got better tips for poor service than they did for excellent service. They also got higher tips than not-so-attractive waitresses no matter what kind of service they gave. When they gave poor service, pretty servers averaged a tip of 20.3 percent; when they gave excellent service it was 17.3 percent. On the other hand, the less attractive women averaged 14.9 percent for excellent service and 11.9 percent for poor service. Also studied was the number of people in the party and whether the bill was paid by credit card or by cash. The best tippers were solitary diners who paid by credit card. They left a tip that averaged 23.7 percent of the bill. Credit card tips overall averaged 15.2 percent compared to a cash tip of 15 percent. Tables of three or five diners left less per person than did tables of four or six. The worst tippers overall were parties of five who paid by cash; they left an average tip of 11.2 percent per person. Said one waitress in the study: "Waitresses have known for a long time that the best way to get good tips is to look as cute and as helpless as possible. The customers feel sorry for you."[49]

In all cases, the size of the tip was greater when a credit card was used for parties of one to six, the largest number studied. May noted that it was commonly believed that diners tipped to reward good service, and withheld or reduced gratuities in response to poor service. In one survey 40 percent of respondents said that if service was inadequate they would refuse to leave a tip; 52 percent claimed they would leave a smaller tip than usual; only 8 percent of respondents claimed they would not alter their standard gratuity. In May's study, the quality of service was evaluated by independent observers and included such items as time elapsed before the customer was greeted and time elapsed between taking an order and the arrival of the food. May's results caused her to conclude "that variables traditionally associated with the speed and efficiency of service do not have a significant impact on tipping." She also mentioned an 86-page paperback published in 1979 by John Begman called *Tips for You,* in which the author gave "common sense" recommendations to tip recipients on how to increase gratuities. Most revolved around the idea of treating the customer like royalty such as greeting warmly, apologizing for mistakes, knowing the menu, being neat, smiling, and so forth. None of those factors mattered, thought May. The factors that really did count, such as group size, method of payment, server attractiveness, and so on, were all beyond the control of the server.[50]

When Boas Shamir conducted his early 1980s study on tippees' attitudes he began with a number of assumptions. He expected tipped employees to perceive a closer relationship between their efforts and their rewards, and as a result to be more highly motivated than workers in nontipped areas. He also assumed tip recipients' satisfaction with their pay would be higher than that of nontipped employees' because most people believed pay should be based on performance. Lastly, he assumed that tipped workers would experience greater conflict between customer demands and superiors' policy and orders than the nontipped because in the case of the former their dependence on the customer and his power over them was greater. Consequently he expected tipped personnel to be more loyal to customers, adopting the latter's viewpoint more than the nontipped. That would likely bring them into conflict with some of their superiors' demands.[51]

To test these assumptions Shamir had 286 employees at a five-star hotel in Jerusalem fill out questionnaires. Forty percent of those employees received tips as part of their pay; the others were in nontipped positions. Fifty-three percent of tip recipients perceived a relationship between their performance and their earnings versus 38 percent of the nontipped. "However," observed Shamir, "the level of pay satisfaction among tip recipients is not higher, contrary to the hypothesis." There was a greater tendency among tippees to adopt the customers' viewpoint in that 28 percent of them claimed the customer didn't get full value for his money, compared to 13 percent of the nontipped. Shamir found the level of customer-superior conflict to be much higher among tip receivers than among the nonrecipients; recipients held a more favorable attitude toward the customers than the nontipped, but job satisfaction was significantly lower among tip recipients. He thought this was perhaps because of the higher level of customer-superior conflict. Shamir concluded that perhaps "the dependence on the customer is a source of reward or satisfaction. It is also possible that the practice of tipping may produce high motivation but low satisfaction."[52]

Michael Lynn did two studies in the mid–1980s to look at the effects of group size, customer gender, method of payment, and size of the bill on tip size. He determined that tipping was not related to service quality, a server's efforts, a server's gender, a restaurant's atmosphere, or a restaurant's food. With the restaurant industry taking in $500 billion in 1977, he thought it likely that servers alone received some $8 billion in tips that year. Lynn embarked upon his study with the following assumptions:

- tipping adhered to a 15 percent norm
- the percentage tipped per person was inversely related to the number of people at the table
- the percentage tipped was unrelated to the per person bill size
- attractive servers received bigger tips than did less attractive ones
- patrons paying with a credit card left bigger tips than those paying with cash
- the percentage tipped was unrelated to whether the table ordered alcoholic beverages
- the percentage tipped increased with the number of non–task-oriented visits paid to the table by the server
- the percentage tipped was sometimes related to the patron's gender
- all-male groups tipped more than all-female groups
- the percentage tipped was unrelated to observers' ratings of service quality.[53]

The first study was conducted at a low-priced breakfast house in Columbus, Ohio, with 169 dining groups studied. The average bill per person was $3.16 with the average per person tip being 49 cents—15.6 percent. Tables of one tipped 19 percent, going down to a low of 11 percent at tables of four and six. Men tipped a considerably higher percentage than did women, at 17.4 percent versus 9.5 percent. Patrons evaluated the restaurant's service, food, and atmosphere, with a finding inconsistent with the "glow of goodwill" concept, since those customer ratings on food and atmosphere were not predictive of the percentage tipped. Patron ratings of service quality were also not predictive of the amount tipped. Inconsistent with other results, Lynn found that as the size of the per person bill increased, the percentage tipped decreased. For his second study, Lynn looked at 206 dining groups at a moderately high-priced dinner house in Columbus that employed four waiters and five waitresses (all servers were females at the breakfast house). Here the average bill was $13.01 per person with a tip of $2.01—15.5 percent. There was no interaction between gender of server and gender of customer, although overall men tipped more than women, 15.7 percent versus 14.6 percent. Lynn reported the inconsistent finding that dining group size had no effect on the percentage tipped. For both studies the number of checks at a table were unrelated to the percentage tipped, causing Lynn to suggest that servers had nothing to gain or lose by writing separate checks for a group. The variances in percentage tipped by customers paying separate checks was greater between tables than it was within tables with separate checks. That suggested people's tipping decisions conformed to those of others at the same table. Lynn found in this study that per person bill size was unrelated to the size of the tip, unlike his finding from the first study. Those paying with a credit card tipped 16.9 percent, compared to cash payers who left 14.5 percent. Also unrelated to tipping was the amount of effort spent by waiters at a table (the servers rated themselves on that measure). Lynn commented, "It is evident from the analysis that waiters' and waitresses' efforts are not strongly related to the percent their customers tip."[54]

April Crusco investigated the effect on tipping of a server touching a patron. Using about 85 subjects in two Oxford, Mississippi, restaurants, researchers set up conditions where the waitress briefly touched the customer on the hand while returning the change, or briefly touched the patron on the shoulder under the same condition. A third, control, group was not touched at all. Crusco believed that a touch on the hand would produce positive effects toward the waitress and increase the tip size but a touch on the shoulder might not be viewed as positively, especially by males, because such a touch was often used as a sign of dominance by high-status people — servants are not expected to dominate their employer. Thus, she speculated that a shoulder touch might reduce tips compared to a hand touch, more so for men than women diners. However, she found that the tipping rates for the two types of touch did not differ from each other and did not differ according to patron gender. Both those tipping rates were significantly larger than those for the nontouch group. After their meal, patrons filled out a restaurant survey for the study rating the server, restaurant atmosphere, and dining experience. As there were no touch effects in those ratings, Lynn concluded that touch effects could occur without awareness.[55]

Around the same time a similar investigation was conducted by Renee Stephen, who studied 112 pairs of customers in a Greensboro, North Carolina, restaurant. Each pair contained a male and female patron. In 28 cases, after the diners had received their food, the waitress touched the female diner lightly and briefly on the shoulder while asking if everything was all right (female-touch condition); in 28 cases the waitress touched the male in the same fashion with the same question (male touch condition); in 56 cases neither customer was touched while the question was asked (no-touch condition). Average tip in the female-touch condition was 15 percent; in the male-touch condition it was 13 percent; in the no-touch group it was 11 percent — all significant differences. Speculating that

American females responded to touch more positively than American males and that touching the male might arouse jealousy on the part of the female diner, Stephen felt that it would be more profitable for a waitress to touch the female rather than the male. He concluded that "waitresses in the United States may enhance their incomes when they touch the female rather than the male in serving male-female couples." Although he didn't mention Crusco's shoulder-touching dominance ideas, his finding lent support to that theory.[56]

Even errors in the check could apparently cause fluctuations in tipping patterns. In a study analyzing 377 transactions at 288 different restaurants around the country, it was found that when checks were accurate the average tip was 13.3 percent. Overcharged customers left 4.7 percent; when customers found an error in their favor on the tab they tipped 11.5 percent. An average of one check in eight was in error, with 70 percent of those mistakes in the customer's favor.[57]

At a Huntington Beach, California, restaurant in 1988, 42 two-person dining parties were studied eating Sunday brunch, with a constant bill size of $23.21. All were served by the same waitress. For half the group she introduced herself by name saying: "Good morning. My name is Kim, and I will be serving you this morning." In the no-name condition she used the same greeting except "My name is Kim" was omitted. Tipping averaged 23.4 percent in the named condition versus 15 percent from the no-name group. Those who paid by charge card tipped 22.6 percent compared to 15.9 percent for the cash payers. There was no interaction for method of payment and named or no-name conditions.[58]

A study published in 1995 looked at 51 dining parties at an upscale Philadelphia restaurant under three different conditions. One waitress served all the patrons. In the control condition the server delivered the check without writing anything on it. In the thank-you condition she wrote "thank you" on the back of the check, while in the third group the waitress wrote "thank you" and also signed her first name directly below that phrase. For the control group the average tip was 16.28 percent; for the thank-you group it was 18.10 percent; in the thank-you plus name condition it was 18.01 percent. Both the latter groups were significantly different than the control group, but not from each other. Credit card diners left 17.9 percent compared to 17 percent from those paying cash, not a significant difference. Size of the dining party was not related to the percentage tipped. Researcher Bruce Rind observed that if the one waitress in his study had used the thank-you strategy for all the diners, her tips would have increased from $268 to $297, an 11 percent increase. Speculating further Rind noted that for the 1.3 million servers in America, "systematic employment of this technique could mean millions of dollars of additional income annually."[59]

Researcher Michael Lynn returned to study the effects of alcohol consumption on tipping. He did admit that previous studies found no such relationship; the ordering of alcoholic beverages did not alter the percentage tipped, compared to tables that did not order alcohol. Still, Lynn believed such a relationship should exist because alcohol increased prosocial behavior by improving people's moods; that enhanced effect should increase tipping. Arguing that restaurant patrons usually faced strong social pressure to leave a large tip which conflicted with their desire to minimize the cost of eating out, Lynn declared that alcohol decreased people's ability to process information. Therefore, assuming social pressures to tip were the most salient cues in tipping situations, alcohol should increase tips by weakening people's ability to process additional cues that would ordinarily inhibit it. He then studied 207 dining parties at a moderately priced Italian restaurant where he found that alcohol consumption did increase tipping, but the effect of the number of drinks ordered was weak relative to the effects of whether or not the party had any alcoholic drinks. The problem with other studies that found no such relationship may have been that bill size is negatively correlated to tip size and that fact was not taken into account in those previous studies, he thought. Thus Lynn used a different statistical method — the residual tip — to get his results. He claimed that he found the effect of alcohol ordering on tipping was sizably reduced when the percentage of tip was used as the dependent measure. Also the relationship between tipping and number of drinks ordered was almost completely wiped out when the percentage tipped was used. Lynn conveniently ignored the fact that most studies on tipping found that bill size had no effect on the percentage tipped, not the opposite as he decided. This study was an example of a researcher making false assumptions and using inappropriate statistical methods to achieve a result that he believed should exist, before he conducted the study.[60]

Lynn returned yet again with a paper on the effect of server posture on tipping. In his introduction he declared that, from other research, "people tip more the larger their bills" and results of his own study were that "the restaurant's patrons tipped more when their bills were larger." He conveniently took an opposite position in his abovementioned research. Using a waiter and a waitress at different Houston, Texas, eateries, Lynn had his servers approach the patrons either in the normal posture of remaining standing throughout the initial table visit or of squatting down during that first visit (eyes become closer to level, facilitating more direct eye contact, increased friendliness, and so on). For the waiter his average tips when squatting were 17.5 percent compared to 14.9 percent while standing. In the case of the waitress, tips averaged 15 percent when she squatted versus 12 percent for standing visits.[61]

A study by Mary Harris of the University of New Mexico in 1995 focused on the perceptions of servers and customers about factors associated with tipping. A total of 107 servers and 137 customers filled out questionnaires which included having the respondent tick off boxes of 15 factors, defined by the researchers. One finding was that servers indicated that they tipped an average of 17.29 percent while expecting the average customer to tip only 12.17 percent. Results suggested that servers viewed themselves as being more generous tippers than their customers and believing that factors such as friendly service, good suggestions from the waiter, excellent food, quick service of the main course, prompt delivery of the check, an expensive restaurant, customers' drinking, servers' introducing themselves, and payment by credit card led to significantly larger tips, while other factors such as taking a long time to bring the beverage, being seated in a bad location, and being served by a waitress with a flower in her hair led to significantly smaller tips. Customers who had worked as servers at some time in the past said their average tip was 15.89 percent, and believed that others tipped 12.88 percent. Customers who had never been employed as servers said they tipped 13.88 percent while indicating others tipped 12.08 percent. Like the servers, the customers believed factors such as friendly service, good suggestions, excellent food, prompt delivery of the main course and check, a server's self-introduction, and the receipt of separate checks led to larger tips; waiting a long time for a beverage and being seated in a bad location led to smaller tips. Harris' study found no significant gender differences on any variable. It is not surprising that Harris found that factors that could be called conventional wisdom were the ones listed by both servers and customers. Respondents were limited to those preselected by the researchers; it is unlikely that an esoteric factor like the server wearing a flower in her hair would ever be listed in a free-response format. Research such as this forced respondents into a narrow range of responses with the options chosen from previous research that reinforced their importance even though it may not have been warranted.[62]

Boas Shamir offered some thoughts on the process of tipping. In an economic explanation of tipping, a gratuity was simply a payment for something extra, services or effort. Economic theory also assumed recurrent interaction between tipper and recipient and a relation between service quality and size of the tip — yet none existed. In view of that, the lack of repeated interactions and the fact that a basic postulate of economic theory was self-interest meant, to Shamir, that economic theory did not explain the custom. Under social exchange theory, that exchange entailed unspecified obligations. A main function was to establish superordination over others. When something (such as a gift) was given under conditions of unspecified obligations, the recipient felt gratitude or indebtedness toward the giver. In this theory, a tip was given under a voluntary guise but in fact was given under a normative framework where the mutual obligations were not specified exactly. The customer got something more than what he paid for, such as a meal, creating in him a motivation to reciprocate, discharging that obligation allowed him to balance his account and stay out of debt to the service-giver. Failure to clear that debt, under social exchange theory, would put the customers under pressure to repay the service-giver with approval or subordination, which was impossible. To avoid becoming dependent on the service-giver and preventing any possibility of the server's superiority, the customer tipped to escape his obligation and impose his superior identity. Drawbacks to that theory thought Shamir, were the lack of continuity — many single-encounter situations — and that theory led one to expect regular customers to tip more than irregular customers, yet that didn't happen.[63]

Shamir suggested that tipping created or demonstrated status and thus could be satisfying to the giver even in the absence of an audience and in noncontinuous social relationship; ego needs were met with tipping serving to enhance the self-image. When a person gave something over and above the agreed-upon price, the giver may demonstrate to himself and others that he was not fully tapped in the market mechanism. By expressing freedom from the market the customer desired to maintain and demonstrate an internal rather than an external locus of control. Perhaps giving a tip also allowed an image of oneself as a source of gratification to others. Shamir felt that giving a tip might also be an expression of guilt; that is, some people might have felt guilty or at least uneasy when spending money and being served by others.[64]

One person who may have turned that theory on its head was Groucho Marx. The following is from the Marx Brothers film *A Night at the Opera.*

> GROUCHO: Do they allow tipping on the boat?
> STEWARD: Oh, yes sir!
> GROUCHO: Have you got two fives?
> STEWARD: Yes, sir!
> GROUCHO: Well then, you won't need the 10 cents I was going to give you.[65]

Appendix 1

Earnings in Various Occupations

While there are no data specifically recording tip recipients' income, the following can be used as a comparison against the often very exaggerated numbers found in media accounts.

Average Annual Earnings of Full-time Employees, by Selected Industries

Year	Manufacturing	Transportation	Wholesale and Retail Trade	Services	Government
1900	$487	$505	$508	340	584
1905	561	543	561	385	628
1910	651	607	630	447	725
1915	661	711	720	493	753
1920	1532	1645	1270	912	1245
1925	1450	1539	1359	984	1425
1930	1488	1610	1569	1066	1553
1935	1216	1492	1279	873	1292
1940	1432	1756	1382	953	1344
1945	2517	2734	2114	1688	2052
1950	3302	3714	3045	2183	3014
1955	4356	4823	3755	2831	3708
1960	5352	6185	4597	3513	4676
1965	6389	7485	5436	4295	5717
1970	8150	9928	6886	5946	7965

Source: U.S. Bureau of the Census, *Historical Statistic of the United States: Colonial Times to 1970* (Washington, D.C.: 1975), pp. 165–166.

Average Hourly Earnings (All Full-time and Part-time), Private Sector Workforce Only

	1970	1975	1980	1985	1990
Gross hourly earnings	3.23	$4.53	$6.66	$8.57	$10.02
Gross hourly, manufacturing	3.35	4.83	7.27	9.54	10.83
Gross hourly, transportation	3.85	5.88	8.87	11.40	12.96
Gross hourly, wholesale	3.44	4.73	6.96	9.15	10.79
Gross hourly, retail	2.44	3.36	4.88	5.74	6.76
Gross hourly, services	2.81	4.02	5.85	7.90	9.83
Gross hourly, eating and drinking places	*	2.55	3.69	*	4.97

In 1991 the workforce was 45.6 percent female, 10.1 percent black, 7.5 percent Hispanic. In the category of service occupations:

Percentage

	Female	Black	Hispanic
Bartenders	54.0	2.0	2.7
Waiters and waitresses	81.6	4.2	7.1
Cooks, except short order	46.9	18.3	14.4
Short order cooks	28.9	23.3	11.7

Sources: U.S. Bureau of the Census 103rd ed. *Statistical Abstract of the United States 1982–1983,* (Washington, D.C.: 1982), pp. 398, 401.

U.S. Bureau of the Census 112th ed. Statistical Abstract of the United States 1992, (Washington D.C.: 1992), pp. 394, 407, 410.

---

*Data not available

Appendix 2

Laws Against Tipping

Washington State, enacted 1909; repealed 1913.

Sec. 439. Every employee of a public house or public service corporation who shall solicit or receive any gratuity from any guest shall be guilty of a misdemeanor.

Sec. 440. Every person giving any such gratuity mentioned in section 439 shall be guilty of a misdemeanor.
Source: Washington State. *Session Laws, 1909*, Ch. 249, p. 1029.

Mississippi, enacted 1912; repealed 1926.

3235. To prohibit practice of allowing tips in public eating places.— 1. It shall be unlawful in this state for any hotel, restaurant, cafe, dining car railroad company or sleeping car company to knowingly allow any person in its employ to receive any gratuity, commonly known as a "tip," from any patron or passenger; and it shall be unlawful for any patron of any hotel, restaurant, cafe, dining car or any passenger on any railroad train or sleeping car to give to any employee any such gratuity; and it shall be unlawful for any employee of any hotel, restaurant, cafe, dining car railroad company or sleeping car company to receive any gratuity or "tip."

3236. The term "tip" defined.— 2. By gratuity or "tip," as used in this act is meant any extra compensation of any kind which any hotel, restaurant, cafe, dining car railroad company, or sleeping car company, or the manager, officer, or any agent thereof in charge of same, allows to be given an employee, or which any person gives to any employee, or which is received by any employee, and is not a part of the regular charge of the hotel, restaurant, cafe, dining car railroad company or sleeping car company, which is not a part of its regular charge for the thing bought or services rendered, or a part of the service which by contract it is under duty to render. No hotel, restaurant, cafe, dining car railroad company or sleeping car company shall evade this act by adding to the regular charge, directly or indirectly, anything intended for, or to be used, or to be given away as a gratuity or tip to the employee. All charges made by the hotel, restaurant, cafe, dining car railroad company or sleeping car company must be made by it and be in good faith a charge for the service which it renders exclusive of the service which it furnishes through its employees.

3237. Copy of act to be conspicuously posted.—3. Each hotel shall post a copy of this act in the office and in each room, and each restaurant and cafe shall post at least two copies of this act in two conspicuous places in same, and each dining car railroad or sleeping car company doing business within this state, shall post two copies of this act in conspicuous places in each passenger coach or sleeping car.

3238. Penalty for violating provisions of this act.—4. Any hotel, restaurant, cafe, dining car railroad company or sleeping car company, and the manager, officer, or agent of same in charge, violating this act or wilfully or negligently allowing the same to be violated in any way, shall each be subject to a penalty not to exceed one hundred dollars for each tip allowed to be given. If any person shall give any such employee any gratuity or tip, such person shall be subject to a fine of not more than fifty dollars for each offense. If any of the above employees shall receive any gratuity or tip, he shall be subject to a fine or not more than fifty dollars. If the hotel, restaurant, cafe, dining car railroad or sleeping car company fail, neglect, or refuse to post this act as required herein, such hotel, restaurant, cafe, dining car railroad or sleeping car company shall be subject to a fine not to exceed one hundred dollars for every day it shall so fail.

3239. Grand juries to be especially instructed.—5. It shall be the duty of the circuit judges to specially call the attention of the grand jury to the provisions of this act at each term of the court.
Source: William Hemingway, The Annotated Mississippi Code (Indianapolis: Bobbs-Merrill, 1917), pp. 1563–1564.

Arkansas, enacted 1913; repealed 1925.
Tips, unlawful to receive, etc.

Section 2224. It shall be unlawful for any steward, waiter, porter or other employee at any hotel, restaurant, cafe, or eating house in the state of Arkansas to solicit or receive either directly or indirectly; or for any proprietor or manager of any such hotel, restaurant, cafe or eating house, to permit any such steward, waiter, porter or other employee to receive either directly or indirectly from any guest or patron any gift, compensation or honorarium, or gratuity commonly known as a "tip."

Section 2225. It shall be unlawful for any porter or other employee of any sleeping car company or dining car company or corporation or carrier operating any sleeping car or dining car in this State, to receive either directly or indirectly, an gratuity or compensation commonly known as a "tip," and any sleeping or dining car company or any common carrier or corporation operating a sleeping or dining car in this state that permits an employee to accept or receive any gratuity or compensation commonly known as a "tip," shall be guilty of a misdemeanor.

Section 2226. Any person, firm, corporation of common carrier violating any of the provisions of this Act shall be punished by a fine of not less than ten dollars, nor more than twenty-five dollars.

Source: William F. Kirby, *A Digest of the Statutes of Arkansas* (Little Rock: n.p., 1916), p. 683.

Tennessee, enacted 1915; repealed 1925.
Unlawful to give or receive certain tips.

6888a1. Unlawful to permit, give, or receive certain tips.—It shall be unlawful in this state for any hotel, restaurant, cafe, barber shop, dining car railroad company, or sleeping car company to willfully allow any person in its employ to receive any gratuity, commonly known as a "tip" from any patron or passenger, and it shall be unlawful for any patron of any hotel, restaurant, cafe, barber shop, dining car, or any passenger on any railroad train or sleeping car, to give any employee any such gratuity and it shall be unlawful for any employee of any hotel, restaurant, cafe, barber shop, dining car, railroad company or sleeping car company to receive any gratuity or tip.

6888a2. Tip or gratuity is defined.—By "gratuity" or tip, as used in this article, is meant any extra compensation of any kind which any hotel, restaurant, cafe, barber shop, dining car, railroad company or sleeping car company or the manager, officer or any agent thereof, in charge of same, allows to be given an employee or which any person gives to any employee, or which is received by any employee, and is not a part of the regular charge of the hotel, restaurant, cafe, barber shop, dining car, railroad company or sleeping car company for the thing bought or service rendered, or a part of the services which by contract it is under duty to render.

6888a3. No evasion allowed.—No hotel, restaurant, cafe, barber shop, dining car railroad company or sleeping car company shall evade this law by adding to the regular charge, directly or indirectly, anything intended for or to be used or to be given away as a gratuity or tip to the employee. All charges made by the hotel, restaurant, cafe, barber shop, dining car railroad company, or sleeping car company must be made by it in good faith, a charge for the service which it renders, exclusive of the service which it furnishes to it employees.

6888a4. Notice of this law to be conspicuously posted, and synopsis printed on menu cars.—Each hotel shall post notice of this law in the office and in each room, and each restaurant, cafe, and barber shop shall post at least two notices of this law in two conspicuous places in same, and each dining car railroad, or sleeping car company, doing business within this state, shall post two notices of this law in conspicuous places in each sleeping car, and each cafe, hotel or dining car operator shall have printed, in a conspicuous place on their menu cards or bills of fare, the synopsis of the provisions of this law.

6888a5. Fines for violation of this law.—Any hotel, restaurant, cafe, barber shop, dining car railroad, or sleeping car company, and the manager, officer or agent of same in charge, violating this law or willfully allowing the same to be violated in any way, shall each be subject to a penalty of not less than $10 nor more than $50 for each tip allowed to be given. If any person shall give an employee any gratuity or tip, each person shall be subject to a fine of not more than $25 nor less than $5 for each offense. If any of the above employees shall receive any gratuity or tip, he or she shall be subject to a fine of not more than $25 nor less than $5 for each offense. Should any hotel, restaurant, cafe, barber shop, dining car railroad company, or sleeping car company fail, neglect, or refuse to post notice of this law, as required herein, such hotel, restaurant, cafe, barber shop, dining car railroad, or sleeping car company shall be subject to a fine not to exceed $100 for each day it shall fail.

6888a6. Special charge.—It shall be the duty of the circuit judges and the courts of like jurisdiction to especially call the attention of the grand jury to the provisions of this article at each term of the court.

Source: Robert T. Shannon, *A Compilation of the Tennessee Statutes* (Nashville: Tennessee Law Book, 1918), pp. 6221–6222.

South Carolina, enacted 1915; repealed 1922.

An act to prohibit hotels, restaurants, cafes, dining car companies, sleeping car companies and barber shops from allowing tips to be given to employees, and to prohibit employees in hotels, restaurants, cafes, dining cars, railroad companies, sleeping car companies and barber shops from receiving them.

Section 1. Unlawful to allow, give or receive tip.—Be it enacted by the General Assembly of the State of South Carolina, It shall be unlawful in this State for any hotel, restaurant, cafe, dining car company, railroad company, sleeping car company or barber shop, to knowingly allow any person in its employ to receive any gratuity, commonly known as a "tip," from any patron or passenger, and it shall be unlawful for any patron of any hotel, restaurant, cafe, dining car or for any passenger on any railroad train or sleeping car to give to any employee any such gratuity and it shall be unlawful for any employee of any hotel, restaurant, cafe, dining car company, railroad company, sleeping car company or barber shop to receive any such gratuity.

Section 2. Meaning of gratuity or tip — No evasion of act.—By "gratuity," or "tip," as used in this Act, is meant any extra compensation of any kind, which any hotel, restaurant, cafe, dining car, railroad company, sleeping car company or barber shop manager, officer or any agent thereof in charge of the same, allows to be given to an employee or which any person gives to an employee, or which is received by any employee and is not a part of the regular charge of the hotel, restaurant, cafe, dining car, railroad company, sleeping car company, or barber shop, for any part of service rendered, or a part of the service which by contract it is under duty to render. No company or corporation shall evade this Act by adding to the regular charge, directly or indirectly, anything intended for or to be used or to be given away as a gratuity or "tip" to the employee. All charges must be made by the company or proprietor in good faith as a charge for the service it renders, inclusive of the service which it furnishes through employees.

Section 3. Copies of act to be posted.—Each hotel shall post a copy of this Act in each room, and each restaurant, cafe and barber shop, shall post at least two copies of the Act in two conspicuous places in their place of business, and each railroad company shall post two copies of this Act in their waiting rooms and passenger rooms at passenger stations in cities of three thousand inhabitants or more. Each sleeping car and dining car shall have posted therein, at least one copy of this Act.

Section 4. Penalty for failure to post.— Any person or corporation failing to post copies as required shall be fined not less than ten dollars for such failure, and each day of such failure shall constitute a separate and distinct offense, and any person violating any of the other provisions of this Act shall be subject to a fine of not less than ten dollars, or more than one hundred dollars, or be imprisoned for not exceeding thirty days.

Section 5. All laws in conflict with this Act be, and the same are hereby, repealed, and this Act shall take effect on June first, nineteen hundred and fifteen.

Source: South Carolina, *Session Laws 1915*, pp. 262–263.

Iowa, enacted 1915; struck down by state
Supreme Court as unconstitutional, 1919.
Title 24, Ch. 11

Sec. 5028-u. Accepting or soliciting gratuity or tip. Every employee of any hotel, restaurant, barber shop, or other public place, and every employee of any person, firm, partnership, or corporation, or of any public service corporation engaged in the transportation of passengers in this state, who shall accept or solicit any gratuity, tip, or other thing of value or of valuable consideration, from any guest or patron, shall be guilty of a misdemeanor, and upon conviction thereof shall be fined not less than five dollars, or more than twenty-five dollars, or be imprisoned in the county jail for a period not exceeding thirty days.

Sec. 5028-v. Giving or offering gratuity or tip. Every person who shall give or offer any tip or gratuity to any person or employee prohibited from receiving or soliciting the same by the provisions of the preceding section shall be guilty of a misdemeanor and be punished upon conviction as provided by the preceding section.

Sec. 5028-w. Permitting violation of anti-tipping law — failure to post sign. Any person who shall knowingly permit a violation of this act in any place under his control or who shall fail to keep conspicuously posted in every said place under his control a notice bearing the words "No tipping allowed" shall be deemed guilty of a misdemeanor and be punished as provided in section one.

Source: Laws of Iowa 1915, (Des Moines: State Printer, 1915), p. 347.

Notes

Chapter 1

1. Rae L. Needleman, "Tipping as a factor in wages," *Monthly Labor Review* 45 (December 1937): 1303; "Economic effects of tipping," *Gunton's Magazine* 11 (July 1896): 13; Boas Shamir, "Between gratitude and gratuity: An analysis of tipping," *Annals of Tourism Research* 11 (1984): 62.

2. "British baksheesh," *Leisure Hour* 3 (July 4, 1863): 464.

3. Peter T. White, "Tips, tippers and tippees," *New York Times Magazine*, April 8, 1956, p. 64; "Vails or tips," *News-Sheet of the Bribery & Secret Commissions Prevention League* #260 (April 1939): 23; Arthur Gaye, "Baksheesh," *Macmillan's Magazine* 64 (1891): 211.

4. "Earl of Sefton bars tips," *New York Times*, August 25, 1907, p. 1.

5. "Americans blamed for tipping evil," *New York Times*, April 26, 1908, pt. 4, p.2.

6. "Feeing in private houses," *New York Times*, January 28, 1900, p. 8; "The week-end tip," *New York Times*, September 1, 1907, pt. 2, p. 6.

7. Dodie Kazanjian, "Parting gestures," *House & Garden* 160 (June 1988): 188; Amy Vanderbilt and Letitia Baldridge, *The Amy Vanderbilt Complete Book of Etiquette: A Guide to Contemporary Living* (Garden City, NY: Doubleday, 1978).

8. "Pepys on tipping," *New York Times*, September 18, 1927, sec. 8, p. 12; Arthur Gaye, "Baksheesh," pp. 211–212.

9. R.A. Crouch, "Tips," *Cornhill Magazine* 154 (November 1936): 544–545.

10. Oneta Aldrich Wakeford, "Tipping, a national racket?" *American Mercury* 78 (June 1954): 129; M.J. Arlen, "Tips on tipping and tippees," *New York Times Magazine*, May 31, 1964 p. 20; Joanne M. May, "Looking for tips," *Cornell Hotel and Restaurant Administration Quarterly* 20 (February, 1980): 9; "Tipping as practiced by Samuel Johnson," *New York Times Magazine*, September 28, 1930, p. 18.

11. David Streitfeld, "Tip o' the season," *Washington Post*, December 11, 1987, p. C5; Floyd Anderson, "Tips for tippers," *America* 52 (November 24, 1934): 152; Joanne M. May, "Looking for tips," p. 9.

12. Arthur Gaye, "Baksheesh," p. 209; *Oxford English Dictionary* 2nd ed. (Oxford: Clarendon, 1989), vol. 18, p. 134; Boas Shamir, "Between gratitude," p. 60.

13. Alvin F. Harlow, "Our daily bribe," *Forum and Century* 99 (April 1938): 231; "Editor's easy chair," *Harper's Magazine* 127 (July 1913): 312.

14. "Economic effects of tipping," *Grunton's Magazine* 11 (July 1896): 14–15.

15. "Rapid growth of the tipping system," *New York Times*, June 9, 1895, p. 16; "Topics of the Times," *New York Times*, May 9, 1897, p. 22.

16. Edward Bok, "An American nuisance," *Ladies Home Journal* 22 (February 1905): 20.

17. "Tipping," *New York Times*, April 27, 1908, p. 6; Ames Higgins, "The tactful art of tipping," *Outlook* 81 (September 16, 1905): 128; Peter T. White, "Tips," p. 28.

18. "Topics of the Times," *New York Times*, May 9, 1987, p. 22; "The no tip hotel," *New York Times*, October 8, 1909, p. 8.

19. "Tipping," *New York Times*, April 7, 1908, p. 6; "The rambler," *Travel* 21 (June 1913): 40.

20. William R. Scott, *The Itching Palm: A Study of the Habit of Tipping in America* (Philadelphia: Penn, 1916), pp. 147, 150; Samuel Gompers, *Labor in Europe and America* (New York: Harper & Brothers, 1910).

Chapter 2

1. H.C. Bierwirth, "The ethics of tips, fees and gratuities," *Andover Review* 6 (August 1886): 172–173; Arthur Gaye, "Baksheesh," *Macmillan's Magazine* 64 (1891): 210.

2. John Gilmer Speed, "Tips and commissions," *Lippincott's Magazine* 69 (June 1902): 749.

3. "Komura's tips at the Waldorf," *New York Times*, August 9, 1905, p. 6.

4. Elizabeth Banks, "Tips versus social equality and self-respect," *New York Times*, June 11, 1905, pt. 3, p. 7.

5. Ibid.

6. John Gilmer Speed, "Tips and commissions," p. 748.

7. James Samuel Stemons, "Tipping—the other side," *Independent* 55 (March 26, 1903): 726–727.

8. "Tillman gives negro a tip," *New York Times*, August 9, 1907, p. 1; "Tillman's tip," *New York Times*, August 11, 1907, p. 6.

9. Joseph Hatton, "The idler's club," *Idler* 3 (July 1893): 680; "The tip question," *New York Times*, July 30, 1905, p. 6; "Tipping," *Spectator* 100 (April 25, 1908): 662.

10. "The tipping nuisance," *New York Times*, November 3, 1884, p. 3.

11. "The hold-up game," *New York Times*, July 9, 1911, pt. 5, p. 7; "Problems in tips and tipping," *New York Times*, July 30, 1911, pt. 5, p. 11.

12. Joseph Hatton, "The idler's club," p. 677; Ames Higgins, "The tactful art of tipping," *Outlook* 81 (September 16, 1905): 127.

13. "Tipping," *New York Times*, March 24, 1882, p. 5; "Another protest against tipping," *New York Times*, March 26, 1882, p. 5; "The tipping nuisance," *New York Times*, November 3, 1884, p. 3.

14. "British baksheesh," *Leisure Hour* 3 (July 4, 1863): 463; "To fix scale of tips," *New York Times*, October 3, 1909, p. 2; "Tipping," *New York Times*, September 28, 1909, p. 8.

15. "The tipping nuisance," *New York Times*, November 3, 1884, p. 3; "Rapid growth of the tipping system," *New York Times*, June 9, 1895, p. 16; Joseph Hatton, "The idler's club," p. 681; Servitor, "The philosophy of tipping," *Canadian Magazine* 36 (April 1911): 536.

16. Robert Sloss, "The way of the waiter," *Harper's Weekly* 52 (January 11, 1908): 21.

17. John Kendrick Bangs, "Table d'hote talks," *Harper's Weekly* 55 (March 11, 1911): 12–13.

18. "100 tip hungry waiters arrested," *New York Times*, June 23, 1918, p. 7.

19. Elizabeth Banks, "Tips versus social equations."; "The hold-up game," *New York Times*, July 9, 1911, pt. 5, p. 7.

20. "Tipping here and in Europe," *New York Times*, August 8, 1895, p. 1.

21. "The pourboire in danger," *The Nation* 65 (August 26, 1897): 163; "To fix the scale of tips," *New York Times*, October 3, 1909, p. 2; John Gilmer Speed, "Tips and commissions," p. 678.

22. "The common sense of tipping," *Spectator* 91 (October 29, 1904): 631; Joseph Hatton, "The idler's club," p. 678.

23. "The hold-up game," *New York Times*, July 9, 1911, pt. 5, p. 7.

24. "The hotel tip trust," *New York Times*, October 12, 1906, p. 6.

25. "Tip trust losing its grip on hats," *New York Times*, November 27, 1910, p. 10.

26. "Tipping is illegal," *New York Times*, February 6, 1912, p. 1.

27. "Suit over hatboy's tips," *New York Times*, September 7, 1916, p. 3.

28. "We endure from lack of courage," *New York Times*, August 31, 1917, p. 6.

29. Rae L. Needleman, "Tipping as a factor in wages," *Monthly Labor Review* 45 (December 1937): 1313.

30. "Tips really don't go to tiptakers," *New York Times*, May 5, 1914, p. 10.

31. William R. Scott, *The Itching Palm: A Study of the Habit of Tipping in America* (Philadelphia: Penn, 1916), pp. 105–107.

32. Ibid., pp. 111–112.

33. "Put on blacklist for demanding tips," *New York Times*, August 9, 1908, pt. 3, p. 1.

34. "Untipped waiters mutinied," *New York Times*, August 26, 1908, p. 7.

35. "Put on blacklist,"; "Plaint of the steward," *New York Times*, February 20, 1910, pt. 5, p. 5.

36. "Hard times for ocean stewards," *New York Times*, August 22, 1909, pt 5, p. 7.

37. Ibid.

38. "No easy way to stop tipping," *New York Times*, August 31, 1908, p. 6.

39. Ames Higgins, "The tactful art of tipping," *Outlook* 81 (September 16, 1905): 125; "Problems in tips and tipping," *New York Times*, July 30, 1911, pt. 5, p 11; Louise Hayter Birchall, "How much shall I tip," *Canadian Magazine* 39 (October 1912): 553, 555.

40. "British baksheesh," p. 464; Arthur Gaye, "Baksheesh," *Macmillan's Magazine* 64 (1891): 212.

41. "Taft an anti-tipper," *New York Times*, June 20, 1908, p. 2; "Taft and tips," *New York Times*, June 21, 1908, pt. 2, p. 10.

42. "Rockefeller tips 5 cents," *New York Times*, December 10, 1908, p. 1; "Problems in tips and tipping," *New York Times*, July 30, 1911, pt. 5, p. 11.

43. "Regulating tips," *Scribner's Magazine*, 45 (February 1909): 252.

44. Joseph Hatton, "The idler's club," p. 680; "Tipping in Berlin," *New York Times*, July 14, 1912, pt. 4, p. 4; "Paris tipping excessive," *New York Times*, June 15, 1913, pt. 3, p. 3.

45. "Tipping to go on," *New York Times*, November 15, 1908, pt. 3, p. 2; "The scale of tips," *New York Times*, August 1, 1906, p. 8.

46. "The hold-up game,"; William R. Scott, *The Itching Palm*, pp. 8, 18, 22.

47. "Topics of the Times," *New York Times*, November 21, 1899, p. 6.

48. "Economic effects of tipping," *Gunton's Magazine* 11 (July 1896): 16–17.

49. William R. Scott, *The Itching Palm*, pp. 23–24.

Chapter 3

1. John Gilmer Speed, "Tips and commissions," *Lippincott's Magazine* 69 (June 1902): 749; "Club lifts ban on tips," *New York Times*, January 17, 1914, p. 6.

2. "The no tip hotel," *New York Times*, October 8, 1909, p. 8; Frank X. Finnegan, "Tipping as a fine art," *Travel* 16 (February 1911): 172.

3. "Tipless London," *Independent* 75 (July 10, 1913): 111.

4. "Komura's tips at the Waldorf," *New York Times*, August 9, 1905, p. 6; "Tips in the bill in one hotel now," *New York Times*, February 17, 1913, p. 6.

5. "Editor's easy chair," *Harper's Magazine* 127 (July 1913): 313.

6. "No-tip barber shop soon stared out," *New York Times*, May 1, 1908, p. 5.

7. "For tipless barbers," *New York Times*, September 18, 1910, p. 5.

8. "Will regulate tips," *New York Times*, November 1, 1908, p.4.

9. "Regulating tips," *Scribner's Magazine* 45 (February 1909): 251–252.

10. "To fix scale of tips," *New York Times*, October 3, 1909, p. 2.

11. "Pay the tips in your bills," *New York Times*, May 12, 1912, pt. 3, p. 5.

12. "Trying to stop tipping," *New York Times*, April 22, 1913, p. 1; "Swiss tip reform fails," *New York Times*, July 20, 1913, pt. 3, p. 3.

13. "Topics of the Times" *New York Times*, August 24, 1907, p. 6.

14. Edward Bok, "An American nuisance," *Ladies Home Journal* 22 (February 1905): 20; Richard Strouse, "Notes on tips, tippers and tippees," *New York Times Magazine*, July 17, 1949, p. 23; "Organize to stop tipping," *New York Times*, November 23, 1906, p. 9.

15. "Begin war on tip system," *New York Times*, November 4, 1911, p. 22; "An appeal likely to be heard," *New York Times*, November 4, 1911, p. 12.

16. "Told to quit tipping," *New York Times*, January 2, 1912, p. 7.

17. "Tipless hotels," *New York Times*, March 24, 1912, pt. 3, p. 14; "The tipping evil," *New York Times*, February 9, 1914, p. 6.

18. "Drummers in war on tips," *New York Times*, June 28, 1913, p. 1; William R. Scott, *The Itching Palm: A Study of the Habit of Tipping in America* (Philadelphia: Penn, 1916), pp. 40–41.

19. Rae L. Needleman, "Tipping as a factor in wages," *Monthly Labor Review* 45 (December 1937): 1312.

20. William R. Scott, *The Itching Palm*, pp. 160–165.

21. Ibid., pp. 166–167.

22. "Economic effects of tipping," *Gunton's Magazine* 11 (July 1896): 14; "Wages and tipping," *The Public* 21 (September 7, 1918): 1138,

23. "Waitresses plead for tips," *New York Times*, June 22, 1915, p. 24.

24. "Hotel porters out, strike for tips," *New York Times*, May 30, 1907, p. 18.

25. "May abolish tips," *New York Times*, April 25, 1909, p. 12.

26. "Boston may cut off tips," *New York Times*, December 27, 1911, p. 1.

27. "Waiters weaken on no-tip crusade," *New York Times*, January 27, 1912, p. 20.

28. "Waiters want anti-tip law," *New York Times*, October 19, 1913, pt. 2, p. 13.

29. "Hotel men in war on prohibitionists," *New York Times*, April 15, 1914, p. 8.

30. "Spread of idleness alarms Berlin," *New York Times*, December 24, 1918, p. 2.

31. "Waiter refused a tip," *New York Times*, August 18, 1908, p. 1.

32. "Ushers strike for tips," *New York Times*, November 1, 1919, p. 8.

33. "Economic effects of tipping," *Gunton's Magazine* 11, (July 1896): 15–16.

34. William R. Scott, *The Itching Palm*, pp. 150–157.

35. "The reclamation of the tip," *Outlook* 87 (October 26, 1907): 373–374.

36. "Recognition of tipping," *New York Times*, October 30, 1912, p. 12.

37. "Controller opposes tips," *New York Times*, April 9, 1913, p. 2.

38. "Tipping," *New York Times*, April 4, 1910, p. 8; "Tipping and its remedy," *New York Times*, January 23, 1911, p. 6.

39. "Law to cut down tips," *New York Times*, January 21, 1911, p. 1.

40. "Tipping a St. Louis misdemeanor," *New York Times*, July 27, 1913, pt. 2, p. 7; "Federal bill to abolish tips," *New York Times*, June 25, 1914, p. 4.

41. Rae L. Needleman, "Tipping as a factor," p. 1313; "Makes tipping a crime," *New York Times*, March 6, 194, p. 13.

42. William R. Scott, *The Itching Palm*, pp. 11–12, 91; "Tipping and the law," *New York Times*, April 16, 1915, p 12; Rae L. Needleman, "Tipping as a factor," p. 1313.

43. "Dunahoo v. Huber," *The Northwestern Reporter* v. 171 (St. Paul: West, 1919), pp. 123–125.

44. Rae L. Needleman, "Tipping as a factor," p. 1314.

45. William R. Scott, "The Itching Palm," pp. 122–128.

46. "Tips," *Spectator* 59 (January 2, 1886): 10.

47. "The common sense of tipping," *Spectator* 91 (October 29, 1904): 630–631.

48. Albert R. Carman, "Tipping—a defence," *Canadian Magazine* 24 (March 1905): 416–418.

49. Robert Sloss, "The way of the waiter," *Harper's Weekly* 52 (January 11, 1908): 21.

50. "Tipping," *Outlook* 110 (May 19, 1915): 121.

51. "Paris benevolence," *New York Times*, December 19, 1910, p. 8.

52. Edward Bok, "An American nuisance," *Ladies Home Journal* 22 (February 1905): 20.

53. "The question of tipping," *New York Times*, November 19, 1899, p. 10; "Tipping," *New York Times*, November 16, 1899, p. 6.

54. "Tipping as a source of happiness," *New York Times*, November 6, 1909, p. 8.

55. "Regulating tips," *Scribner's Magazine* 45 (February 1909): 252.

56. Arthur Gaye, "Baksheesh," *Macmillan's Magazine* 64 (1891): 212; Lady Grove, "Hotels as homes?" *Critic* 41 (October 1902): 356; Littel McClune, "When not to tip," *Lippincott's Magazine* 91 (April 1913): 510; Frank X. Finnegan, "Tipping as a fine art," p. 170.

57. Arthur Gaye, "Baksheesh," p.211; "Refuse to stop tipping," *New York Times*, April 6, 1913, pt. 3, p. 2.

58. "The tip question," *New York Times*, July 30, 1905, p. 6; "Editor's easy chair," *Harper's Magazine* 127 (July 1913): 311–312; "Tipping," *Spectator* 100 (April 25, 1908): 662.

59. "The pourboire in danger," *The Nation* 65 (August 26, 1897): 163.

60. H.C. Bierwirth, "The ethics of tips, fees, and gratuities, "*Andover Review* 6 (August 1886): 166–168.

61. William R. Scott, *The Itching Palm*, pp. 7, 36–37.

62. Ibid., pp. 38, 42–43.

63. Ibid., pp. 50, 58, 69–70, 75.

Chapter 4

1. "Bought auto with tips, "*New York Times*, January 17, 1920, p. 4.

2. "Sophie and her tips," *The Nation* 110 (January 31, 1920): 133.

3. "Sees peril in tips," *New York Times*, January 23, 1925, p. 7.

4. "A drive against tipping," *World's Work* 40 (July 1920): 230.

5. "Pullman porters fight on tipping," *New York Times*, July 23, 1928, p. 8.

6. "Tipping," *Life* 21 (July 15, 1946): 30.

7. Clara Laughlin, "Hobo signs reach Europe," *New York Times*, April 21, 1927, p. 35: James F. Roche, "Random notes of travelers," *New York Times*, May 19, 1935, sec. 9, p. 21.

8. "Traveler tires of tipping," *New York Times*, August 26, 1922, pt. 9, p. 14.

9. "The crime of not tipping," *New York Times*, August 31, 1922, p. 14.

10. Rose C. Feld, "Tickling America's outstretched palm" *New York Times*, February 1, 1925, sec. 4, p. 2.

11. Alvin F. Harlow, "Our daily bribe," *Forum and Century* 99 (April 1938): 232; Juliet Danziger, "He also serves — maybe," *New York Times Magazine*, August 28, 1933, p. 19.

12. "Gets no tip, fined $2," *New York Times*, August 23, 1927, p. 38.

13. "American woman saves self after being pushed overboard," *New York Times*, April 28, 1933, p. 19.

14. Bernhard Ragner, "Itching palms of Paris," *New York Times*, December 6, 1925, sec. 4, p. 17.

15. "Tips expected in France by workers of many types," *New York Times*, December 13, 1925, pt. 10, p. 24.

16. "French may go non-tipping," *Variety*, September 10, 1930, p. 1; "Struggles in France," *New York Times*, June 14, 1936, sec. 4, p. 6; F.J. Philip, "Blum regime acts to end tipping evil," *New York Times*, June 13, 1937, sec 4, p. 4.

17. "Admits girls pay $10 a week for job," *New York Times*, May 1, 1928, p. 31.

18. Charles W. Ferguson, "Will that be all, sir?" in *Magazine Essays of Today* ed. Elias Lieberman (New York: Prentice–Hall, 1935), p. 152.

19. "Clemenceau's book stirs trepidation," *New York Times*, December 15, 1929, sec. 3, p. 1.

20. "To bare tip-taking employers," *New York Times*, February 23, 1939, p. 16.

21. "Sues tipping trust to recover $25,000," *New York Times*, January 11, 1920, pt. 2, p. 1; H.A. Lamb, "Can tips be abolished?" *New York Times*, July 4, 1920, pt. 7, p. 2.

22. "Bill prohibiting kickback of tips," *Variety*, February 19, 1947, p. 43; "Tipping," *Life* 21 (July 15, 1946): 30.

23. Charles W. Ferguson, "Will that be all, sir?" p. 154; Howard Whitman, "How much shall I tip?" *Woman's Home Companion* 66 (September 1939): 8.

24. "Porters assail tipping," *New York Times*, November 27, 1927, sec. 10, p. 3; "Assails Pullman tipping," *New York Times*, October 26, 1927, p. 2.

25. "Pullman porters open union fight," *New York Times*, June 24, 1928, p. 22; "Porters tips put at $25 net a month," *New York Times*, July 30, 1928, p. 32.

26. Floyd Anderson, "Tips for tippers," *America* 52 (November 24, 1934): 152; Catherine MacKenzie, "Tips are smaller but tipping persists," *New York Times Magazine*, December 31, 1933, p. 6.

27. "Railroad bars tips in its dining cars," *New York Times*, June 8, 1946, p. 1.

28. "No tipping," *New York Times*, April 20, 1947, sec 2, p. 13.

29. "Dining car tips barred on Chinese rail system," *New York Times*, January 6, 1935, p. 20.

30. Howard Whitman, "How much shall I tip?" *Woman's Home Companion* 66 (September 1939): 8; "Tipping," *Life* 21 (July 15, 1946): 30; Richard Strouse, "Notes on tips, tippers and tippees," *New York Times Magazine*, July 178, 1949, pp. 15, 22.

31. "Pullman porters say the day of the lavish tip has passed," *New York Times*, August 17, 1924, sec. 8, p. 2; "Mrs. Roosevelt a leader in tipping on dining cars," *New York Times*, February 2, 1939, p. 21.

32. Al Stump, *Cobb: A Biography* (Chapel Hill, NC: Algonquin Books, 1994), p. 242; Helen Bullitt Lowry "Pity the poor Pullman porter," *New York Times*, October 24, 1920, pt. 3, p. 12.

33. Joanne M. May, "Looking for tips," *Cornell Hotel and Restaurant Administration Quarterly* 20 (February 1980): 9.

34. "Pullman porters say the day."

35. Helen Christine Bennett, "Fr-R-Ront!" *Saturday Evening Post* 199 (June 11, 1927): 44, 46.

36. "Reform in dining pleases maitres," *New York Times*, March 5, 1935, p. 21.

37. Meyer Berger, "Tippers are stiffs or sports," *New York Times Magazine*, October 4, 1936, p. 24.

38. Charles W. Ferguson, "Will that be all, sir?" p. 156.

39. R.A. Crouch, "Tips," *Cornhill Magazine* 154 (November 1936): 545, 547; "Mrs. Roosevelt a leader."

40. Francis Donovan, *The Woman Who Waits* (Boston: Badger), 1920, p. 200.

41. Dwight MacDonald, "Your waiter looks at you," *Harper's Magazine* 182 (April 1944): 519–520.

42. Fred Sparks, "Headwaiter, Esq.," *Colliers* 118 (November 23, 1946): 40.

43. "Tickling America's Outstretched palm,"; Helen Christine Bennett, "Fr-R-Ront!" p. 41.

44. "10 per cent service charge in tipless cafe," *New York Times*, February 19, 1922, pt. 2, p. 1.

45. Alvin F. Harlow, "Our daily bribe," *Forum and Century* 99 (April 1938): 233; Fred Sparks, "Headwaiter, Esq.," p. 26; Richard Strouse, "Notes on tips," p. 22.

46. Rae L. Needleman, "Tipping as a factor in wages," *Monthly Labor Review* 45 (December 1937): 1305–1307.

47. Ibid., p. 1309.

48. Ibid., p. 1309–1310.

49. Fred Davis, "The cabdriver and his fare," *American Journal of Sociology* 65 (September 1959): 161.

50. John P. Henderson, "Gratuities as a source of income in the lodging industry," *Business Trends* 13 (Summer 1965): 7.

Chapter 5

1. "Tipless hotel has long waiting list," *New York Times*, September 18, 1927, sec. 8, p. 12.

2. "Tipless hotel's success," *New York Times*, October 29, 1922, pt. 9, p. 10; "A non-tipping hotel," *New York Times*, December 30, 1924, p. 16; Helen Christine Bennett, "To tip or not to tip?" *American Magazine* 108 (December 1929): 69–70.

3. "Germany abolishes weak war beer," *New York Times*, October 3, 1920, pt. 10, p. 14.

4. "Columbia bans tipping," *New York Times*, November 2, 1930, p. 16.

5. "The no-tipping plan," *Reader's Digest* 28 (March 1936): 104.

6. "Shall we abolish tipping?" *Reader's Digest* 33 (October 1938): 107.

7. "A no-tip hotel," *New York Times*, June 5, 1921, pt. 6, p. 7; "Scientific tipping," *New York Times*, September 3, 1922, pt. 6, p. 8.

8. "Tries not tipping in a no-tip hotel," *New York Times*, June 5, 1922, p. 6.

9. Will Payne, "Tips," *Saturday Evening Post* 198 (May 15, 1926): 33, 86.

10. "New hotel bans tipping," *New York Times*, October 15, 1929, p. 20.

11. Meyer Berger, "Tippers are stiffs or sports," *New York Times Magazine*, October 4, 1936, p. 8.

12. B.Y. Lee, "Can exorbitant tipping in China be prohibited?" *China Weekly Review*, 71 (December 15, 1934): 92–93.

13. "A spectator's notebook," *Spectator* 173 (September 15, 1944): 236.

14. "Form anti-gimme league," *New York Times*, January 25, 1923, p. 4; "Tippers and tipped," *New York Times*, August 18, 1927, p. 20.

15. "Hotel men say public alone can end tipping," *New York Times*, March 19, 1922, pt. 2, p. 16.

16. "Frenchman uses token in move to press war on tipping evil," *New York Times*, September 18, 1932, sec. 2, p. 3; "The reluctant gratuity," *Commonweal* 16 (September 28, 1932): 500; Meyer Berger, "Tippers are stiffs," p. 24.

17. "Income tax includes tips," *New York Times*, November 16, 1921, p. 13.

18. "Six waiters made $27,000, not $5,000 in tips," *New York Times*, April 7, 1947, p. 25.

19. "Topics of the Times," *New York Times*, February 14, 1921, p. 8; "Anti-tip bill for Massachusetts," *New York Times*, December 20, 1927, p. 27.

20. "Tipping in hotels and restaurants," *Times* (London), November 23, 1936, p. 19.

21. "Anti-tipping bill passed in France," *New York Times*, June 5, 1937, p. 19.

22. "Tipping in Italy," *New York Times*, April 3, 1927, sec. 9, p. 15; F. Roche, "Random notes of travelers," *New York Times*, May 19, 1935, sec. 9, p. 21; "No tipping in Hungary," *New York Times*, July 5, 1936, sec. 10, p. 12; "Czech order end to tipping," *New York Times*, May 30, 1948, p. 8.

23. "Army in Europe repeats aim to ban cigarette tip," *New York Times*, October 29, 1946, p. 12.

24. "Coolidge fixes 60 cents a day tip limit," *New York Times*, August 28, 1926, p. 1; Meyer Berger, "Tippers are stiffs," p. 24.

25. "Bars waiters' tips in claim for injury," *New York Times*, May 25, 1930, p. 30; "Massachusetts court holds tips are wages under compensation act," *Monthly Labor Review* 45 (December 1937): 1315, 1318.

27. Ibid., p. 1320; "10%," *Literary Digest* 123 (July 10, 1937): 5–6.

28. Rae L. Needleman, "Tipping as a factor," p. 1320; "Says tips are not wages," *New York Times*, September 17, 1941, p. 25.

29. "Barbers accept tip estimates," *New York Times*, August 9, 1946, p. 14; Richard Strouse, "Notes on tips, tippers and tippees," *New York Times Magazine*, July 17, 1949, p. 22.

30. Rae L. Needleman, "Tipping as a factor," p. 1319.

31. Ibid., pp. 1319–1320; "To tip or not to tip," *New York Times*, October 14, 1933, p. 14.

32. "Opposes amendment," *New York Times*, February 8, 1938, p. 7.

33. "State minimum-wage law," *Monthly Labor Review* 57 (September 1943): 555–556; "Tips as wages under Fair Labor Standards Act," *Monthly Labor Review* 54 (April 1942): 996–997.

34. Harold Denny, "Growth of tipping in Soviet scored," *New York Times*, May 23, 1936, p. 7; "Tipping," *Literary Digest* 122 (December 19, 1936): 31.

35. "Tipping," *Times* (London), June 3, 1947, p. 2; Richard Strouse, "Notes on tips," p. 22.

36. "Is tipping liked or compelled?" *New York Times*, December 3, 1924, p. 20; Meyer Berger, "Tippers are stiffs," p. 24.

37. Rose C. Feld, "Tickling America's outstretched palm" *New York Times*, February 1, 1925, sec. 4, p. 2.

38. "Bordeaux waiters strike to abolish tips," *New York Times*, July 29, 1936, p. 2.

39. "Swiss waiters fight tips," *New York Times*, August 14, 1921, p. 2.

40. "Says union forces high building costs," *New York Times*, July 21, 1927, p. 23; "State barbers ban tips," *New York Times*, August 17, 1927, p. 5.

41. "Bill regulating distribution of tips urged," *New York Times*, July 4, 1920, pt. 7, p. 2.

42. H.A. Lamb, "Can tips be abolished?" *New York Times*, July 4, 1920, pt. 7, p. 2.

43. "Waiters condemn tips," *New York Times*, November 9, 1927, p. 22.

44. "Opposition of organized labor to the tipping system," *Monthly Labor Review* 25 (October 1927): 717.

45. Ibid., p. 718.

46. Ibid.

47. Rae L. Needleman, "Tipping is a factor," pp. 1311–1312.

48. "Sharp drop in tips laid to end of OPA," *New York Times*, January 4, 1947, p. 12.

49. "Attacks hotel tipping," *New York Times*, March 13, 1922. p. 6.

50. "Tipping," *New Republic* 23 (July 28, 1920): 244–245.

51. "The hated habit of tipping," *Literary Digest* 95 (October 1, 1927): 21.

52. "Russians like tips," *New York Times*, May 25, 1936, p. 18; Rae L. Needleman, "Tipping as a factor," p. 1304.

53. "Tipping," *New Statesman and Nation* 19 (March 30, 1940).

54. Dwight MacDonald, "Your waiter looks at you," *Harper's Magazine* 182 (April 1941): 518.

55. "To tip or not to tip," *Fortune* 18 (August 1938): 75–76.

56. "How do you feel about tipping?" *Woman's Home Companion* 75 (January 1948): 14.

57. . Leo P. Crespi, "The implications of tipping in America," *Public Opinion Quarterly* 11, no. 3 (1947): 424, "Tipping," *Life*, 21 (July 15, 1946): 30.

58. Ibid., pp. 425–426

59. Ibid., pp. 427–429.

60. Ibid., pp. 430–431.

61. Ibid., p. 432.

62. Ibid., pp. 433–434.

63. Ibid., pp. 434–435.

64. H.A. Haring, "Three classes of labor to avoid," *Industrial Management* 62 (December 1921): 370–371.

65. Ibid.

66. "Miss Anderson urges abolition of tipping," *New York Times*, December 29, 1940, p. 24.

67. "Talking it over," *Rotarian* 57 (August 1940): 2.

68. Clyde Brion Davis, "Tips," *Atlantic Monthly* 178 (September 1946): 126–127.

Chapter 6

1. Peter T. White, "Tips, tippers and tippees," *New York Times Magazine*, April 8, 1956, p. 28.

2. Mort Weisginger, "I'm sick of waiters," *Coronet* 36 (June 1954): 32–34.

3. Stuart Wood, "You can't stop tipping," *American Mercury* 83 (September 1956): 11–15.

4. Peter T. White, "Tips, tippers and tippers," p. 67; "Dock worker loses tipping threat case," *New York Times*, March 25, 1962, p. 13.

5. "State's help asked in walkout," *New York Times*, May 22, 1967, p. 85.

6. John A. Patton, "Down with tipping," *Saturday Evening Post* 237 (February 29, 1964): 6, 8; "Sluggish tipping," *Wall Street Journal*, August 17, 1964, p. 8.

7. "Transport news and notes," *New York Times*, October 22, 1967, p. 86.

8. O.A. Battista, "To tip or not to tip," *Catholic Digest* 15 (December 1950): 57; Mort Weisinger, "What happens when you don't tip," *Coronet* 34 (July 1953): 24.

9. Blanche Holland, "May I take your coat, please," *American Mercury* 78 (June 1954): 39–41.

10. Mort Weisinger, "What happens," p. 25; Carlisle Bargeron, "Tips, incidentals, etc.," *Nation's Business* 39 (February 1951): 86.

11. "Transport news of interest here," *New York Times*, February 1, 1956, p. 62.

12. "Holland-America will end tipping entirely in April," *New York Times*, October 16, 1967, p. 89; "Ship line widens no-tipping policy," *New York Times*, November 19, 1967, sec. 10 p. 31; "No-tip holiday cruises," *Times* (London), April 4, 1968, p. 2; Carry on tipping," *Times* (London), July 9, 1968, p. 8.

13. "Travel tips," *Time* 62 (October 26, 1953): 42.

14. Carol Lane, "Tips for touring," *Travel* 103 (April 1955): 44; Howard Greig, "Tips, tippers and tippees," p. 64; "Tips on tipping, *New York Times*, June 26, 1956, p. 24.

15. "When to tip, and what," *Changing Times* 10 (May 1956): 34; "A guide to tipping," *Good Housekeeping* 144 (June 1957): 50–51; "Here's your tip sheet," *Travel* 109 (April 1958): 60–61; Howard Greig, "Tipping in Britain," *Holiday* 23 (April 1958): 119.

16. Jennifer Colton, "The answer to Christmas tipping," *Good Housekeeping* 131 (December 1950): 49ff.

17. Ralph Bass, "What's the right tip?" *Coronet* 49 (January 1961): 38–41.

18. Frances Kiltun, "The intelligent woman traveler," *Madamoiselle* 64 (March 1967): 203–204; "The 1965 tourists' guide to the fine art of tipping," *New York Times*, February 28, 1965, sec. 12, pp. 13–14; "Tips on tipping," *Christian Century* 82 (June 2, 1965): 727; Jean Sprain, *All About Tipping* (McFadden Bartell, 1965).

19. Mort Weisinger, "What Happens," p. 24; "Dime tips by Yankees prohibited by Stengel," *New York Times*, March 9, 1955, p. 32.

20. O.A. Battista, "To tip or not to tip," p. 59; "10 percent is not enough," *New York Times*, October 26, 1952, sec. 10, p. 3.

21. "That tightrope—tipping!" *Travel* 99 (April 1953): 37.

22. Peter T. White, "Tips, tippers and tippees," p. 28.

23. "How much, for whom?" *Newsweek* 49 (May 27, 1957): 116.

24. "The outstretched palm," *Time* 77 (July 23, 1961): 44–45.

25. Gay Talese, "Tourists' tipping dismays tippees," *New York Times*, August 27, 1964, p. 55.

26. "How much, for whom?," 114.

27. Craig Claiborne, "Built-in tips is favored by waiters," *New York Times*, November 12, 1962, P. 34; M.J. Arlen, "Tips on tipping and tippees," *New York Times Magazine*, May 31, 1964, p. 37.

28. Oneta Aldrich Wakeford, "Tipping, a national racket?" *American Mercury* 78 (June 1954): 128; Stuart Wood, "You can't stop tipping,": 11.

29. John P. Henderson, "Gratuities as a source of income in the lodging industry," *Business Topics* 13 (Summer 1965): 8–11, 18–21.

30. George Stelluto, "Wages in eating and drinking places in 27 areas," *Monthly Labor Review* 85 (May 1962): 518–519; George Stelluto, "Wages in eating and drinking places, June 1963," *Monthly Labor Review* 87 (May 1964): 544–546.

Chapter 7

1. Mort Weisinger, "What happens when you don't tip," *Coronet* 34 (July 1953): 27; "Ban on tips is dropped by Chock Full o' Nuts," New York Times, December 4, 1967, p. 22.
2. "White House tipping isn't done," *New York Times*, December 17, 1958, p. 1.
3. "Changes in an old custom," *Times* (London), October 27, 1953, 1953, p. 4; Art Buchwald, "Tips on tips," *Mademoiselle* 38 (April 1954): 92–93; Hans Koningsberger, "Pourboire or trinkgelt of mancia," *New York Times Magazine*, April 17, 1960, pp. 67–68.
4. "Banquet waiters sue the Waldorf," *New York Times*, March 29, 1952, p. 1; "Waiters lose hotel tip suit," *New York Times*, May 27, 1955, p. 10.
5. Robert Sylvester, "Why they behave like waiters," *Holiday* 24 (December 1958): 37; "Sluggish tipping," *Wall Street Journal*, August 17, 1964, p. 8.
6. R.D. Musser, "An answer to the tipping problem," *Cornell Hotel and Restaurant Administration Quarterly* 8 (1968): 99–100.
7. "Bostonian sells tips on tipping," *New York Times*, November 27, 1959, p. 36; "The outstretched palm," *Time* 77 (June 23, 1961): 45.
8. "State's help asked in walkout," *New York Times*, May 22, 1967, p. 85.
9. "No tips? Mixed reception to a campaign," *Times* (London), April 6, 1966, p. 7.
10. "No tips drive welcomed," *Times* (London), January 21, 1967, p. 7.
11. Mark Donald, "Anti-tipping drive in low-low gear," *New York Times*, April 23, 1967, sec. 10. p. 29.
12. "Anti-tipping drive," *New York Times*, May 21, 1967, sec. 10, p. 3.
13. Edward Ranzal, "Tax fraud charged on tips at Waldorf," *New York Times*, April 25, 1956, p. 14.
14. "Ex-Waldorf waiter is jailed for taxes," *New York Times*, April 25, 1956, p. 14; "2d Waldorf waiter faces tax charges," *New York Times*, July 6, 1956, p. 1; "Tax fraud admitted," *New York Times*, August 7, 1956, p. 28; "The real rich," *Time* 68 (July 16, 1956): 15.
15. "Tax indictments name 15 waiters," *New York Times*, October 31, 1956, p. 35; "Two headwaiters fined," *New York Times*, December 12, 1956, p. 80.
16. "Hotel head waiter jailed in tax fraud," *New York Times*, March 12, 1958, p. 21; "Headwaiter jailed," *New York Times*, March 15, 1960, p. 26.
17. "$17,280 tax evasion laid to headwaiter," *New York Times*, March 15, 1960, p. 26.
18. "Waiters on tips plot charge," *Times* (London), December 19, 1959, p. 4.
19. Carlisle Bargeron, "Tips, incidentals, etc." *Nation's Business* 39 (February 1951): 86; "No tips," *Times* (London), April 14, 1966, p. 13; Peter T. Waite, "Tips, tippers and tippees." *New York Times*, April 8, 1956, p. 28.
20. Oneta Aldrich Wakeford, "Tipping, a national racket?" *American Mercury* 78 (June 1954): 128; "Restaurant rise discouraged," *New York Times*, November 29, 1956, p. 23; "Bootblacks hurt as 35-cent shine cuts business," *New York Times*, January 22, 1967, p. 43.
21. "Waiter tips figured at 2 billion a year," *New York Times*, March 24, 1950, p. 30.
22. "Patrons force tipping, hotel man tells hearing," *New York Times*, February 2, 1956, p. 7; "The itching palm," *New York Times*, February 3, 1956, p. 22.
23. "Unions want tips rated as wages," *New York Times*, January 10, 1960, p. 37.
24. John P. Henderson, "Gratuities as a source of income in the lodging industry," *Business Topics* 13 (Summer 1965): 8–11.

25. Ibid., p. 11–12.

26. "Monthly reports of tips required for U.S. taxes," *New York Times*, December 31, 1965, p. 25.

27. "Waiters dispute U.S. on tip rate," *New York Times*, April 7, 1965, p. 1.

28. "Izvestia opens campaign against tipping in Soviet," *New York Times*, August 13, 1954, p. 2; "Tipping still in vogue, Soviet paper concedes," *New York Times*, January 13, 1958, p. 3; "Soviet paper assails tipping," *New York Times*, February 16, 1959, p. 23.

29. "The old tribute," *Time* 74 (November 16, 1959): 41.

30. "State's help asked in walkout," *New York Times*, May 22, 1967, p. 85; "Insult me, comrade," *Newsweek* 73 (April 14, 1969): 112.

31. "How much, for whom?" *Newsweek* 49 (May 27, 1957): 116; M.J. Arlen "Tips on tipping and tippees," *New York Times Magazine*, May 31, 1964, p. 37.

32. John P. Henderson, "Gratuities as a source," p. 8.

33. "Tipping," *Cornell Hotel and Restaurant Quarterly* 8 (1968): 44–45.

34. "Reform of tipping," *New York Times*, May 20, 1951, sec. 2, p. 30.

35. "Waiters at Waldorf strike 90 minutes," *New York Times*, May 14, 1962, pp. 1,50.

36. "Changes in an old custom," *Times* (London), October 27, 1953, p. 4.

37. "Waiters, counting tips, sign no-rise pay pact," *New York Times*, January 13, 1960, p. 10.

38. "10 Catskill unions back hotels in opposing higher pay for service employees," *New York Times*, November 30, 1966, p. 35.

39. Mort Weisinger, "What happens when you don't tip," p. 24; Peter T. White, "Tips, tippers and tippees," p. 28; "How much, for whom?" *Newsweek* 49 (May 27, 1957): 116.

40. Victor H. Grohmann, "Tipping in American-plan resorts," *Cornell Hotel and Restaurant Administration Quarterly* 8 (1968): 47–50; John A. Patton, "Down with tipping," *Saturday Evening Post* 237 (February 29, 1964): 6.

41. "Sluggish Tipping," *Wall Street Journal*, August 17, 1964, p. 8.

42. "Beggers?" *Newsweek* 49 (May 27, 1957): 116.

43. Craig Claiborne, "Food: why tip for poor service?" *New York Times*, December 21, 1959, p. 31.

44. Ralph Bass, "What's the right tip?" *Coronet* 49 (January 1961): 41; Hans Koningsberger, "Pourboire or trinkgelt or mancia," *New York Times Magazine*, April 17, 1960, p. 68.

45. "A handbook for handouts," *New York Times*, August 14, 1960, sec. 2, p. 38; Peter T. White, "Tips, tippers and tippees," p. 67.

46. Gilbert Millstein, "Who tips what and why," *New York Times Magazine*, January 10, 1960, p. 26.

47. John A. Patton, "Down with tipping," *Saturday Evening Post* 237 (February 29, 1964): 6.

48. Robert L. Karen, "Some factors affecting tipping behavior," *Sociology and Social Research* 47 (October 1961): 71–74.

Chapter 8

1. Paul A. Camp, "Some tips on tipping," *Chicago Tribune*, October 5, 1986, sec. 13, p. 29; Wallace Immen, "A low amount better than no amount," *Globe & Mail*, September 22, 1990, p. A15; Ella Brennan, "Tip credit controversy," *Restaurant Business* 86 (August 10, 1987): 16.

2. Colman McCarthy, "No tipping," *Washington Post*, January 2, 1982, p. A19.

3. "A rivalry at airports," *New York Times*, February 28, 1988, p. 48.

4. "Court rules arguing about tips isn't a cabby's job," *New York Times*, February 14, 1979, p. B9; "Big tips raise prices of a cab," *New York Times*, February 3, 1977, p. 37.

5. "Diners stabbed, waiter held," *New York Times*, January 17, 1989, p. B7; "Slain pair cheap, trial told," *Vancouver Sun*, December 8, 1995, p. A3.

6. "Give staff its tips, restaurant is told," *New York Times*, August 9, 1985, p. B3.

7. "Travel notes," *New York Times*, March 12, 1972, sec. 10, p. 4.

8. Paul Grimes, "Correct tipping will help make the passage smoother," *New York Times*, October 14, 1979, sec. 10, p. 25; Betsy Wade, "Calming the jitters about tipping on cruises," *New York Times*, November 1, 1987, sec. 10, p. 3.

9. "Cruise is canceled by a labor dispute," *New York Times*, November 13, 1973, p. 89.

10. "How much to tip," *Fortune* 83 (May 1971): 94: Colin Leinster, "Playing the tipping game," *Fortune* 112 (November 11, 1985): 175ff.

11. "A few tips on shipboard tipping," *Travel/Holiday* 172 (September, 1989): 12; Dan Carlinsky, "In tipping, too, the take is down," *New York Times*, June 22, 1975, sec. 3, p. 2.

12. "Tipping for beauty services," *Glamour* 80 (September 1982): 225; "Everything you wanted to know about beauty tipping (but were afraid to ask)," *Glamour* 93 (January 1995): 156–159.

13. Ron Alexander, "The quandry of Christmas tipping," *New York Times*, December 17, 1981, p. C1; Peter Kerry, "Holiday tipping," *New York Times*, December 16, 1982, p. C1; "Guidepost," *New York Times*, December 9, 1989, p. 32; Ken Sheets, "The art of the tip," *Kiplinger's Personal Finance Magazine* 48 (December 1994): 123.

14. Sylvia Porter, "You and your money," *Ladies Home Journal* 98 (December 1981): 68; Ruth J. Katz, "Tip sheet," *New York* 22 (December 18, 1989): 54ff.; "The great tipping robbery," *Travel/Holiday* 152 (July 1979): 37–38.

15. Colman McCarthy, "No tipping."

16. "Making a list," *Sports Illustrated* 75 (August 5, 1991): 16.

17. William A. Krause, "The decline and fall of the great American tip," *New York Times*, January 13, 1974, sec. 10, p. 1.

18. "Bartenders tally the best tippers," *Washington Post*, March 18, 1980, p. A15.

19. Paul Schreiber, "Lounge lizards, doctors are among worst tippers, bartenders say," *Winnipeg Free Press*, November 13, 1991, p. C29.

20. "Quebecers are big tippers," *Canadian Hotel & Restaurant* 69 (November, 1991): 13.

21. Bill Granger, "Why women are such lousy tippers," *Chicago Tribune*, February 21, 1988, sec. 10, p. 8.

22. Paul Feldman, "Waitress' suit accuses 2 posh restaurants of sex bias in hiring," *Los Angeles Times*, March 16, 1990. P. B3.

23. Charles M. O'Connor, "Wages and tips in restaurants and hotels," *Monthly Labor Review* 94 (July 1971): 47–51.

24. Harry B. Williams, "Wages and tips in hotels and motels," *Monthly Labor Review* 98 (March 1975): 60–63.

25. "Wages and tips in hotels and motels," *Monthly Labor Review* 103 (December 1980): 60; Donald G. Schmitt, "Tips," *Monthly Labor Review* 108 (July 1985): 50–51.

26. Suellen Butler, "Working for tips," *Sociological Quarterly* 22 (Winter 1981): 16.

27. "The palm crossed with silver," *New York Times*, July 13, 1989, p. 22.

28. Gene Bourg, "Eating out," *Times Picayune* (New Orleans), March 13, 1990, pp. C1, C6.

Chapter 9

1. "Chock Full o' Nuts shops revert to original no-tipping policy," *New York Times*, July 6, 1974, p. 21.

2. Kathy Seal, "No-tipping policy highlights hotels' service," *Hotel & Motel Management* 210 (September 18, 1995): 8.

3. Bernard Levin, "Tipping: where I beg to differ," *Times* (London), March 19, 1981, p. 14.

4. Frank Prial, "Restaurant tipping," *New York Times*, March 12, 1973, p. B13; Paul Grimes, "Knowing when and how much to tip," *New York Times*, March 22, 1981, sec. 10, p. 5.

5. "Knowing when and how much to tip"; Laurent Belsie, "Will waiters' tips slip when owners' profits dip?" *Christian Science Monitor*, May 23, 1988, p. 3.

6. "Service charges gain as tips are taxed," *New York Times*, April 13, 1988, p. C8; Peter Berlinski, "Tipping should go: yes or no?" *Restaurant Business* 87 (May 20, 1988): 16.

7. "Straw poll results: operators speak out," *Restaurant Business* 87 (July 20, 1988): 116, 118; "Service charges gain as tips are taxed," *New York Times*, April 13, 1988, p. C8.

8. "Travel notes," *New York Times*, July 7, 1974, sec. 10, p. 5.

9. "Tipper's revenge," *Time* 104 (August 26, 1974): 61; "Knowing when and how much to tip."

10. Dan Carlinsky, "In tipping, too the take is down," *New York Times*, June 22, 1975, sec. 3, p. 2; Arlene Vigoda, "Tight budgets won't put clamps on tipping," *USA Today*, December 6, 1990, p. 9A.

11. Tippers International, a few sheets of paper mailed in response to a letter for information about the group.

12. Tippers Anonymous, a few sheets of paper mailed in response to a letter for information about the group.

13. Tracy Thompson, "Palm waiters sentenced for not reporting $145,000 in tips," *Washington Post*, June 16, 1989, p. C4.

14. Stephanie Manfield, "IRS puts tax bite on young waitresses' tips," *Washington Post*, June 16, 1979, p. C1.

15. "They hid their tips in San Francisco," *Restaurant Hospitality* 76 (October 1992): 36.

16. "Payment of full wage urged to waiters and waitresses," *New York Times*, April 27, 1974, p. 63.

17. Philip Shabecoff, "House votes minimum wage rise," *New York Times*, September 16, 1977, p. 1; "Senate votes $2.65 minimum pay for 1978," *New York Times*, October 7, 1977, p. 1; Conferees agree on $1.05 rise in minimum pay by '81," *New York Times*, October 15, 1977, p. 10.

18. Advertisement, *Washington Post*, July 26, 1977, p. B12.

19. "No easy answers," *Restaurant Business* 79 (June 1, 1980): 114, 116, 123.

20. Michael Edgerton, "IRS targets undeclared tip income," *Chicago Tribune*, December 7, 1982, sec. 3, p. 9; Marjorie Hunter, "Intense restaurant lobbying is reflected in tax proposals," *New York Times*, August 15, 1982, pp. 1, 24.

21. Marcel R. Escoffier, "The new tip-reporting law," *Cornell Hotel and Restaurant Administration Quarterly* 23 (February 1983): 8-0.

22. Michael Edgerton, "IRS targets;" Marcel R. Escoffier, "The new tip-reporting law," p. 11.

23. Alfred T. Demaria, "Legal implications," *Restaurant Business* 87 (September 1, 1988): 180–181.

24. "For the record," *Washington Post*, November 25, 1983, p. A22; "Tip tax rule brings suit," *New York Times*, January 18, 1984, p. D10; "Waiter and I.R.S. gird to do battle over tips," *New York Times*, February 21, 1984, p. D1; "Final regs ease tip reporting rules," *Journal of Taxation* 59 (October 1983): 282.

25. Alfred T. Demaria, "Tips for tipped employees," *Restaurant Business* 87 (February 10, 1988): 118; "Tipping legislation stirs anger in the restaurant," *Wall Street Journal*, May 24, 1988, p. 1.

26. Peter Weaver, "The IRS is on the trail of unreported tips," *Nation's Business* 82 (November 1994): 74.

27. "Restaurants, IRS call truce," *Wall Street Journal*, August 24, 1995, p. A1.

28. "California's 2-tier wage will stand — for now," *San Francisco Chronicle*, July 8, 1988, p. A7.

29. "Tipping takes a trip," *Time* 130 (August 3, 1987): 32.

30. "Chinese warned not to take tips," *Chicago Tribune*, August 19, 1987, sec. 1, p. 14.

31. Liu Zhuoye, "Tipping experiment in Tianjin," *Beijing Review* 32 (May 8, 1989:31–33.

32. "Consumer attitudes toward tipping," *Cornell Hotel and Restaurant Administration Quarterly* 19 (August 1978): 3; Wendy Cole, "Leaving tips," *Time* 133 (February 27, 1989): 54.

33. David Streitfeld, "Tip o' the season," *Washington Post*, December 11, 1987, p. C5.

34. "Tax report," *Wall Street Journal*, August 23, 1989, p. A1.

35. "Tips on tipping," *Consumer Reports Travel Letter* 11 (October 1995): 227–229.

36. Frank J. Prial, "Restaurant tipping," *New York Times*, March 12, 1973, p. B13.

37. Joanne M. May, "Looking for tips," *Cornell Hotel and Restaurant Administration Quarterly* 20 (February 1980): 10.

38. Wallace Immen, "A low amount better than no amount," *Globe & Mail*, September 22, 1990, p. A15; Ann Landers, "Anger below tipping line," *Los Angeles Times*, December 4, 1989, p. E7.

39. Andy Rooney, "Why tipping trips me up," *Chicago Tribune*, December 24, 1981, p. C1.

40. Emily Card, "Tips on tipping," *Ms* 14 (August 1985): 14–15.

41. Alexander Cockburn, "Tipping in America," *House and Garden* 157 (June 1985): 86.

42. Zachary Citron, "Waiting for nodough," *New Republic* 200 (January 2, 1989): 9–10.

43. James M. Degen, "Do tips still motivate?" *Restaurant Business* 80 (May 1, 1981): 332, 334.

44. Seth Lubove, "Token appreciation," *Forbes* 154 (November 21, 1994): 20.

45. John Berendt, "The case against tipping," *Esquire* 122 (Septemb er 1994): 60, 62.

46. Michael Kinsley, "Yuppies and the servant problem," *Time* 142 (July 5, 1993): 68.

47. Stephen Freeman, "Diffusion of responsibility and restaurant tipping," *Per-*

sonality and Social Psychology Bulletin 1 (Fall 1975): 584–586; "The waiter's lament," *Psychology Today* 9 (April 1976): 28–29.

48. "What tips tippers to tip," *Psychology Today* 14 (June 1980): 98.

49. Joanne M. May, "Looking for tips," pp. 6–8, 12–13; "Beauty and the tips," *Washington Post*, June 8, 1980, p. B8.

50. Joanne M. May, "Looking for tips."

51. Boas Shamir, "A note on tipping and employee perceptions and attitudes," *Journal of Occupational Psychology* 56 no. 3 (1983): 255–256.

52. Ibid., pp. 256–258.

53. Michael Lynn, "The psychology of restaurant tipping," *Journal of Applied Social Psychology* 14 no. 6 (1984): 549–550.

54. Ibid., pp. 551–559.

55. April H. Crusco, "The Midas touch: the effects of interpersonal touch on restaurant tipping," *Personality and Social Psychology Bulletin* 10 (December 1984): 512–515.

56. Renee Stephen, "The effect on tipping of a waitress touching male and female customers," *Journal of Social Psychology* 126 (February 1986): 142.

57. David Streitfeld, "Tip o' the season."

58. Kimberly Garrity, "Effect of server introduction on restaurant tipping," *Journal of Applied Social Psychology* 20, no. 2 (1990): 168.

59. Bruce Rind, "Effect of server's 'Thank you' and personalization on restaurant tipping," *Journal of Applied Social Psychology* 25, no. 9 (1995): 747–749.

60. Michael Lynn, "The effects of alcohol consumption on restaurant tipping," *Personality and Social Psychology Bulletin* 14 (March 1988): 87–90.

61. Michael Lynn, "Effect of server posture on restaurant tipping," *Journal of Applied Social Psychology* 23, no. 8 (April 16, 1993): 678–683.

62. Mary B. Harris, "Waiters, customers, and service: some tips about tipping," *Journal of Applied Social Psychology* 25, no. 8 (1995): 727–741.

63. Boas Shamir, "Between gratitude and gratuity: An analysis of tipping," *Annals of Tourism Research*, 11 (1984): 63–67.

64. Ibid., pp. 69–70.

65. David Streitfeld, "Tip o' the season."

Bibliography

"Admits girls pay $10 a week for job." *New York Times*, May 1, 1928, p. 31.

"Advertisement." *Washington Post*, July 26, 1977, p. B12.

Alexander, Ron. "The quandary of Christmas tipping." *New York Times*, December 17, 1981, p. C1.

"American woman saves self after being pushed overboard," *New York Times*, April 28, 1933, p. 19.

"Americans blamed for tipping evil." *New York Times*, April 26, 1908, pt. 4, p. 2.

Anderson, Floyd. "Tips for tippers." *America* 52 (November 24, 1934): 151–153.

"Another protest against tipping." *New York Times*, March 26, 1882, p. 5.

"Anti-tip bill for Massachusetts," *New York Times*, December 20, 1927, p. 27.

"Anti-tipping bill passed in France." *New York Times*, June 5, 1937, p. 19.

"Anti-tipping drive." *New York Times*, May 21, 1967, sec. 10, p. 3.

"An appeal likely to be heard." *New York Times*, November 4, 1911, p. 12.

Arlen, M.J. "Tips on tipping and tippees." *New York Times Magazine*, May 31, 1964, pp. 20, 37.

Armstrong, John. "Serving the gentry." *American Mercury* 14 (August 1928): 392.

"Army in Europe repeats aim to ban cigarette tip." *New York Times*, October 29, 1946, p. 12.

"Assails Pullman tipping." *New York Times*, October 26, 1927, p. 2.

"Attacks hotel tipping." *New York Times*, March 13, 1922, p. 6.

"Ban on tips is dropped by Chock Full o' Nuts." *New York Times*, December 4, 1967, p. 22.

Bangs, John Kendrick. "Table d'hote talks." *Harper's Weekly* 55 (March 11, 1911): 12–13.

Banks, Elizabeth. "Tips versus social equality and self-respect." *New York Times*, June 11, 1905, sec. 3, p. 7.

"Banquet waiters sue the Waldorf," *New York Times*, March 29, 1952, p. 1.

"Barber arrested for taking a tip." *New York Times*, August 7, 1915, p. 6.

"Barbers accept tip estimate." *New York Times*, August 7, 1915, p. 6.

Bargeron, Carlisle. "Tips, incidentals, etc." *Nation's Business* 39 (February 1951): 84–86.

"Bars waiters' tips in claim for injury." *New York Times*, May 25, 1930, p. 30.

"Bartenders tally the best tips," *Washington Post*, March 18, 1980, p. A15.

Bass, Ralph. "What's the right tip?" *Coronet* 49 (January 1961): 38–41.

Battista, O.A. "To tip or not to tip." *Catholic Digest* 15 (December 1950): 57–59.

"Beauty and the tips." Washington Post, June 8, 1980, p. B8.

"Beggars?" *Newsweek* 49 (May 17, 1957): 116.

"Begin war on tip system." *New York Times*, November 4, 1911, p. 22.

Belsie, Laurent. "Will waiters' tips slip when owners' profits dip?" *Christian Science Monitor*, May 23, 1988, p. 3.

Bemberger, Werner. "Ship line widens no-tipping policy." *New York Times*, November 19, 1967, sec. 10, p. 31.

Bennett, Helen Christine. "Fr-R-Ront!" *Saturday Evening Post* 199 (June 11, 1927): 41ff.

_____. "To tip or not to tip?" *American Magazine* 108 (December 1929): 69–70.

Berendt, John. "The case against tipping," *Esquire* 122 (September 1994): 60, 62.

Berger, Meyer, "Tippers are stiffs or sports," *New York Times*, October 4, 1936, sec. 7, pp. 8, 24.

Berlinski, Peter. "Tipping should go: yes or no?" *Restaurant Business* 87 (May 20, 1988): 16.

Bierwirth, H.C. "The ethics of tips, fees and gratuities." *Andover Review* 6 (August 1886): 265–173.

"Bill prohibiting kickback of tips." *Variety*, February 19, 1947, p. 43.

"Bill regulating distribution of tips urged." *New York Times*, April 21, 1929, sec. 3, p. 1.

Birchall, Louise Hayter. "How much shall I tip?" *Canadian Magazine* 39 (October 1912): 552–556.

Blumenthal, Ralph. "Big tips raise price of a cab." *New York Times*. February 3, 1977, p. 37.

Bok, Edward. "An American nuisance." *Ladies Home Journal* 22 (February 1905): 20.

"Bootblacks hurt as 35-cent shine cuts business." *New York Times*, January 22, 1967, p. 43.

"Bordeaux waiters strike to abolish tips." *New York Times*, July 29, 1936, p. 2.

"Boston may cut off tips." *New York Times*, December 27, 1911, p. 1.

"Bought auto with tips." *New York Times*, January 17, 1920, p. 4.

Bourg, Gene. "Eating out." *Times Picayune* (New Orleans), March 13, 1990, pp. C1, C6.

"Brazilian hotel workers ask abolition of tipping." *New York Times*, November 4, 1936, p. 26.

Brennan, Ella, "Tip credit controversy." *Restaurant Business* 86 (August 10, 1987): 16.

"British baksheesh." *Leisure Hour* 3 (July 4, 1863): 463–464.

Buchwald, Art. "Tips on tips." *Mademoiselle* 38 (April, 1954): 92–93+

Butler, Suellen. "Working for tips." *The Sociological Quarterly* 22 (Winter 1981): 15–27.

"California's 2-tier wage will stand — for now." *San Francisco Chronicle*, July 8, 1988, p. A7.

Camp, Paul A. "Some tips on tipping." *Chicago Tribune*, October 15, 1986, sec. 13, p. 29.

Card, Emily. "Tips on tipping." *Ms* 14 (August 1985): 14–15.

Carlinsky, Dan. "In tipping, too, the take is down." *New York Times*, June 22, 1975, sec. 3, p. 2.

Carman, Albert R. "Tipping — a defence." *Canadian Magazine* 24 (March 1905): 416–418.

"Carry on tipping." *Times* (London), July 9, 1968, p. 8.

"Changes in an old custom." *Times* (London), October 27, 1953, p. 4.

"Chinese warned not to take tips." *Chicago Tribune*, August 19, 1987, sec. 1, p. 14.

"Chock Full o' Nuts shops revert to original no-tipping policy." *New York Times*, July 6, 1974, p. 21.

Citron, Zachary. "Waiting for nodough." *New Republic* 200 (January 2, 1989): 9–10.

Claiborne, Craig. "Food: shy tip for poor service?" *New York Times*, December 21, 1959, p. 31.

_____. "Built–in tip is favored by waiters." *New York Times*, November 12, 1962, p. 34.

"Clemenceau's book stirs trepidation." *New York Times*, December 15, 1929, sec. 3, p. 1.

"Club lifts ban on tips." *New York Times*, January 17, 1914, p. 6.

Cockburn, Alexander. "Tipping in America." *House & Garden* 157 (June 1985): 80ff.

Cole, Wendy. "Leaving tips," *Time* 133 (February 27, 1989): 54.

Colton, Jennifer. "The answer to Christmas tipping." *Good Housekeeping* 131 (December 1950): 49ff.

"Columbia bans tipping." *New York Times*, November 2, 1930, p. 16.

"The common sense of tipping." *Spectator* 91 (October 29, 1904): 630–631.

"Conferees agree on $1.05 rise in minimum pay by '81." *New York Times*, October 15, 1977, p. 10.

"Consumer attitudes toward tipping." *Cornell Hotel and Restaurant Quarterly* 19 (August 1978): 3.

"Controller opposes tips." *New York Times*, April 9, 1913, p. 2.

"Coolidge fixes 60 cents a day tip limit." *New York Times*, August 28, 1926, p. 1.

Copeland, George H. "Reform of tipping." *New York Times*, May 20, 1951, sec. 2, p. 30.

"Court rules arguing about tips isn't a cabby's job." *New York Times*, February 14, 1979, p. B9.

Crespi, Leo P. "The implications of tipping in America." *Public Opinion Quarterly* 11 no. 3, (1947): 424–435.

"The crime of not tipping." *New York Times*, August 31, 1922, p. 14.

Crouch, R.A. "Tips." *Cornhill Magazine* 154 (November 1936): 541–548.

"Cruise is canceled by a labor dispute." *New York Times*, November 13, 1973, p. 89.

Crusco, April H. "The Midas touch: The effects of interpersonal touch on restaurant tipping." *Personality and Social Psychology Bulletin* 10 (December 1984): 512–517.

"Czechs order end to tipping." *New York Times*, May 30, 1948, p. 8.

Danziger, Juliet. "He also serves — maybe." *New York Times*, August 13, 1944, pp. 20–21, magazine sec.

Davis, Clyde Brion. "Tips." *Atlantic Monthly* 178 (September 1946): 126–127.

David, Fred. "The cabdriver and his fare." *American Journal of Sociology* 65 (September 1959): 158–165.

Degen, James M. "Do tips still motivate?" *Restaurant Business* 80 (May 1, 1981): 332ff.

Demaria, Alfred T. "Tips for tipped employees." *Restaurant Business* 87 (February 10, 1988): 110ff.

_____. "Legal implications." *Restaurant Business* 87 (September 1, 1988): 180–181.

Denny, Harold. "Growth of tipping in Soviet scored." *New York Times*, May 23, 1936, p. 7.

"Dime tips by Yankees prohibited by Stengel." *New York Times*, March 9, 1955, p. 32.

"Diners stabbed, waiter held." *New York Times*, January 17, 1989, p. B7.

"Dining car tips barred on Chinese rail system." *New York Times*, January 6, 1935, p. 20.

"Dock worker loses tipping threat case," *New York Times*, March 25, 1962, p. 13.

Donald, Mack. "Anti-tipping drive in low-low gear." *New York Times*, April 23, 1967, sec. 10, p. 29.

Donovan, Francis. *The Woman Who Waits* (Boston: Badger, 1920).

"A drive against tipping." *World's Work* 40 (July 1920): 230.

"Drummers in war on tips." *New York Times*, June 28, 1913, p. 1.

"Dunahoo v. Huber." *The Northwest Reporter v. 171* (St. Paul: West, 1919), pp. 123–125.

"Earl of Sefton bars tips." *New York Times*, August 25, 1907, p. 1.

"Economic effects of tipping." *Gunton's Magazine* 11 (July 1896): 13–19.

Edgerton, Michael. "IRS targets undeclared tip income." *Chicago Tribune*, December 7, 1982. Sec. 3, p. 9.

"Editor's easy chair." *Harper's Magazine* 127 (July 1913): 3120–313.

Escoffier, Marcel R. "The new tip-reporting law." *Cornell Hotel and Restaurant Administration Quarterly* 23 (February 1983): 8–14.

"Everything you wanted to know about beauty tipping (but were afraid to ask)." *Glamour* 93 (January 1995): 156–159.

"Ex-Waldorf waiter is jailed for taxes." *New York Times*, April 25, 1956, p. 14.

"Federal bill to abolish tips." *New York Times*, June 25, 1914, p. 4.

"Feeing in private houses." *New York Times*, January 28, 1900, p. 8.

Feld, Rose C. "Tickling America's outstretched palm." *New York Times*, February 1, 1925, sec. 4, p. 2.

Feldman, Paul. "Waitresses' suit accuses 2 posh restaurants of sex bias in hiring." *Los Angeles Times*, March 16, 1990, p. B3.

Ferguson, Charles W. "Will that be all, sir?" in Elias Lieberman, ed., *Magazine Essays of Today* (New York: Prentice-Hall, 1935), pp. 151–158.

"A few tips on shipboard tipping." *Travel/Holiday* 172 (September 1989): 12.

"Fight income tax on tips." *New York Times*, November 16, 1921, p. 13.

"Final regs ease tip reporting rules." *Journal of Taxation* 59 (October 1982): 282–283.

Finnegan, Frank X. "Tipping as a fine art." *Travel* 16 (February 1911): 170–172.

"For the record." *Washington Post*, November 25, 1983, p. A22.

"For tipless barbers." *New York Times*, September 18, 1910, p. 5.

"Form anti-gimme league." *New York Times*, January 25, 1923, p. 4.

Freeman, Stephen. "Diffusion of responsibility and restaurant tipping." *Personality and Social Psychology Bulletin* 1 (Fall 1975): 584–587.

"French may go non-tipping." *Variety*, September 10, 1930, p. 1.

"Frenchman uses token in move to press war on tipping evil." *New York Times*, September 18, 1932, sec. 2, p. 3.

Garrity, Kimberly. "Effect of server introduction on restaurant tipping." *Journal of Social Psychology* 20, no. 2 (1990): 168–172.

Gaye, Arthur. "Baksheesh," *Macmillan's Magazine* 64 (1891): 206–213.

"Germany abolishes weak war beer." *New York Times*, October 3, 1920, pt. 10, p. 14.

"Gets no tip, fined $2." *New York Times*, August 23, 1927, p. 38.

"Give staff its tips, restaurant is told." *New York Times*, August 9, 1985, p. B3.

Granger, Bill. "Why women are such lousy tippers," *Chicago Tribune*, February 21, 1988, sec. 10, p. 8.

"The great tipping robbery." *Travel/Holiday* 152 (July 1979): 37–38.

Greig, Howard. "Holiday travel tips." *Holiday* 15 (May 1954): 79.

_____. "Tipping in Britain." *Holiday* 23 (April 1958): 119.

Grimes, Paul. "Correct tipping will help make the passage smoother." *New York Times*, October 154, 1979, sec. 10, p. 25.

Grohmann, H. Victor. "Tipping in American-plan resorts." *Cornell Hotel and Restaurant Administration Quarterly* 8 (1968): 47–50.

Grove, Lady. "Hotels as homes?" *Critic* 41 (October 1902): 355–357.

"A guide to tipping." *Good Housekeeping* 144 (June 1957): 50– 51.

"Guidepost." *New York Times*, December 9, 1989, p. 32.

"A handbook for handouts." *New York Times*, August 14, 1960, sec. 2, p. 38.

"Hard times for ocean stewards." *New York Times*, August 22, 1909, pt. 5, p. 7.

Haring, R.A. "Three classes of labor to avoid." *Industrial Management* 62 (December 1921): 370–373.

Harlow, Alvin F. "Our daily bribe." *Forum and Century* 99 (April 1938): 231–235.

Harris, Mary B. "Waiters, customers and service: some tips about tipping." *Journal of Applied Social Psychology* 25, no. 8 (1995): 725–744.

"The hated habit of tipping." *Literary Digest* 95 (October 1, 1927): 21.

Hatton, Joseph. "The Idler's club." *Idler* 3 (July 1893): 674–682.

"Headwaiter jailed." *New York Times*, October 15, 1960, p. 48.

Hemingway, William. *The Annotated Mississippi Code* (Indianapolis: Bobbs-Merrill, 1917), pp. 1573–1564.

Henderson, John P. "Gratuities as a source of income in the lodging industry." *Business Topics* 13 (Summer 1965): 7–22.

"Here's your tip sheet." *Travel* 109 (April 1958): 60–61.

Higgins, Ames. "The tactful art of tipping." *Outlook* 81 (September 16, 1905): 125–129.

"Hobo signs reach Europe." *New York Times*, April 21, 1927, p. 35.

"The hold-up game." *New York Times*, July 9, 1911, pt. 5, p. 7.

"Holland-American will end tipping entirely in April." *New York Times*, October 16, 1967, p. 89.

Holland, Blanche. "May I take your coat, please." *American Mercury* 78 (June 1954): 38–41.

"Hotel head waiter jailed in tax fraud." *New York Times*, March 12, 1958, p. 21.

"Hotel men in war on prohibitionists." *New York Times*, April 15, 1914, p. 8.

"Hotel men say public alone can end tipping." *New York Times*, March 19, 1922, pt. 2, p. 16.

"Hotel porters out, strike for tips." *New York Times*, May 30, 1907, p. 18.

"The hotel tip trust." *New York Times*, October 12, 1906, p. 6.

"How do you feel about tipping?" *Woman's Home Companion* 75 (January 1948): 14.

"How much, for whom?" *Newsweek* 49 (May 27, 1957): 114, 116.

"How much to tip." *Fortune* 83 (May 1971): 94.

Hunter, Marjorie. "Intense restaurant lobbying is reflected in tax proposals." *New York Times*, August 15, 1982, pp. 1, 24.

Immen, Wallace. "A low amount better than no amount." *Globe & Mail*, September 22, 1990, p. A15.

"Income tax includes tips." *New York Times*, February 18, 1920, p. 6.

"Insult me, comrade." *Newsweek* 73 (April 14, 1969): 112.

"Is tipping liked or compelled?" *New York Times*, December 3, 1924, p. 20.

"The itching palm." *New York Times*, February 3, 1956, p. 22.

"Izvestia opens campaign against tipping in Soviet." *New York Times*, August 13, 1954, p. 2.

Karen, Robert L. "Some factors affecting tipping behavior." *Sociology and Social Research* 47 (October 1962): 68–74.

Katz, Ruth J. "Tip sheet." *New York* 22 (December 18, 1989): 54ff.

Kanzanjian, Dodie. "Parting gestures." *House & Garden* 160 (June 1988): 188ff.

Kerr, Peter. "Holiday tipping." *New York Times*, December 16, 1982, p. C1.

Kinsley, Michael. "Yuppies and the servant problem" *Time* 142 (July 5, 1993): 68.

Kirby, William F. *A Digest of the Statutes of Arkansas* (Little Rock: n.p., 1916), p. 683.

Koltun, Frances. "The intelligent woman traveler." *Mademoiselle* 64 (March 1967): 203–204.

"Komura's tips at the Waldorf." *New York Times*, August 9, 1905, p. 6.

Koningsberger, Hans. "Pourboire or trinkgelt or mancia." *New York Times Magazine*, April 17, 1960, p. 35ff.

Krauss, William A. "The decline and fall of the great American tip." *New York Times*, January 13, 1974, sec. 10, p. 1.

Lamb, H. A. "Can tips be abolished?" *New York Times*, July 4, 1920, pt. 7, p. 2.

Landers, Ann. "Anger below tipping line." *Los Angeles Times*, December 4, 1989, p. E7.

Lane, Carol. "Tips for touring," *Travel* 103 (April 1955): 44.

"Law to cut down tips." *New York Times*, January 21, 1911, p. 1.

Laws of Iowa 1915 (Des Moines: State Printer, 1915), p. 347.

Lee, B.Y. "Can exorbitant tipping be prohibited?" *China Weekly Review* 71 (December 15, 1934): 92–93.

Leinster, Colin. "Playing the tipping game." *Fortune* 112 (November 11, 1985): 175ff.

Levin, Bernard. "Tipping: where I beg to differ." *Times* (London), March 19, 1981, p. 14.

Liu, Zhuoye. "Tipping experiment in Tianjin." *Beijing Review* 32 (May 8, 1989): 31–33.

Lowery, Helen Bullitt. "Pity the poor Pullman porter." *New York Times*, October 24, 1920, pt. 3, p. 12.

Lubove, Seth. "Token appreciation." *Forbes* 154 (November 21, 1994): 20.

Lynn, Michael. "The effect of alcohol consumption of restaurant tipping." *Journal of Applied Social Psychology* 14, no. 6 (1984): 549–561.

_____. "The effects of alcohol consumption on restaurant tipping." *Personality and Social Psychology Bulletin* 14 (March 1988): 87<EN91.

_____. "Effect of server posture on restaurant tipping." *Journal of Applied Social Psychology* 23, no. 8 (1993): 678–685.

MacDonald, Dwight. "Your waiter looks at you." *Harper's Magazine* 182 (April 1944): 517–522.

MacKenzie, Catherine. "Tips are smaller but tipping persists." *New York Times Magazine*, December 31, 1933, pp. 6, 11.

"Makes tipping a crime." *New York Times*, March 6, 1914, p. 13.

"Making a list." *Sports Illustrated* 75 (August 5, 1991): 16.

Mansfield, Stephanie. "IRS puts tax bite on young waitresses' tips." *Washington Post*, June 16, 1979, p. C1.

"Massachusetts court holds tips are wages under Compensation Act." *Monthly Labor Review* 33 (August 1931): 311–313.

"May abolish tips." *New York Times*, April 25. 1909, p. 12.

May, Joanne M. "Looking for tips." *Cornell Hotel and Restaurant Administration Quarterly* 20 (February 1980): 6–13.

McCarthy, Colman. "No tipping." *Washington Post*, January 2, 1982, p. A19.

McClune, Littel. "When not to tip." *Lippincott's Magazine* 91 (April 1913): 510.

Millones, Peter. "10 Catskill unions back hotels in opposing higher pay for service employees." *New York Times*, November 30, 1966, p. 35.

Millstein, Gilbert. "Who tips what and why." *New York Times Magazine*, January 10, 1960, p. 26.

"Miss Anderson urges abolition of tipping." *New York Times*, December 29, 1940, p. 24.

"Monthly reports of tips required for U.S. taxes." *New York Times*, December 31, 1965, p. 25.

Moreau, Dan. "The modern art of tipping." *Changing Times* 44 (July 1990): 51–52.

"Mrs. Roosevelt a leader in tipping on dining cars." *New York Times*, February 2, 1939, p. 21.

Musser, R.D. "An answer to the tipping problem." *Cornell Hotel and Restaurant Administration Quarterly* 8 (1968): 99–101.

Needleman, Rae L. "Tipping as a factor in wages." *Monthly Labor Review* 45 (December 1937): 1303–1322.

"New hotel bans tipping." *New York Times*, October 15, 1929, p. 20.

"The 1965 tourist's guide to the fine art of tipping." *New York Times*, February 18, 1965, sec. 12, pp. 13–14.

"No easy answers." *Restaurant Business* 79 (June 1, 1980): 114ff.

"The no tip hotel." *New York Times*, October 8, 1909, p. 8.

"A non-tipping hotel." *New York Times*, December 30, 1924, p. 16.

"Not easy to stop tipping." *New York Times*, August 31, 1908, p. 6.

"No-tip barber shop soon starved out." *New York Times*, May 1, 1908, p. 5.

"No-tip holiday cruises." *Times* (London), April 4, 1968, p. 2.

"A no-tip hotel." *New York Times*, June 5, 1921, pt. 6, p. 7.

"No tipping." *New York Times*, April 20, 1947, sec. 2, p. 13.

"No tipping in Hungary." *New York Times*, July 5, 1936, sec. 10, p. 12.

"The no-tipping plan." *Reader's Digest* 28 (March 1936): 104.

"No tips." *Times* (London), April 14, 1966), p 13.

"No tips drive welcomed." *Times* (London), January 21,1967), p. 7.

"No tips? Mixed reception to a campaign." *Times* (London), April 6, 1966, p. 7.

O'Connor, Charles M. "Wages and tips in restaurants and hotels." *Monthly Labor Review* 94 (July 1971): 57–71.

"The old tribute." *Time* 74 (November 16, 1959): 41.

"100 tip-hungry waiters arrested." *New York Times*, June 23, 1918, p. 7.

"Opposes amendment." *New York Times*, June 23, 1918, p. 7.

"Opposes amendment." *New York Times*, February 8, 1939, p. 7.

"Opposition of organized labor to the tipping system." *Monthly Labor Review* 25 (October 1927): 717–720.

"Organize to stop tipping." *New York Times*, November 23, 1906, p. 9.

"Outstanding issues." *Vancouver Sun*, February 27, 1990, p. C8.

"The outstretched palm." *Time* 77 (June 23, 1961): 44–45.

"The palm crossed with silver." *New York Times*, July 13, 1989, p. 22.

"Paris benevolence." *New York Times*, December 19, 1910, p. 8.

"Paris tipping excessive." *New York Times*, June 15, 1913, pt. 3, p. 3.

"Patrons force tipping, hotel man tells hearing." *New York Times*, February 2, 1956, p. 7.

Patton, John A. "Down with tipping." *Saturday Evening Post* 237 (February 29, 1964): 6, 8.

"Pay the tips in your bill." *New York Times*, My 12, 1912, pt. 3, p. 5.

"Payment of full wages urged to waiters and waitresses." *New York Times*, April 27, 1974, p. 63.

Payne, Will. "Tips." *Saturday Evening Post* 198 (May 15, 1926): 33, 86.

"Pepys on tipping." *New York Times*, September 18, 1927, sec. 8, p. 12.

Philip, F.J. "Blum regime acts to end tipping evil." *New York Times*, June 13, 1937, sec. 4, p. 4.

"Plaint of the steward," *New York Times*, February 20, 1910, p. 5, p. 5.

Porter, Sylvia. "You and your money." *Ladies Home Journal* 98 (December 1981): 68.

"Porters assail tipping." *New York Times*, November 27, 1927, sec. 10, p. 3.

"Porters' tips put at 25 net a month." *New York Times*, July 30, 1928, p. 32.

"The pourboire in danger." *The Nation* 65 (August 26, 1897): 163.

Prial, Frank J. "Restaurant tipping." *New York Times*, March 12, 1973, p. B13.

"Problems in tips and tipping." *New York Times*, July 30, 1911, pt. 5, p. 11.

"Pullman porters' fight on tipping." *New York Times*, July 23, 1928, p. 8.

"Pullman porters open union fight." *New York Times*, June 24, 1928, p. 22.

"Pullman porters say the day of the lavish tip has passed." *New York Times*, August 17, 1924, sec. 8, p. 2.

"Put on blacklist for demanding tips." *New York Times*, August 9, 1908, pt. 3, p. 1.

"Quebecers are big tippers." *Canadian Hotel & Restaurant* 69 (November 1991): 13.

"The question of tipping." *New York Times*, November 19, 1899, p. 10.

Ragner, Bernhard. "Itching palm of Paris." *New York Times*, December 6, 1925, sec. 4, p. 17.

"Railroad bars tips in its dining cars." *New York Times*, June 8, 1946, p. 1.

"The rambler." *Travel* 21 (June 1913): 40.

Ranzal, Edward. "Tax fraud charged on tips at Waldorf." *New York Times*, January 21, 1956, pp. 1, 14.

"Rapid growth of the tipping system" *New York Times*, June 9, 1895, p. 16.

Rasking, A.H. "Unions want tips rated as wages." *New York Times*, January 10, 1960, p. 37.

"The real rich." *Time* 68 (July 16, 1956): 15.

"The reclamation of the tip." *Outlook* 87 (October 26, 1907): 373–374.

"Recognition of tipping." *New York Times*, October 30, 1912, p. 12.

"Reform in dining pleases maitres." *New York Times*, March 5, 1935, p. 21.

"Refuse to stop tipping." *New York Times*, April 6, 1913, pt. 3, p. 2.

"Regulating tips." *Scribner's Magazine* 45 (February 1909): 251–252.

"The reluctant gratuity." *Commonweal* 16 (September 28, 1932): 500.

"Restaurant rise discouraged." *New York Times*, November 29, 1956, p. 23.

"Restaurants, IRS call truce." *Wall Street Journal*, August 24, 1995, p. A1.

Rind, Bruce. "Effect of server's 'thank you' and personalization on restaurant tipping." *Journal of Applied Social Psychology* 25, no. 9 (1995): 745–751.

"A rivalry at airports," *New York Times*, February 28, 1988, p. 48.

Roche, James F. "Random notes of travelers," *New York Times*, May 19, 1935, sec. 9, p. 21.

"Rockefeller tips 5 cents." *New York Times*, December 10, 1908, p. 1.

Rooney, Andy. "Why tipping trips me up." *Chicago Tribune*, December 24, 1981, sec. C, p. 1.

"Russians like tips." *New York Times*, May 25, 1936, p. 18.

"Says tips are not wages." *New York Times*, September 17, 1941, p. 25.

"Says union forces high building costs." *New York Times*, July 21, 1927, p. 23.

"The scale of tips." *New York Times*, August 1, 1906, p. 8.

Schmitt, Donald G. "Tips." *Monthly Labor Review* 108 (July 1985): 50–51.

Schreiber, Paul "Lounge lizards, doctors are among worst tippers, bartenders say." *Winnipeg Free Press*, November 13, 1991, p. C29.

"Scientific tipping." *New York Times*, September 3, 1922, pt. 6, p. 8.

Scott, William R. *The Itching Palm: A Study of the Habit of Tipping in America* (Philadelphia: Penn, 1916).

Seal, Kathy. "No-tipping policy highlights hotels' service." *Hotel & Motel Management* 210 (September 18, 1995): 8.

"2d Waldorf waiter faces tax charges." *New York Times*, July 6, 1956, p. 1.

"Sees peril in tips." *New York Times*, January 23, 1925, p. 7.

"Service charges gain as tips are taxed." *New York Times*, April 13, 1988, p. C8.

Servitor. "The philosophy of tipping." *Canadian Magazine* 36 (April 1911): 533–538.

"$17,280 tax evasion laid to headwaiter." *New York Times*, March 15, 1960, p. 26.

Shabad, Theodore. "Bostonian sells tips on tipping." *New York Times*, November 27, 1959, p. 36.

Shabecoff, Philip. "House votes minimum wage rise." *New York Times*, September 16, 1977, p. 1.

"Shall we abolish tipping?" *Reader's Digest* 33 (October 1938): 107–110.

Shamir, Boas. "A note on tipping and employee perceptions and attitudes." *Journal of Occupational Psychology* 56, no. 3 (1983): 255–259.

_____. "Between gratitude and gratuity: an analysis of tipping." *Annals of Tourism Research* 11 (1984): 59–78.

Shannon, Robert T. *A Compilation of the Tennessee Statutes* (Nashville: Tennessee Law Book, 1918), pp. 6221–6222.

"Sharp drop in tips laid to end of OPA." *New York Times*, January 4, 1947, p. 12.

Sheets, Ken. "The art of the tip." *Kiplinger's Personal Finance Magazine* 48 (December 1994): 123.

"Six waiters made $17,000, not $5,000 in tips." *New York Times*, April 7, 1947, p. 25.

"Slain pair cheap, trial told." *Vancouver Sun*, December 8, 1995, p. A3.

Sloss, Robert. "The way of the waiter." *Harper's Weekly* 52 (January 11, 1908): 20–22.

"Sluggish tipping." *Wall Street Journal*, August 17, 1964, pp. 1, 8.

"Sophie and her tips." *The Nation* 110 (January 31, 1920): 133.

South Carolina. *Session Laws, 1915*, no. 161, pp. 262–263.

"Soviet paper assails tipping." *New York Times*, February 16, 1959, p. 23.

Sparks, Fred. "Headwaiter, esq." *Collier's* 118 (November 23, 1946): 26ff.

"A spectator's notebook." *Spectator* 173 (September 15, 1944): 236.

Speed, John Gilmer. "Tips and commissions." *Lippincott's Magazine* 69 (June 1902): 742–750.

"Spread of idleness alarms Berlin." *New York Times*, December 24, 1918, p. 2.

"State barbers ban tips." *New York Times*, August 17, 1927, p. 5.

"State minimum-wage law." *Monthly Labor Review* 57 (September 1943): 55–556.

"State's help asked in walkout." *New York Times*, May 22, 1967, p. 85.

Stelluto, George. "Wages in eating and drinking places in 27 areas, June 1961." *Monthly Labor Review* 85 (May 1961): 517–519.

_____. "Wages in eating and drinking places, June 1963." *Monthly Labor Review* 87 (May 1964): 544–548.

Stemons, James Samuel. "Tipping — the other side." *Independent* 55 (March 26, 1903): 725–729.

Stephen, Renee. "The effect on tipping of a waitress touching male and female customers." *The Journal of Social Psychology* 126 (February 1986): 141–142.

"Straw poll results: operators speak out." *Restaurant Business* 87 (July 20, 1988): 116ff.

Streitfeld, David. "Tip o' the season." *Washington Post*, December 11, 1987, p. C5.

Strouse, Richard. "Notes on tips, tippers and tippees." *New York Times Magazine*, July 17, 1949, pp. 15, 22–23.

"Struggles in France." *New York Times*, June 14, 1936, sec. 4, p. 6.

Stump, Al. *Cobb: A Biography* (Chapel Hill, N.C.: Algonquin Books, 1994.)

"Sues tipping trust to recover $25,000." *New York Times*, January 11, 1920, pt. 2, p. 1.

"Suit over hautboy's tips." *New York Times*, September 7, 1916, p. 3.

"Swiss tip reform fails." *New York Times*, July 20, 1913, pt. 3, p. 3.

"Swiss waiters fight tips." *New York Times*, August 14, 1921, p. 2.

Sylvester, Robert. "Why they behave like waiters." *Holiday* 24 (December 1958): 30ff.

"Taft an anti-tipper." *New York Times*, June 20, 1908, p. 2.

"Taft and tips." *New York Times*, June 21, 1908, pt. 2, p. 10.

Talese, Guy. "Tourists' tipping dismays tippees." *New York Times*, August 27, 1964, p. 55.

"Talking it over." *The Rotarian* 57 (August 1940): 2.

"Tax fraud admitted." *New York Times*, August 7, 1956, p. 28.

"Tax indictments name 15 waiters." *New York Times*, October 31, 1956, p. 35.

"Tax report." *Wall Street Journal*, August 23, 1989, p. A1.

"10 per cent is not enough." *New York Times*, October 16, 1952, sec. 10, p. 3.

"10 per cent service charge in tipless cafe." *New York Times*, February 19, 1922, pt. 2, p.1.

"10%." *Literary Digest* 123 (July 10, 1937): 5–6.

"That tightrope — tipping!" *Travel* 99 (April 1953): 37.

"They hid their tips in San Francisco." *Restaurant Hospitality* 76 (October 1992): 36.

Thompson, Tracy. "Palm waiters sentenced for not reporting $145,000 in tips." *Washington Post*, June 16, 1989, p. C4.

"Tillman gives negro a tip." *New York Times*, August 9, 1907, p. 1.

"Tillman's tip." *New York Times*, August 11, 1907, p. 6.

"The tip question." *New York Times*, July 30, 1905, p. 6.

"Tip tax rule brings suit." *New York Times*, January 18, 1984, p. D10.

"Tip trust losing its grip on hats." *New York Times*, November 27, 1910, p. 10.

"Tipless hotel has long waiting list." *New York Times*, September 18, 1927, sec. 8, p. 12.

"Tipless hotels." *New York Times*, March 24, 1912, pt. 3, p. 14.

"Tipless hotel's success." *New York Times*, October 29, 1922, pt. 9, p. 10.

"Tipless London." *Independent* 75 (July 10, 1913): 110–111.

"Tippers and tipped." *New York Times*, August 18, 1927, p. 20.

Tippers Anonymous, literature mailed out.

Tippers International, literature mailed out.

"Tipper's revenge." *Time* 104 (August 26, 1974); 61.

"Tipping." *New York Times*, March 24, 1882, p. 5.

"Tipping." *New York Times*, November 16, 1899, p. 6.

"Tipping." *Spectator* 100 (April 25, 1908): 662–663.

"Tipping." *New York Times*, April 27, 1908, p. 6.

"Tipping." *New York Times*, September 28, 1909, p. 8.

"Tipping." *New York Times*, April 4, 1910, p. 8.

"Tipping." *Outlook* 1110 (May 19, 1915): 121.

"Tipping." *New Republic* 23 (July 28, 1920): 244–245.

"Tipping." *Literary Digest* 122 (December 19, 1936): 31.

"Tipping." *New Statesman and Nation* 19 (March 30, 1940): 426–427.

"Tipping." *Life* 21 (July 15, 1946): 30.

"Tipping." *Times* (London), June 3, 1947, p. 2.

"Tipping." *Cornell Hotel and Restaurant Administration Quarterly* 8 (1968): 43–50.

"Tipping a St. Louis misdemeanor." *New York Times*, July 27, 1913, pt. 2, p. 7.

"Tipping and its remedy." *New York Times*, January 23, 1911, p. 6.

"Tipping and the law." *New York Times*, April 16, 1915, p. 12.

"Tipping as a source of happiness." *New York Times*, November 6, 1909, p. 8.

"Tipping as practiced by Samuel Johnson." *New York Times*, September 28, 1930, sec. 5, p. 18.

"The tipping evil." *New York Times*, February 9, 1914, p. 6.

"Tipping for beauty services." *Glamour* 80 (September 1982): 225.

"Tipping here and in Europe." *New York Times*, August 8, 1895, p. 11.

"Tipping in Berlin." *New York Times*, July 14, 1912, pt. 4, p. 4.

"Tipping in hotels and restaurants." *Times* (London), November 23, 1936, p. 19.

"Tipping in Italy." *New York Times*, April 3, 1927, sec. 9, p. 15.

"Tipping is illegal." *New York Times*, February 6, 1912, p. 1.

"Tipping legislation stirs anger in the restaurant." *Wall Street Journal*, May 24, 1988, p. 1.

"The tipping nuisance." *New York Times*, November 3, 1884, p. 3.

"Tipping still in vogue, Soviet paper concedes." *New York Times*, January 13, 1958, p. 3.

"Tipping takes a trip." *Time* 130 (August 3, 1987): 32.

"Tipping to go on." *New York Times*, November 15, 1908, pt. 3, p. 2.

"Tips." *Spectator* 59 (January 2, 1886): 10.

"Tips as wages under Fair Labor Standards Act." *Monthly Labor Review* 54 (April 1947): 996–997.

"Tips expected in France by workers of many types." *New York Times*, December 13, 1925, pt. 10, p. 24.

"Tips in the bill in one hotel now." *New York Times*, February 17, 1913, p. 6.

"Tips on tipping." *New York Times*, June 26, 1956, p. 24.

"Tips on tipping." *Christian Century* 82 (June 2, 1965): 727.

"Tips on tipping." *Consumer Reports Travel Letter* 11 (October 1995): 227–229.

"Tips really don't go to tiptakers." *New York Times*, May 5, 1914, p. 10.

"To bare tip-taking employers." *New York Times*, February 23, 1939, p. 16.

"To fix scale of tips." *New York Times*, October 3, 1908, p. 2.

"To tip or not to tip." *New York Times*, October 14, 1933, p. 14.

"To tip or not to tip." *Fortune* 18 (August 1938): 75–76.

Tolchin, Martin. "Senate votes $2.65 minimum pay for 1978." *New York Times*, October 7, 1977, p. 1.

"Told to quit tipping." *New York Times*, January 2, 1912, p. 7.

"Topics of the Times." *New York Times*, May 9, 1897, p. 22.

"Topics of the Times." *New York Times*, November 21, 1899, p. 6.

"Topics of the Times." *New York Times*, August 24, 1907, p. 6.

"Topics of the Times." *New York Times*, February 14, 1921, p. 8.

"Transport news and notes." *New York Times*, October 22, 1967, p. 86.

"Transport news of interest here." *New York Times*, February 1, 1956, p. 62.

"Travel notes." *New York Times*, March 12, 1972, sec. 10, p. 4.

"Travel notes." *New York Times*, July 7, 1974, sec. 10, p. 5.

"Travel tips." *Time* 62 (October 26, 1953): 42.

"Traveler tires of tipping." *New York Times*, August 26, 1922, pt. 9, p. 14.

"Tries not tipping in a no-tip hotel." *New York Times*, June 5, 1922, p. 6.

Trumball, Robert. "Waiters dispute U.S. on tip rate." *New York Times*, April 7, 1964. P. 1.

"Trying to stop tipping." *New York Times*, April 22, 1913, p. 1.

"Two headwaiters fined." *New York Times*, December 12, 1956, p. 80.

"Untipped waiters mutinied." *New York Times*, August 26, 1908, p. 7.

U.S. Bureau of the Census. *Historical Statistics of the United States: Colonial Times to 1970.* Washington, 1975.

U.S. Bureau of the Census. *Statistical Abstract of the United States, 1982–1983, 103rd ed.* Washington, 1982.

U.S. Bureau of the Census. *Statistical Abstract of the United States, 1992, 112th ed.* Washington, 1992.

"Ushers strike for tips." *New York Times*, November 1, 1919, p. 8.

"Vails or tips." *News-Sheet of the Bribery & Secret Commissions Prevention League* #260 (April 1939): 23.

Vigoda, Arlene. "Tight budgets won't put clamps on tipping." *USA Today*, December 6, 1990, p. 9A.

Wade, Betsy. "Calming the jitters about tipping on cruises." *New York Times*, November 1, 1987, sec. 10, p. 3.

"Wages and tipping." *The Public* 21 (September 7, 1918): 1138–1139.

"Wages and tips in hotels and motels." *Monthly Labor Review* 103 (December 1980): 60.

"Waiter refused a tip." *New York Times*, August 18, 1908, p. 1.

"Waiter tips figured at 2 billion a year." *New York Times*, March 24, 1950, p. 30.

"Waiters and I.R.S. gird to do battle over tips." *New York Times*, February 21, 1984, p. D1.

"Waiters at Waldorf strike 90 minutes." *New York Times*, May 14, 1962, pp. 1, 50.

"Waiters condemn tips." *New York Times*, November 9, 1927, p. 22.

"Waiters, counting tips, sign no-rise pay pact." *New York Times*, January 13, 1960, p. 10.

"The waiter's lament." *Psychology Today* 9 (April 1976): 28–29.

"Waiters lose hotel tip suit." *New York Times*, May 27, 1955, p. 10.

"Waiters on tips plot charge." *Times* (London), December 19, 1959, p. 4.

"Waiters plead for tips." *New York Times*, June 22, 1915, p. 24.

"Waiters want anti-tip law." *New York Times*, October 19, 1913, pt. 2, p. 13.

"Waiters weaken on no-tip crusade." *New York Times*, January 27, 1912, p. 20.

Wakeford, Oneta Aldrich. "Tipping, a national racket?" *American Mercury* 78 (June 1954): 127–129.

Washington State. *Session Laws, 1909*, chapter 249, p. 1029.

"We endure for lack of courage." *New York Times*, August 31, 1917, p. 6.

Weaver, Peter. "The IRS is on the trail of unreported tips." *Nation's Business* 82 (November 1994): 74.

"The week-end tip." *New York Times*, September 1, 1907, pt. 2, p. 6.

Weisinger, Mort. "What happens when you don't tip." *Coronet* 34 (July 1953): 24–28.

_____. "I'm sick of waiters." *Coronet* 36 (June 1954): 32–35.

"What tips tippers to tip." *Psychology Today* 14 (June 1980): 98.

"When to tip, and what." *Changing Times* 10 (May 1956): 34.

White House tipping isn't done." *New York Times*, December 17, 1958, p. 1.

White, Peter T. "Tips, tippers and tippees." *New York Times Magazine*, April 8, 1956, pp. 28, 64, 67.

Whitman, Howard. "How much shall I tip?" *Woman's Home Companion* 66 (September 1939): 8.

"Will regulate tips." *New York Times*, November 11, 1908, p. 4.

Williams, Harry B. "Wages and tips in hotels and motels." *Monthly Labor Review* 98 (March 1975): 60–63.

Wood, Stuart. "You can't stop tipping." *American Mercury* 83 (September 1956): 11–15.

Index